FIG. 9. — Monnaie de cuivre de Justinien, datée de AD.

Translation: Copper currency of Justinian, date of 538

[Emperor Justinian I, AD 527-565, Holding the Cross with the World as Her Seat]
"I saw a woman sit upon a scarlet coloured beast." Rev. 17:3.

Charles Diehl, *Justinien et la Civilisation Byzantine* (Paris: Rue Bonaparte, 1901), 18.

AD 538 Source Book

Heidi Heiks

TEACH Services, Inc.
www.TEACHServices.com

**PRINTED IN
THE UNITED STATES OF AMERICA**

The author assumes full responsibility for the accuracy
of all facts and quotations as cited in this book.

Copyright © 2010 TEACH Services, Inc.
ISBN-13: 978-1-57258-630-7
Library of Congress Control Number: 2010931970

Published by
TEACH Services, Inc.
www.TEACHServices.com

To
Robin

My constant helpmate,
and best friend.

CONTENTS

FOREWORD

The year A.D. 538 was a landmark year for the beginning of the fulfillment of an important time prophecy that spans the Middle Ages. It is essential, therefore, that those who follow the historicist method of interpreting prophecy establish this fixed point as firmly as possible. Brother Heiks has done precisely that with this present study of the important events that occurred and documents what were developed that year. His related studies of A.D. 508 and A.D. 1798 are also recommended to complete this trilogy of important historical-prophetic studies.

William H. Shea, MD, Ph.D.
Former Professor: Old Testament Department
Seminary, Andrews University
Former Associate: Biblical Research Institute
General Conference of Seventh-day Adventists

* * * * * * *

Heidi Heiks has produced and completed as promised a most thorough and timely study on the historical/prophetic dimensions of these four years. In many respects it is an original contribution, anchoring with great scholarly precision the reliability of the significance of these four dates.

It will be a great read, not only for fellow scholars across the academic landscape, but equally so for the thoughtful layperson that enjoys documentation that guarantees deeper assurance in critical biblical study. It surely will not compete with anything else on the market.

Anyone familiar with historical research will be gratified with the author's care and devotion to unvarnished facts and his articulateness in translating from the original languages. Perhaps someone somewhere will take issue with some aspect of this research. But if so, he would have to demolish the brick-by-brick structure that the author has constructed—and that seems to be an unlikely achievement.

I was especially grateful for his writing style—his force, careful transitions, and absence of pretentiousness. This is an unexpected achievement in the world of scholarship. I predict that many teachers and pastors will use these three volumes as a basis for many church-sponsored study groups. I can't imagine an Adventist church that will overlook the power flowing through these pages.

One of the most impressive features that make these books so timely and relevant is the linkage of the historical facts with the biblical anchorage and Ellen White's commentary. I found this three-fold connection to be rewarding and gratifying—not because I had hoped to find it so, but to see how deep this linkage is.

Many good men and women have supported the century-old interpretation that the "daily" refers to paganism, rather than Christ's ministry in heaven. They have seen, for them, good reasons for this position. However, it seems to me that they will find this understanding worthy of further consideration.

I am a wiser man after reading these books, not only for clearer reasons to see validity in 508, 538, 1798 and 1843, but also for the careful details describing the temporary demise of the papacy in 1798.

Herbert Edgar Douglass, Th.D.
Professor: Pacific Union College,
President: Atlantic Union College
Associate editor: Review and Herald
Vice President: Pacific Press
Lincoln Hills, California

* * * * * * *

The apocalyptic books of Daniel and Revelation have received a variety of interpretations throughout church history. Of the three major schools of interpretation, historicism, futurism and preterism, historicism is the oldest, and until the nineteenth century it was the dominant school of interpretation. It can be traced back to some of the church fathers like Irenaeus, Hippolytus, and Jerome. It was taught by Joachim of Floris (1130-1202) in the twelfth century and became the standard interpretation of expositors until the time of the Counter Reformation.

Historicists believe in the divine inspiration of the book of Daniel, that it was written in the sixth century B.C., and that its main prophecies cover the period from the Babylonian Empire to the second coming of Christ. Historicists generally agree that the four empires of Daniel 2 and 7 represent the kingdoms of Babylon, Medo-Persia, Greece, and Rome, and that the Little Horn in Daniel 7 is the papacy. A third factor common to all is their use of the year-day principle in interpreting most, if not all, the time prophecies in Daniel? A last point on which there is general agreement among historicists is the prophecy in Daniel 9:24-27. All historicist commentators agree that the focus of this prophecy is Jesus Christ and that He fulfilled it in His incarnation.

Because historicists believe that the prophecies of Daniel and Revelation are fulfilled throughout the history, and particularly throughout the history of the Christian church, historical sources confirming the fulfillment of these prophecies are extremely important to historicist interpreters. The three volumes by Heidi Heiks contain not only a large amount of primary source material illustrating how the prophecies of Daniel and Revelation were fulfilled in history, they also provide important background information.

The backbone for the interpretation of the time prophecies found in Daniel and Revelation (3½ times, 1260, 1290, 1335 days and 42 months) is the year-day principle. The main points in support of it can be summarized as follows:[1]

---

[1] See Desmond Ford, *Daniel* (Nashville: Southern Publishing Association, 1978), 300-305 and William H. Shea, *Selected Studies on Prophetic Inter-pretation*, Revised edition, DARCOM, 7 vols. (Silver Spring, MD: Biblical Research Institute, 1992), 1:67-104.

1) Since the visions in Daniel 7 and 8 are largely symbolic, with a number of different beasts representing important historical empires (7:3-7; 8:3-5, 20-21), the time periods (7:25; 8:14) should also be seen as symbolic.

2) The fact that the visions deal with the rise and fall of known empires in history which existed for hundreds of years indicates that the prophetic time periods must also cover long time periods.

3) In Daniel 7 the four beasts which together account for a reign of at least one thousand years are followed by the little horn power. It is the focus of the vision since it is most directly in opposition to God. Three and a half literal years for the struggle between the little horn and the Most High are out of proportion to the comprehensive scope of salvation history portrayed in this vision. The same applies to Revelation 12:6 and 14 where the one thousand and two hundred and sixty prophetic days or three and a half times cover most of the history between the First and Second Advents.

4) According to the context, the expressions "time, times, and half a time" (Dan 7:25; 12:7; Rev 12:14), "forty-two months" (Rev 11:2; 13:5), and "one thousand two hundred and sixty days" (Rev 11:3; 12:6) all apply to the same time period, but the natural expression "three years and six months" is not used once. The Holy Spirit seems, in a manner, to exhaust all the phrases by which the interval could be expressed, excluding always that one form which would be used of course in ordinary writing, and is used invariably in Scripture on other occasions, to denote the literal period. This variation is most significant if we accept the year-day system, but quite inexplicable on the other view[2]

5) The prophecies in Daniel 7-8, and 10-12 lead up to the "time of the end" (8:17; 11:35, 40; 12:4, 9) which is followed by the resurrection (12:2) and the setting up of God's everlasting kingdom (7:27). Literal time periods of a few years are not capable of reaching anywhere near the time of the end. Therefore, these prophetic time periods

[2] T.R. Birks, *The Two Later Visions of Daniel: Historically Explained* (London: Seeley, Burnside, and Seeley, 1846), 352.

should be seen as symbolic, standing for long periods of actual time.

6) In Numbers 14:34 and Ezekiel 4:6 God deliberately used the day for a year principle as a teaching device.

7) In Dan 9:24-27 the 70-week time prophecy met its fulfillment at the exact time, if we use the year-day principle to interpret it. Many interpreters, who in other apocalyptic texts do not use the year-day principle, recognize that the 70 weeks are in fact "weeks of years" reaching from the Persian period to the time of Christ. Thus the pragmatic test in Daniel 9 confirms the validity of the year-day principle.

The historicist method of interpretation is used by the angel in Daniel 7 and 8, explaining the various beast symbols as representing a sequence of political powers in history. Hence, it rests on a solid biblical and historical foundation; and in spite of what some may claim, it is not an outdated method belonging to the past but a valid principle of interpreting apocalyptic prophecies today. Heidi Heiks has put together an impressive array of historical material. One may disagree with his comments and interpretations of the sources, but one can hardly argue with the historical material itself. Students of prophetic history will find an abundance of information to facilitate the interpretation of the apocalyptic prophecies of Daniel and Revelation.

Gerhard Pfandl Ph.D.
Associate Director: Biblical Research Institute
General Conference of Seventh-day Adventists

****

PREFACE

How Important Will It Be to Know What We Believe?

"Every position of truth taken by our people will bear the criticism of the greatest minds; the highest of the world's great men will be brought in contact with truth, and therefore every position we take should be critically examined and tested by the Scriptures. Now we seem to be unnoticed, but this will not always be. Movements are at work to bring us to the front, and if our theories of truth can be picked to pieces by historians or the world's greatest men, it will be done. We must individually know for ourselves what is truth, and be prepared to give a reason of the hope that we have with meekness and fear, not in a proud, boasting self-sufficiency, but with the spirit of Christ. We are nearing the time when we shall stand individually alone to answer for our belief. Religious errors are multiplying and entwining themselves with Satanic power about the people. There is scarcely a doctrine of the Bible that has not been denied."[3]

"I have been shown that many who profess to have a knowledge of present truth know not what they believe. They do not understand the evidences of their faith. They have no just appreciation of the work for the present time. When the time of trial shall come, there are men now preaching to others who will find, upon examining the positions they hold, that there are many things for which they can give no satisfactory reason. Until thus tested they knew not their great ignorance. And there are many in the church who take it for granted that they understand what they believe; but, until controversy arises, they do not know their own weakness. When separated from those of

---

[3] Ellen White, *Letter 6*, 1886.

like faith and compelled to stand singly and alone to explain their belief, they will be surprised to see how confused are their ideas of what they had accepted as truth. Certain it is that there has been among us a departure from the living God and a turning to men, putting human in place of divine wisdom. "God will arouse His people; if other means fail, heresies will come in among them, which will sift them, separating the chaff from the wheat . . . . This light should lead us to a diligent study of the Scriptures and a most critical examination of the positions which we hold. God would have all the bearings and positions of truth thoroughly and perseveringly searched, with prayer and fasting. Believers are not to rest in suppositions and ill defined ideas of what constitutes truth. Their faith must be firmly founded upon the word of God so that when the testing time shall come . . . they may be able to give a reason for the hope that is in them, with meekness and fear. "Agitate, agitate, agitate. The subjects which we present to the world must be to us a living reality. . . . As a people we are called individually to be students of prophecy. . . . Through prayerful study clearer light may be obtained, which can be brought before others."[4]

". . . If God has ever spoken by me, the time will come when you will be brought before councils, and every position of truth which you hold will be severely criticized. The time that so many are now allowing to go to waste should be devoted to the charge that God has given us of preparing for the approaching crisis."[5]

"Those who endeavor to obey all the commandments of God will be opposed and derided. They can stand only in God. In order to endure the trial before them, they must understand the will of God as revealed in His word; they can honor Him only as they have a right conception of His character, government, and purposes, and act in accordance with them. None but those who have fortified the

[4] Ellen White, *Testimonies for the Church*, (Boise, ID: Pacific Press, 1948), 5:707-708.
[5] Ibid., 717.

mind with the truths of the Bible will stand through the last
great conflict. . . ."[6]

"There is no Bible sanctification for those who cast a
part of the truth behind them. . . ."[7]

Correct information is first and foremost if our spiritual experience
is to bear the fruits of sanctification, because error never sanctifies.
Without the right information, we cannot make the right decisions,
and if we have the wrong doctrine, we will have the wrong experience.

[6] Ellen White, *The Great Controversy,* (Nampa, ID: Pacific Press, 1911), 593-594.
[7] Ellen White, *Review and Herald,* May 6, 1862.

INTRODUCTION

Today many people, including scholars, count the prophetic historic dates of A.D. 508, 538, 1798, 1843, and 1844 as error, offering new interpretations that are historically and theologically untenable. These new views have resulted in confusion and division within Seventh-day Adventism. As Scripture warns us that we are soon to answer for our faith before the wise men of the world, we must know that "we have not followed cunningly devised fables." All of the objections raised by those who have tried to move the 1260-, 1290-, 1335- or 2300-year dates to sometime in the future (or renounce them altogether) instead of calculating the longest of the prophetic periods of Daniel to the autumn of 1844, can now, by documentation, be officially refuted. This documentation, much of it from primary sources, comes from historians and witnesses whom the world, as a whole, accepts as authoritative voices. Some of them lived and wrote during the reign of Justinian. Civil and ecclesiastical annals from those time periods will declare their truths, as well. Many of these sources are rare or largely inaccessible volumes, unfamiliar to much of the academic world. In addition, some of the most respected Byzantine historians in Europe who corroborated these facts have been consulted and have even given their consent to be quoted. Most importantly, the Catholics themselves have given their official sanction and imprimatur to these facts which will be demonstrated from their very own published works. Finally, Biblical verses and the writings of Ellen White are cited to confirm and support the historical applications here presented and, in turn, the reliable recorded history attests to their accuracy and trustworthiness. The purpose of this book, then, is to document our application and interpretation of certain scriptural and historical events of A.D. 538 as the fulfillment of prophecy found in the books of Daniel and Revelation. What began as an investigation into the accuracy of the historicist interpretation has ended in an accumulation of evidence that firmly validates that view. From the primary sources, we will piece together all the specifications of this prophetic puzzle. Fundamental issues surrounding those dates will be shown to be the following: the union of church and state, the increasing influence of the church over the state, and their combined efforts through various channels to abrogate freedom of conscience and nullify the gospel and the government or law of God. The true Antichrist of the Apocalypse and its methods will be exposed for the world to see:

> "There will be one fierce struggle before the man of sin shall be disclosed to this world—who he is and what has been his work."[8]

Seven times this prophetic time period of 1260 years is mentioned in Daniel and Revelation and, in every instance, one and the same event is identified. By repetition, God established and emphasized it with further details:

> Daniel 7:25 "And he shall speak *great* words against the most High, and shall wear out the saints of the most High, and think to change times and laws: and they shall be given into his hand until a time and times and the dividing of time."

> Daniel 12:7 "And I heard the man clothed in linen, which *was* upon the waters of the river, when he held up his right hand and his left hand unto heaven, and sware by him that liveth for ever that *it* shall *be* for a time, times, and an half; and when he shall have accomplished to scatter the power of the holy people, all these *things* shall be finished."

> Revelation 11:2 "But the court which is without the temple leave out, and measure it not; for it is given unto the Gentiles: and the holy city shall they tread under foot forty *and* two months."

> Revelation 11:3 "And I will give *power* unto my two wit-

---

[8] Ellen White, *Selected Messages,* (Hagerstown, MD: Review and Herald, 1980), 3:426.

nesses, and they shall prophesy a thousand two hundred and threescore days, clothed in sackcloth."

Revelation 12:6 "And the woman fled into the wilderness, where she hath a place prepared of God, that they should feed her there a thousand two hundred *and* threescore days."

Revelation 12:14 "And to the woman were given two wings of a great eagle, that she might fly into the wilderness, into her place, where she is nourished for a time, and times, and half a time, from the face of the serpent."

Revelation 13:5 "And there was given unto him a mouth speaking great things and blasphemies; and power was given unto him to continue forty *and* two months."

Ellen White specifically affirms those time prophecies' application and relevance in history.

"The forty and two months are the same as the 'time and times and the dividing of time,' three years and a half, or 1260 days, of Daniel 7—the time during which the papal power was to oppress God's people. This period, as stated in preceding chapters, began with the supremacy of the papacy, A.D. 538, and terminated in 1798."[9]

These and other scriptures will be referenced and diagnosed when and where appropriate to our study. In addition, our study will show that the Bible does not teach that the temporal sovereignty of the Papacy or the Primacy of the Popes is the reference point for the commencement of the 1260-year prophecy; consequently, neither do we advocate that faulty premise. The first possible year that can be attributed to the temporal power of the Papacy is undisputedly A.D. 754, not 538. Similarly, it cannot be accurately stated that the Primacy of the Popes began in A.D. 538. Neither does the Bible say that the pope was continually the "Head of all the Holy Churches" for 1260 years. The Bible does, however, paint a picture of persecution during this 1260-year period, but, for the sake of God's people, the gospels of

[9] Ellen G. White, *The Great Controversy*, (Nampa, ID: Pacific Press, 1911), 439.

Matthew and Mark predict a shortening of this activity. (See Matthew 24:22, 29 and Mark 13:24) Therefore, the actual time period falls short of the 1260 years. To say that 1798 was the first time a pope had been exiled or killed is simply not true. Furthermore, the death of Pope Pius VI in Valance, France on August 29, 1799, cannot be the event that dictates the termination of the prophecy, as that would extend the prophecy to 1261 years and would, therefore, go outside of the prophetic period. By now, the inquisitive mind of the reader is no doubt asking, then, "1260 years of what?" In order to discover the answer to this all-encompassing question, we must begin with the same foundational premise found in the Bible. But first, we will clarify and establish some necessary Biblical fundamentals.

I have focused on a Seventh-day Adventist readership, from academia to local churches to whom these several topics are not unfamiliar. It is hoped that the information presented will lead to unity among us. The research has been presented before the most versed, scholarly minds of our faith in order to demonstrate that the applications made on the combined basis of historical and prophetic literature will stand the test of investigation. This gathering and compilation of the primary historical sources, with its translation of the Latin, Greek French, German and Italian, will serve Seventh-day Adventism with the needed Biblical integrity she must display to the world as she is commissioned to present the last invitation of mercy to a perishing world. Our Biblical and historical interpretation will provide Seventh-day Adventism with a solid foundation for the four prophetic periods of Daniel, so we may boldly, correctly and without reserve proclaim the Four Angels' messages of Revelation 14:6-12, 18:1-5. Furthermore, we believe all the necessary information has been provided in these three volumes (Vol. 1, *A.D. 508 Source Book,* Vol. 2, *A.D. 538 Source Book,* and Vol. 3, *A.D. 1798 1843 Source Book*) to forever eliminate long-standing error and confusion within Seventh-day Adventism regarding those dates and the prophetic events linked to them. When all doubt is removed, unanimity is attainable. Then, with a unified front, we can present to the world a united message.

This thesis uses the day-for-a-year principle for interpreting prophecy which is supported by Ezekiel 4:6 and Numbers 14:34. Due to space limitations and a bibliography of over one hundred pages, I must refer the reader to my website at www.thesourcehh.org to view the sources used for these three volumes. One will there find all the sources listed in PDF format under their appropriate designated year in alphabetical order along with translated papal letters of the 5th and 6th century, primary documents, books, maps, articles and so much more. However, the reader will find in the footnotes of this book a most thorough description of the source cited, as well. All emphasis mine unless otherwise noted. Scripture references are taken from the King James Version of the Bible.

I am forever indebted to Darcie Litton, my copy editor, for all her endless hours of critique and constructive criticism which gave this work its final veracity.

Special gratitude to Gerhard Pfandl Ph.D., Associate Director of the Biblical Research Institute of the General Conference of Seventh-day Adventists, for his critique and valuable suggestions.

I humbly confess that without the aid of the Holy Spirit and the direct working of my guardian angel this massive project would have never been completed. I could spend hours giving an account of heaven's direct intervention throughout these past six years during which I gained a living experience that will stay with me for the rest of my life. It is, therefore, my hope and sincere prayer that the information provided will be a confirmation and fortification for all in the coming crisis.

Heidi Heiks, former international Christian editor, college educator, and speaker for *The People of the Book* radio program, has written numerous articles and books.

Heidi Heiks

****

1

The Government of God verses the Government of Satan

This foundational premise of *religious liberty*, one of the main *keys* that unlock our understanding in rightly interpreting the four prophetic periods of Daniel in relationship to the government of God, is now to be presented in our study. Ellen White directs our minds to the primary purpose for which heaven gave us these four prophetic periods found in the book of Daniel. The central theme and premise that lie behind them can best be summarized from the following:

> "Satan wished to change the *government of God*, to fix his own *seal* to the rules of God's kingdom. Christ would not be brought into this desire, and here the warfare against Christ *commenced* and waxed strong."[1]

We want Ellen White to expand on this concept of the *government of God*:

> "The principles of the character of God were the foundation of the education constantly kept before the heavenly angels. These principles were goodness, mercy and love. Self-evidencing light was to be recognized and freely accepted by all who occupied a position of trust and power. *They must accept God's*

[1] Ellen White, *Manuscript Releases*, (Silver Spring, Maryland: E.G. White Estate, 1993), 16:180.

principles and convince all who were in the service of God, through the presentation of truth and justice and goodness, [that] this was the only power to be used. Force must never come in. All who thought that their position gave them power to command their fellow men and control conscience, must be deprived of their position. These principles are to be the great foundation of education in every administration on the earth. In every church the rules given by God are to be observed and respected. God has enjoined this. His government is to be moral. Nothing is to be done from compulsion. Truth is to be the prevailing power. All service is to be done willingly and for love of the service of God. All who are honored with positions of influence are to represent God, for when [361] officiating they act in the place of God. In everything their actions must correspond with the importance of their position. The higher the position, the more distinctly will self-sacrifice be revealed, if they are fit for the office.

Satan's representations against the government of God, and his defense of those who sided with him, were a constant accusation against God. These murmurings and complaints were groundless. Yet God allowed Satan to work out his theories. He could have handled Satan and all his sympathizers as easily as one can pick up a pebble and cast it to the earth. But by this he would have given a precedent for the violence of man which is so abundantly shown in our world in the compelling principles. The Lord's principles are not of this order. All the compelling power is found under Satan's government. God would not work on this line. He would not give the slightest encouragement for any human being to set himself up as God over another human being, and cause him mental or physical suffering. This principle is wholly of Satan's creation.

In the councils of heaven it was decided that principles must be acted upon which would not at once destroy Satan's power, for it was His purpose to place things upon an eternal basis of security. Time must be given for Satan to develop the principles which were the foundation of his government. The heavenly universe must see the principles which Satan declared were supe-

rior to God's principles, worked out. God's order must be contrasted with the new order after Satan's devising. The corrupting principles of Satan's rule must be revealed. The principles of righteousness expressed in God's law must be demonstrated as unchangeable, eternal, perfect.
. . . . [362] *The Lord allowed Satan to go on and demonstrate his principles.* God did establish Himself, and He carried the worlds unfallen and the heavenly universe with Him, but at a terrible cost. His only begotten Son was given up as Satan's victim. The Lord Jesus Christ revealed a character entirely opposite to that of Satan. As the high priest laid [off] his gorgeous pontifical robes, and officiated in the white linen dress of a common priest, so Christ emptied Himself and took the form of a servant, and offered sacrifice, Himself the priest, Himself the victim.

By causing the death of the Sovereign of heaven, Satan defeated his own purposes. The death of the Son of God made the death of Satan unavoidable. Satan was allowed to go on until his administration was laid open before the worlds unfallen and before the heavenly universe. By shedding the blood of the Son of God, he uprooted himself [from sympathy], and was seen by all to be a liar, a thief, and a murderer."[2]

"From the very beginning of the great controversy in heaven it has been Satan's purpose to overthrow the law of God. It was to accomplish this that he entered upon his rebellion against the Creator, and though he was cast out of heaven he has continued the same warfare upon the earth. To deceive men, and thus lead them to transgress God's law, is the object which he has steadfastly pursued. Whether this be accomplished by casting aside the law altogether, or by rejecting one of its precepts, the result will be ultimately the same. He that offends "in one point," manifests contempt for the whole law; his influence and example are on the side of transgression; he becomes "guilty of all." James 2:10.

---

[2] Ellen White, *Manuscript Releases*, (Silver Spring, Maryland: E.G. White Estate, 1993), 18:360-62.

In seeking to cast contempt upon the divine statutes, Satan has perverted the doctrines of the Bible,
and errors have thus become incorporated into the
faith of thousands who profess to believe the Scriptures. The last great conflict between truth and error is
but the final struggle of the long-standing controversy
concerning the law of God. Upon this battle we are
now entering—a battle between the laws of men and
the precepts of Jehovah, between the religion of the
Bible and the religion of fable and tradition."[3]

This warfare of Satan on the government of God is
vividly portrayed from the following scriptures contrast-
ing the two:

Isaiah 14:12 "How art thou fallen from heaven, O
Lucifer, son of the morning! *how* art thou cut down to
the ground, which didst weaken the nations!"
Isaiah 14:13 "For thou hast said in thine heart, I
will ascend into heaven, I will exalt my throne above
the stars of God: I will sit also upon the mount of the
congregation, in the sides of the north:"
Isaiah 14:14 "I will ascend above the heights of the
clouds; I will be like the most High."

Ezekiel 28:2 "Son of man, say unto the prince of
Tyrus, Thus saith the Lord GOD; Because thine heart is
lifted up, and thou hast said, I am a God, I sit in the
seat of God, in the midst of the seas; yet thou art a
man, and not God, though thou set thine heart as the
heart of God:"

As we have seen, *time* must be given for Satan to develop the principles which were to be the foundation of
his government, the government of force. The heavenly
universe, we were told, must see these principles which
Satan declared were superior to God's principles,

---

[3] Ellen White, *The Great Controversy* (Nampa, ID: Pacific Press, 1911),
582.
See also Ellen White, *The Desire of Ages*, (Nampa ID: Pacific Press,
1940), 762-3.

worked out. God's order must be contrasted with the new order after Satan's devising. The corrupting principles of Satan's rule must be revealed. The principles of righteousness expressed in God's law must be demonstrated as unchangeable, eternal, and perfect. We have been forewarned in order to endure the trial before us. God's people must be in harmony with the principles of His government and act in accordance with them if they are to have any hope in standing through the last great conflict:

> "Those who endeavor to obey all the commandments of God will be opposed and derided. They can stand only in God. In order to endure the trial before them, they must understand the will of God as revealed in His word; they can honor Him only as they have a right conception of His character, government, and purposes, and act in accordance with them. None but those who have fortified the mind with the truths of the Bible will stand through the last great conflict."[4]

In order to honor our Heavenly Father regardless of our trials and to ultimately stand in His presence, we must have "a right conception of His *character, government* and *purposes*, and act in accordance with them." We believe His *character* and *purposes* are clearly understood by all, but what does Inspiration mean by His *government*? It becomes imperative, then, that we fully take in these principles, for in so doing we will have found the key that unlocks the foundational premise that underlies the four prophetic periods as found in the book of Daniel. Isaiah, speaking of Christ, said:

> "For unto us a child is born, unto us a son is given: and the *government* shall be upon his shoulder: and his name shall be called Wonderful, Counsellor, The mighty God, The everlasting Father, The Prince of Peace. Of the increase of his government and peace there shall be no end, upon the throne of David, and upon his kingdom, to order it, and to establish it with judgment and with justice from henceforth even for

---

[4] Ellen White, *The Great Controversy*, (Nampa, ID: Pacific Press, 1911), 593-4.

ever. The zeal of the LORD of hosts will perform this."
Isaiah 9:6-7.

Christ came to show us the Father; that would include His character and principles of government. If we
are at last to find a place among the heavenly throng, we
will have first developed His character and accepted
those principles here, living daily in accordance with
them, for we have been informed that it is "the highest
crime to rebel against the government of God."[5] Fortunately, we are not left to flounder in speculation as to
what constitutes the government of God. Inspiration has
minutely defined of what that government consists:

   1. "The law of love being the foundation of the
government of God. . . ."[6]

   2. "Justice and mercy are the foundation of the
law and government of God."[7]

   3. "The law of God is the foundation of his
Government in Heaven and in earth."[8]

   "Christ would have all understand the events of his
   second appearing. The judgment scene will take place
   in the presence of all the worlds; for in this judgment
   the government of God will be vindicated, and his law
   will stand forth as 'holy, and just, and good.' Then
   every case will be decided, and sentence will be passed
   upon all. Sin will not then appear attractive, but will
   be seen in all its hideous magnitude. All will see the relation in which they stand to God and to one another."[9]

   4. "The government of God is not, as Satan would
make it appear, founded upon a blind submission, an
unreasoning control. It appeals to the intellect and the

[5] Ellen White, *Spirit of Prophecy*, (Hagerstown, MD: Review and Herald, 1870), 1:22.
[6] Ellen White, *The Great Controversy*, (Nampa, ID: Pacific Press, 1911), 493.
[7] Ibid., 503.
[8] Ellen White, *Signs of the Times*, March 30, 1888.
[9] Ellen White, *Review and Herald*, September 20, 1898.

conscience. 'Come now, and let us reason together,' is the Creator's invitation to the beings He has made (Isaiah 1:18). God does not force the will of His creatures. He cannot accept an homage that is not willingly and intelligently given. He desires that all the inhabitants of the universe shall be convinced of His justice in the final overthrow of rebellion and the eradication of sin. He purposes that the real nature and direful effects of sin shall be clearly manifested to their bitter end that all may be assured of the wisdom and justice of the divine government."[10]

"The perfectly saved will be perfectly free. Throughout eternity they will do just what they please, because they please to do just what makes liberty and joy possible. Now, as to the relation of the state to the conscience of man. Christ found men enslaved to kings and to priests. . . After having made men free to sin, that the internal principle of love might work itself out in outward acts of righteousness unhindered by force. . . ."[11]

Hence, we see that His government consists of love, justice, mercy, His law, and freedom of choice. Divinely-ordained free will, acknowledged in the concept of religious liberty, constitutes the government of God.

The scriptures present clear instruction regarding the path the church must take in the conflict between tolerance and intolerance:

"And it came to pass, when the time was come that he should be received up, he stedfastly set his face to go to Jerusalem, and sent messengers before his face: and they went, and entered into a village of the Samaritans, to make ready for him. And they did not receive him, because his face was as though he would go to Jerusalem. And when his disciples James and John saw this, they said, Lord, wilt thou that we command fire to come down from heaven, and consume them, even as Elias did? But he turned, and rebuked them, and said, Ye know not

---

[10] Ellen White, *Bible Training School*, December 1, 1908.
[11] Ellen White, *The Watchman*, May 1, 1906.

what manner of spirit ye are of. For the Son of man is not come to destroy men's lives, but to save them. . . ." Luke 9:51–56.

It was on the matter of intolerance that the church was sternly rebuked. The disciples were reminded of the power which alone was to govern their lives, namely the Holy Spirit:

"James and John, Christ's messengers, were greatly annoyed at the insult shown to their Lord [when the Samaritans refused hospitality to Jesus, because his face was set to go to Jerusalem]. They were filled with indignation because He had been so rudely treated by the Samaritans whom He was honoring by His presence. They had recently been with Him on the mount of transfiguration, and had seen Him glorified by God, and honored by Moses and Elijah. This manifest dishonor on the part of the Samaritans, should not, they thought, be passed over without marked punishment.

"Coming to Christ, they reported to Him the words of the people, telling Him that they had even refused to give Him a night's lodging. They thought that a grievous wrong had been done Him, and seeing Mount Carmel in the distance, where Elijah had slain the false prophets, they said, 'Wilt Thou that we command fire to come down from heaven, and consume them, even as Elias did?' They were surprised to see that Jesus was pained by their words, and still more surprised as His rebuke fell upon their ears, 'Ye know not what manner of spirit ye are of. For the Son of man is not come to destroy men's lives, but to save them.' And He went to another village."[12]

The hellish principles behind an attempt to control the conscience are rarely touched upon today, but the

---

[12] Ellen White, *The Desire of Ages*, (Nampa, ID: Pacific Press, 1940), 487.

people of God will experience their full impact in the very near future. When we, as a people, fully take in the concepts of religious liberty that are foundational to the government of God, we will have a powerful testimony for the truth that cannot be overthrown. It must be understood and proclaimed that faith itself demands freedom.

When the conscience is controlled through force, faith ceases to be faith. Love disappears and the motive for obedience then becomes fear. It is only through religious freedom that faith can find its fullest potential and expression. Faith, therefore, has its best protection in religious liberty. In an unrestricted religious environment, where one's faith is not governed by mandatory limitations or coercion, faith is an unlimited and voluntary "choice in action." Faith is free to be expressed in the choices one makes regarding the invitation and, in fact, every aspect of the gospel:

> Revelation 22:17 "And the Spirit and the bride say, Come. And let him that heareth say, Come. And let him that is athirst come. And whosoever will, let him take the water of life freely."

In fact, religious liberty and true faith are mutually dependent upon one another. Whoever endangers or restricts religious liberty threatens or restricts truth itself, for truth is forever unfolding to the one who lives and walks by faith. When the soul is prevented from seeking where it will, when it is demanded that the individual conform to certain religious doctrines or practices, when the mind is subjugated to another human being, no true spiritual growth can occur. The religious experience will be dwarfed or stalled. And with no living experience, there can be no character development, and thus no sanctification. Hence, Satan wins.

> "Some will be convicted [by faith] and [by faith] will heed the words spoken to them in love and tenderness. They will acknowledge that the *truth is the very*

thing they need to set them free from the slavery of sin
and the bondage of worldly principles. There are
opened before them themes of thought, fields for action that they had never comprehended."[13]

Only living faith leads to spiritual growth. A formality
of religious exercises contributes to nothing but an external experience, which is valueless with God. It is faith
alone that, above all other considerations, makes men
free because only in free exercise of faith—freedom to believe and follow as suits the heart of each—can man be
the free moral agent God created him to be. Paul exem-
plified that principle in 1 Corinthians 9:19, referring to
himself as "free from all men.":

> "It is not God's purpose to coerce the will. Man
> was created a free moral agent. Like the inhabitants of
> all other worlds, he must be subjected to the test of
> obedience; but he is never brought into such a position
> that yielding to evil becomes a matter of necessity."[14]

It is only by a clear understanding of this matter for
ourselves that we will properly proclaim the second and
fourth angels' messages of Revelation 14 and 18, thus
fulfilling our divine commission during the final crisis.
Therefore, "let every man be fully persuaded in his own
mind." Romans 14:5:

> "The exercise of force is contrary to the principles
> of God's government; He desires only the service of
> love; and love cannot be commanded; it cannot be won
> by force or authority. Only by love is love awakened."[15]

> "It is no part of Christ's mission to compel men to
> receive Him. It is Satan, and men actuated by his

[13] Ellen White, *Medical Ministry*, (Nampa, ID: Pacific Press, 1963), 244.
[14] Ellen White, *Patriarchs and Prophets*, (Nampa, ID: Pacific Press, 1958), 331-2.
[15] Ellen White, *The Desire of Ages*, (Nampa, ID: Pacific Press, 1940), 22.

spirit, that seek to compel the conscience. Under a pretense of zeal for righteousness, men who are confederate with evil angels bring suffering upon their fellow men, in order to convert them to their ideas of religion; but Christ is ever showing mercy, ever seeking to win by the revealing of His love.

"He can admit no rival in the soul, nor accept of partial service; but He desires only voluntary service, the willing surrender of the heart under the constraint of love. There can be no more conclusive evidence that we possess the spirit of Satan than the disposition to hurt and destroy those who do not appreciate our work, or who act contrary to our ideas. Every human being, in body, soul, and spirit, is the property of God. Christ died to redeem all. Nothing can be more offensive to God than for men, through religious bigotry, to bring suffering upon those who are the purchase of the Saviour's blood."[16]

Clearly, then, we can see that those who are in harmony with the government of God will never coerce the will of another to achieve their ends. God's way is to *"draw all men unto"* Himself, (Jeremiah 31:3, John 12:32) to *"receive"* us (Luke 18:17). When we *"choose"* (Joshua 24:15) to *"turn"* unto Him (Ezekiel 33:11) and *"come unto"* Him (Matthew 11:28) we may do so *"freely"* (Revelation 22:17). His ways and methods allow only for freedom of choice.

On the other hand, those who have enlisted under the government of Satan have no scruples about bringing suffering upon those whom they cannot control:

"Compelling power is found only under Satan's government."[17]

Therefore, his subjects are ever ready to use force in any or all its various forms to compel others to accept their bigoted ideas of religion. This is why Inspiration says:

---

[16] Ibid., 487–8.
[17] Ibid., 759.

"Force is the last resort of every false religion."[18]

Luther himself, who had firsthand experience with this spirit of intolerance, said:

"Even this is an evil zeal, not from God but from the devil."[19]

"God never forces the will or the conscience; but Satan's constant resort—to gain control of those whom he cannot otherwise seduce—is compulsion by cruelty. Through fear or force he endeavors to rule the conscience and to secure homage to himself. To accomplish this, he works through both religious and secular authorities, moving them to the enforcement of human laws in defiance of the law of God."[20]

"'Whereunto,' asked Christ, 'shall we liken the kingdom of God? or with what comparison shall we compare it?' Mark 4:30. He could not employ the kingdoms of the world as a similitude. In society He found nothing with which to compare it. Earthly kingdoms rule by the ascendancy of physical power; but from Christ's kingdom every carnal weapon, every instrument of coercion, is banished."[21]

This is the instruction and mandate for the born-again Christian whether we be laity, independent, conference, academic, or any other Christian community or church throughout the world.

A contributor to *The Southern Watchman* wrote in summation:

"All slavery, physical, moral, and intellectual, comes from breaking that law. Liberty is found only in obedi-

---

[18] Ellen White, *Seventh-day Adventist Bible Commentary*, (Washington D.C: Review and Herald, 1980), 7:976.
[19] Luther, *Sermon on Luke 9:51*, (1537); Weimar ed., t. 45, p. 407.
[20] Ellen White, *The Great Controversy*, (Nampa, ID: Pacific Press, 1911), 591.
[21] Ellen White, *The Acts of the Apostles*, (Nampa, ID: Pacific Press, 1911), 12.

ence to it. . . . His will becomes ours, and with Christ we delight to do His will, because His law is in our hearts. Here is perfect liberty. The perfectly saved will be perfectly free. Throughout eternity they will do just what they please, because they please to do just what makes liberty and joy possible. Now, as to the relation of the state to the conscience of man. Christ found men enslaved to kings and to priests. . . . After having made men free to [from] sin, that the internal principle of love might work itself out in outward acts of righteousness unhindered by force, . . . has God given to any human authority the right to take away that freedom, and so thwart His plans? He has commanded all men to worship Him and obey His precepts, and this command applies to each individual personally; but has He ever commanded any man or set of men to compel others to worship Him, or to act even outwardly as if they worshiped Him? To ask these questions is to answer them emphatically in the negative. . .

When Peter, as a member of the Christian church, sought to defend the truth by the sword, Jesus, pointing to His Father as the Church's only source of power, said, 'Put up again thy sword into its place; for all they that take the sword [i.e., in religious matters] shall perish with the sword.' [Mat. 26:52] The tares are to be allowed to grow with the wheat until the harvest. Then God will send forth His angels to gather out the tares and burn them. No human effort of arbitrary force can be used in rooting them out, lest in the act the wheat shall be rooted also. [Mat. 13:30] Again Jesus said, 'My kingdom is not of this world, if my kingdom were of this world, then would my servants fight.' [Jn. 18:36] Every civil law has the power of the sword back of it. If it is right to make law, then it is right to enforce it. In denying to the church the power of the sword, Jesus therefore forbade the church to ask the state for laws enforcing religious beliefs and observances. Paul understood this when he said, 'The weapons of our warfare are not carnal, but mighty through God to the pulling down of strongholds.' [2 Cor. 10:4] The early church, strong only in the power of God, triumphed grandly, even over the opposing forces of a false religion, upheld by the state. Only when she allied herself with the state, seeking its aid, did she deny her God, lose her power, and darken the world into a night of a thousand years. The present effort of the church to get the state to enforce the observance of Sunday, and to introduce the teaching of Christianity into state schools, is but a revival of the pagan and papal doctrine of force in religious things, and as such it is antichristian."[22]

Unfortunately, as will be seen, many so-called members of Christendom have chosen their own way, rejecting the plain teachings of Jesus and his last instructions to the Christian church on this vital subject of toleration found in the New Testament. The Bible is abundantly clear and if we err here, it is with eyes wide open. "For all they that take the sword [i.e., in religious matters] shall perish with the sword." (Matthew 26:52) May we all be so settled on this eternal issue that we cannot be moved.

All will be found on only one of the two sides of this issue. Whether we be individuals, churches, or states of any civil entities, we are under one of the two governments. Christ illustrated this Biblical concept at the creation of the world. In Genesis God set up a voting booth, if you will, for all to choose whom he would serve:

> Genesis 2:16 "And the LORD God commanded the man, saying, Of every tree of the garden thou mayest freely eat:"
> Genesis 2:17 "But of the tree of the knowledge of good and evil, thou shalt not eat of it: for in the day that thou eatest thereof thou shalt surely die."

Fortunately for man, he was given a second chance as to whom he would serve and under what government he would freely cooperate. It is here that we have failed to see the forest because we have been standing in the middle of the woods for too long. Like all stories in the Bible,

---

[22] George Fifield, *The Southern Watchman*, May 1, 1906.

as well as in the prophecies, there is a big picture that we often overlook.

The central theme and focus behind all these accounts given in the Bible is the ongoing controversy over the two warring ideologies, the government of God verses the government of Satan. With our fuller understanding of God's government, we are now equipped to see the big picture. Fallen humanity now illustrates this ongoing warfare to the entire universe as each individual enlists under one of two governments. All now should be able to see with clearer vision the big picture behind the following illustrations. We begin by viewing the bigger picture concept which is clearly illustrated in the account of Adam and Eve:

> "*The law of God existed before the creation of man or else Adam could not have sinned.* After the transgression of Adam the principles of the law were not changed, but were definitely arranged and expressed to meet man in his fallen condition. The angels were governed by it [the law]. Satan fell because he transgressed the principles of *God's government.* After Adam and Eve were created, God made known to them His law. It was not then written, but was rehearsed to them by Jehovah."[23]
>
> "Our first parents were not left without a warning of the danger that threatened them. Heavenly messengers opened to them the history of Satan's fall and his plots for their destruction, unfolding more fully the nature of the *divine government, which the prince of evil was trying to overthrow.* It was by disobedience to the just commands of God that Satan and his host had fallen. How important, then, that Adam and Eve should honor that law by which alone it was possible for order and equity to be maintained.
>
> The law of God is as sacred as God Himself. It is a revelation of His will, a transcript of His character, the expression of divine love and wisdom. The harmony of creation depends upon the perfect conformity of all be-

---

[23] Ellen White, *The Faith I Live By*, (Hagerstown, MD: Review and Herald, 2000), 80.

ings, of everything, animate and inanimate, to the law of the Creator. God has ordained laws for the government, not only of living beings, but of all the operations of nature. Everything is under fixed laws, which cannot be disregarded. But while everything in nature is governed by natural laws, man alone, of all that inhabits the earth, is amenable to moral law. To man, the crowning work of creation, God has given power to understand His requirements, to comprehend the justice and beneficence of His law, and its sacred claims upon him; and of man unswerving obedience is required."[24]

Another example illustrating this conflict between these two ideologies is taken from the account of Cain and Abel:

"*Abel did not try to force Cain* to obey God's command. It was *Cain, inspired by Satan and filled with wrath, who used force. Furious because he could not compel Abel to disobey God,* and because God had accepted Abel's offering and refused his, which did not recognize the Saviour, Cain killed his brother.

The two parties represented by Cain and Abel will exist till the close of this earth's history. The well-doer, the obedient man, does not war against the transgressor of God's holy law. But those who do not respect the law of God oppress and persecute their fellow-men. They follow their leader, who is an accuser of God and of those who are made perfect through obedience."[25]

"God set the seventh day apart as the day of his rest. *But the man of sin has set up a false sabbath, which the kings and merchants of the earth have accepted and exalted above the Sabbath of the Bible. In doing this they have chosen a religion like that of Cain, who slew his brother Abel.* Cain and Abel both offered sacrifice to God. Abel's offering was accepted because

---

[24] Ellen White, *Patriarch and Prophets*, (Nampa, ID: Pacific Press, 1958), 52.
[25] Ellen White, *Signs of the Times*, March 21, 1900.

he complied with God's requirements. Cain's was rejected because he followed his own human inventions. Because of this he became so angry that he would not listen to Abel's entreaties or to God's warnings and reproofs, but slew his brother. By accepting a spurious rest day the churches have dishonored God. The people of the world accept the falsehood, and are angry because God's commandment keeping people do not respect and reverence Sunday."[26]

The story of Moses and Pharaoh is far more than just the plagues falling on Egypt. Its primary issue illustrates again the conflict between the two governments:

"Moses and Aaron were God's representatives to a bold, defiant king, and to impenitent priests, hardened in rebellion, who had allied themselves to evil angels. Pharaoh and the great men of Egypt were not ignorant in regard to the wise *government of God*. A bright light had been shining through the ages, pointing to God, to his righteous government, and to the claims of his law. Joseph and the children of Israel in Egypt had made known the knowledge of God. Even after the people of Israel had been brought into bondage to the Egyptians, not all were regarded as slaves. Many were placed in important positions, and these were witnesses for God."[27]

. . . ."Now the great controversy was fully entered upon; for months the warfare between the Prince of Life and the prince of darkness was carried on. The same work which Satan began in heaven he carried on upon the earth,—the powers of darkness warring against the mandate of Jehovah, the king of Egypt in controversy with the Monarch of heaven."[28]

While the Bible contains numerous examples on this wise, we shall share just one more on this account in the rebellion of Korah:

---

[26] Ellen White, *The Kress Collection*, 147-8.
[27] Ellen White, *Youth Instructor*, April 8, 1897.
[28] Ibid., April 15, 1897.

"In the rebellion of Korah is seen the working out, upon a narrower stage, of the same spirit that led to the rebellion of Satan in heaven. It was pride and ambition that prompted Lucifer to complain of the *government of God*, and to seek the overthrow of the order which had been established in heaven. Since his fall it has been his object to infuse the same spirit of envy and discontent, the same ambition for position and honor, into the minds of men. He thus worked upon the minds of Korah, Dathan, and Abiram, to arouse the desire for self-exaltation and excite envy, distrust, and rebellion. Satan caused them to reject God as their leader, by rejecting the men of God's appointment. Yet while in their murmuring against Moses and Aaron they blasphemed God, they were so deluded as to think themselves righteous, and to regard those who had faithfully reproved their sins as actuated by Satan."[29]

These visual aids should bring the following quote into a new perspective:

"'Whereunto,' asked Christ, 'shall we liken the kingdom of God? or with what comparison shall we compare it?' Mark 4:30. He could not employ the kingdoms of the world as a similitude. In society He found nothing with which to compare it. Earthly kingdoms rule by the ascendancy of physical power; but from Christ's kingdom every carnal weapon, every instrument of coercion, is banished."[30]

Spiritual things are spiritually discerned and if we were now to look a little closer, we would see this theme woven through every fiber of the Bible. It is no wonder fallen humanity has not fully comprehended this underlying principle which is throughout the Bible. Heaven has declared, as we have already seen, that these two governments must be exhibited for the entire universe to

---

[29] Ellen White, *Patriarch and Prophets*, (Nampa, ID: Pacific Press, 1958), 403.

[30] Ellen White, *The Acts of the Apostles*, (Nampa, ID: Pacific Press, 1911), 12.

see, and in so doing Satan is revealed for what he is, "the god of forces" Daniel 11:38. Here is another double symbolism, "the god of forces" primarily represents Satan it is, in a secondary sense, a symbol of civil entities that restrict liberty of conscience.

> "The heavenly universe must see the principles which Satan declared were superior to God's principles, worked out. God's order must be contrasted with the new order after Satan's devising. The corrupting principles of Satan's rule must be revealed."[31]

Our understandings in life are generally all dependent upon what we have seen, heard, and experienced. When Christ could find nothing in society with which to compare the kingdom of God, it becomes apparent how fallen mortals could have so easily missed the mark.

With this Biblical premise solidly established as to what the government of God is in contrast to that of the government of Satan, we are now ready to illustrate the next phase of our study:

> "Those who will not accept the light in regard to the law of God will not understand the proclamation of the first, second, and third angels' messages."[32]

By rightly connecting the government of God as the underlying theme of the 1260, 1290, 1335, and the 2300-day/year prophecies in the book of Daniel, we will have established the Biblical premise that solidifies our prophetic interpretations and understandings for the A.D. 508, 538, 1798, and 1843 dates. For a Biblical study of A.D. 1844, the 2300-day/year prophetic period with an exposition on Daniel 8:9-14, see my book, *The "Daily" Source Book*. We begin our study to fully validate that the 538 date under inquiry as being trustworthy and true.

---

[31] Ellen White, *Manuscript Releases*, (Silver Spring, Maryland: E.G. White Estate, 1993), 18:361.

[32] Ellen G. White, *Testimonies to Ministers and Gospel Workers* (Nampa, ID: Pacific Press, 1962), 115.

2

The Ten Horns

In order to diagnose carefully the given specifications and clauses of the ten horns emerging after A.D. 476 which are interrelated to the "little horn" in the book of Daniel, we must contend with the given text of the Bible that directly introduces our topic. As with the fourth beast of Daniel 7 and its ten horns, the great statue of Daniel 2 is likewise a symbol all the way to its toes. Again, our first work is to identify and interpret aright each clause and symbol of the following scriptures directly related to the ten toes as well as to the ten horns:

> Daniel 2:40 "And the fourth kingdom shall be strong as iron: forasmuch as iron breaketh in pieces and subdueth all *things*: and as iron that breaketh all these, shall it break in pieces and bruise.

> Daniel 2:41 "And whereas thou sawest the feet and [ten] toes, part of potters' clay, and part of iron, the kingdom shall be divided; but there shall be in it of the strength of the iron, forasmuch as thou sawest the iron mixed with miry clay.

> Daniel 2:42 "And *as* the toes of the feet *were* part of iron, and part of clay, *so* the kingdom shall be partly strong, and partly broken.

> Daniel 2:43 "And whereas thou sawest iron mixed with miry clay, they shall mingle themselves with the seed of men: but they shall not cleave one to another, even as iron is not mixed with clay.

Daniel 2:44 "And in the days of these kings shall the God of heaven set up a kingdom, which shall never be destroyed: and the kingdom shall not be left to other people, *but* it shall break in pieces and consume all these kingdoms, and it shall stand for ever.

Daniel 2:45 "Forasmuch as thou sawest that the stone was cut out of the mountain without hands, and that it brake in pieces the iron, the brass, the clay, the silver, and the gold; the great God hath made known to the king what shall come to pass hereafter: and the dream *is* certain, and the interpretation thereof sure."

Daniel 7:7 "After this I saw in the night visions, and behold a fourth beast, dreadful and terrible, and strong exceedingly; and it had great iron teeth: it devoured and brake in pieces, and stamped the residue with the feet of it: and it *was* diverse from all the beasts that *were* before it; and it had ten horns."

Daniel 7:20 "And of the ten horns that *were* in his head, and *of* the other which came up, and before whom three fell; even *of* that horn that had eyes, and a mouth that spake very great things, whose look *was* more stout than his fellows."

Daniel 7:24 "And the ten horns out of this kingdom *are* ten kings *that* shall arise: and another shall rise after them; and he shall be diverse from the first, and he shall subdue three kings."

Revelation 12:3 "And there appeared another wonder in heaven; and behold a great red dragon, having seven heads and ten horns, and seven crowns upon his heads."

Revelation 13:1 "And I stood upon the sand of the sea, and saw a beast rise up out of the sea, having seven heads and ten horns, and upon his horns ten crowns, and upon his heads the name of blasphemy."

Revelation 17:3 "So he carried me away in the spirit into the wilderness: and I saw a woman sit upon a scarlet coloured beast, full of names of blasphemy, having seven heads and <u>ten horns</u>."

Revelation 17:12 "And the <u>ten horns</u> which thou sawest <u>are ten kings</u>, which have received no kingdom as yet; but receive power as kings one hour with the beast."

In Daniel 7:20, the little horn (papacy) was declared to be "more <u>stout</u> [larger] than his fellows," the ten horns. The meaning behind this is clarified by the antecedent, "whose <u>look</u> *was* more stout than his fellows." "Look" means vision or sight. The central thought being conveyed here by heaven so that we apprehend this characteristic of the identity of the little horn is that her existence or birth was prior to the existence of the ten horns in A.D. 476.

It is evident that the kingdoms representing the ten toes of Daniel 2:40-45 remain so until "the stone was cut out of the mountain without hands, and that it brake in pieces the iron, the brass, the clay, the silver, and the gold. . ." that is, until the second coming of Jesus Christ. The scriptures declare, "In the days of these kings shall the God of heaven set up a kingdom, which shall never be destroyed. . . ." The kingdom of God is not set up or given to Christ until after the books are first opened and then closed in the investigative judgment described in Daniel 7. This event did not commence until October 22, 1844, which may be confirmed from Daniel 8:14.

"Every case had been decided for life or death. While Jesus had been ministering in the sanctuary, the judgment had been going on for the righteous dead, and then for the righteous living. *Christ had received His kingdom*, having made the atonement for His people and blotted out their sins. *The subjects of the kingdom were made up.* The marriage of the Lamb was consummated. *And the kingdom, and the greatness of the kingdom under the whole heaven, was given to Jesus and the heirs of salvation, and Jesus was to reign as King of kings and Lord of lords."*[33]

It is not without significance that the scriptual emphasis of the ten toes of Daniel 2 are at the time of the end in a post-1844 time period when the God of heaven is setting up His kingdom and when the vision (the 2300-day/year prophecy) was to be understood. (Daniel 8:14, 17) The correlation between the ten toes and the ten horns of Revelation 17:12 will be shown to have their application in a post-1844 judgment era, as well. However, the ten horns are then given additional details in Daniel 7 and are also being pictured as coming on the stage of action after the demise of the fourth beast. This is confirmed by the following scriptures:

> Daniel 7:7 "After this I saw in the night visions, and behold a fourth beast, dreadful and terrible, and strong exceedingly; and it had great iron teeth: it devoured and brake in pieces, and stamped the residue with the feet of it: and it *was* diverse from all the beasts that *were* before it; and it had <u>ten horns</u>."

> Daniel 7:8 "I considered the horns, and, behold, there came up among them another little horn, before whom there were three of the first horns plucked up by the roots: and, behold, in this horn *were* eyes like the eyes of man, and a mouth speaking great things."

> Daniel 7:20 "And of the ten horns that *were* in his head, and *of* the other which came up, and before whom three fell; even *of* that horn that had eyes, and a mouth that spake very great things, whose look *was* more stout than his fellows."

> Daniel 7:24 "And the ten horns out of this kingdom *are* ten kings *that* shall arise: and another shall rise after them; and he shall be diverse from the first, and he shall subdue three kings."

---

[33] Ellen White, *Early Writings*, (Washington, D.C: Review and Herald, 1945), 280.

Daniel 7:25 "And he shall speak *great* words against the most High, and shall wear out the saints of the most High, and think to change times and laws: and they shall be given into his hand until a time and times and the dividing of time."

Daniel 7:26 "But the judgment shall sit, and they shall take away his dominion, to consume and to destroy *it* unto the end."

Daniel 7:27 "And the kingdom and dominion, and the greatness of the kingdom under the whole heaven, shall be given to the people of the saints of the most High, whose kingdom *is* an everlasting kingdom, and all dominions shall serve and obey him."

Daniel 7:28 "Hitherto *is* the end of the matter. . ."

This has brought prophetic interpreters to a crossroad. An area of concern which has caused much confusion is whether the ten toes and the ten horns of Daniel and Revelation should be understood in a literal (ten literal kingdoms) or in a symbolic sense (all encompassing). For our answer, we must turn to the scriptures. Daniel gave us a definitive clue as to the answer we seek:

Daniel 2:44 "And in the days of these kings shall the God of heaven set up a kingdom, which shall never be destroyed. . . ."

The phrase "these kings" quite emphatically sets the precedent for our Biblical understanding and interpretation for the ten toes as well as for the ten horns. Ellen White fully understood this concept and correctly interpreted its meaning:

"The so-called Christian world is to be the theater of great and decisive actions. Men in authority will enact laws controlling the conscience, after the example of the papacy. Babylon will make all nations drink of the wine of the wrath of her fornication. Every nation will be involved. Of this time John the Revelator declares: [Revelation 18:3-7, quoted].

"These have one mind, and shall give their power

and strength unto the beast. These shall make war with
the Lamb, and the Lamb shall overcome them: for He
is Lord of lords, and King of kings: and they that are
with Him are called, and chosen, and faithful"
[Revelation 17:13, 14].

"These have one mind." There will be a universal
bond of union, one great harmony, a confederacy of
Satan's forces. "And shall give their power and strength
unto the beast." Thus is manifested the same arbitrary,
oppressive power against religious liberty, freedom to
worship God according to the dictates of conscience, as
was manifested by the papacy, when in the past it persecuted those who dared to refuse to conform with the
religious rites and ceremonies of Romanism.

In the warfare to be waged in the last days there
will be united, in opposition to God's people, all the
corrupt powers that have apostatized from allegiance
to the law of Jehovah. In this warfare the Sabbath of
the fourth commandment will be the great point at
issue; for in the Sabbath commandment the great
Law-giver identifies Himself as the Creator of the
heavens and the earth."[34]

Who are "all the corrupt powers that have apostatized from allegiance to the law of Jehovah"? In order to
find the answer, we must look at the antecedent of "all"
and "these" that "have one mind" and shall establish a
"universal bond of union . . . a confederacy of Satan's
forces. . . And shall give their power and strength unto
the beast." This is found in the verse preceding the Bible
text she just quoted in Revelation 17:13. It is, of course,
found in verse 12:

Revelation 17:12 "And the ten horns which thou
sawest are ten kings, which have received no kingdom as
yet; but receive power as kings one hour with the beast."

34 Ellen White, *Manuscript Releases*, (Silver Spring, Maryland: E.G.
White Estate, 1993), 19:242-3.

The "these" of Revelation 17:13 that form a "universal bond of union" is none other than the "ten horns" of
Revelation 17:12, and "these kings" of Daniel 2:44 are
the same "kings" of Revelation 17:12 that exist until the
second coming of Jesus Christ. Ellen White further clarifies:

> "As America, the land of religious liberty, shall
> unite with the papacy in forcing the conscience and
> compelling men to honor the false sabbath, the people
> of *every country on the globe will be led to follow her ex-
> ample*."[35]

> "Foreign nations will follow the example of the
> United States. Though she leads out, yet the same cri-
> sis will come upon our people *in all parts of the
> world*."[36]

What numerical value does Ellen White attach to this
"universal bond of union"? With "every country on the
globe" included, its symbolic meaning is obvious and, indeed, all encompassing. But, more importantly, what numerical value does the Bible attach to this universal
bond of union in Revelation17:12? Revelation 13:3 tells
us that after the deadly wound is healed:

> ". . . . all the world wondered after the beast."

The apparent meaning of the text renders it "every
country on the globe." As to the number of countries existing in our world, little has changed since October 22,
1844. At present there are over 200 kingdoms/nations/
horns. Based upon the Bible and the Spirit of Prophecy,
this "universal bond of union" enforces indisputably a
symbolic interpretation for the ten toes and ten horns
found in the prophecies of Daniel and Revelation. The
number "ten" in the Bible is easily designated as an all

---

[35] Ellen White, *Testimonies for the Church*, (Boise, ID: Pacific Press,
1948), 6:18.
[36] Ibid., 395.

inclusive symbol. This is illustrated by the parable of the ten virgins:

> "Then shall the kingdom of heaven be likened unto ten virgins, which took their lamps, and went forth to meet the bridegroom." Matthew 25:1.

The parable of the ten virgins is a symbol of the church:

> "As Christ sat looking upon the party that waited for the bridegroom, He told His disciples the story of the ten virgins, by their experience illustrating the experience of the church that shall live just before His second coming."[37]

It has never been disputed, and rightly so, that there are only ten people in God's universal church today; hence, the all inclusive symbolic interpretation is readily apparent. When heaven placed the emphasis of the ten toes of Daniel 2 in the post-era of October 22, 1844, any just cause for a literal interpretation to be applied to the ten horns was removed. The Bible does not support both a symbolic and literal view of the ten toes/horns. We cannot say the number ten is symbolic at the consummation and at its commencement the number ten is taken to be literal. This would be confusion compounded. Thus, the Biblical interpretation is established and supported by the Bible and Spirit of Prophecy. This, therefore, clears the air of the many inconsistencies of those who claim that the ten horns in Daniel 7:7, 20, 24 are ten literal kings.

To begin with, there were far more than ten literal kings to be found within the borders of the Western Roman Empire in A.D. 476. Here is a partial list:

> Alemanni, Basques, Belgi, Burgundians, Dacians, Franks, Gauls, Helvetii, Heruli, Iberians, Italians, Libyans, Lombards, Ostrogoths, Saxons, Slavic, Vandals, Visigoths.

---

[37] Ellen White, *Christ Object Lessons*, (Washington, D.C: Review and Herald, 1941), 406.

Even those tribes that invaded the Western Roman Empire numbered more than ten:

Allemanni, Burgundians, Celts, Franks, Gauls, Germani, Heruli, Huns, Lombards, Moors, Ostrogoths, Quodi, Suevi, Vandals, Visigoths.

Since there were more than ten tribes found within the borders of the Western Roman Empire in A.D. 476 and more than ten tribes that invaded the ancient Roman Empire, a literal interpretation of ten kings in no way stands the test of investigation. More than this, it would have to be shown that the ten literal kings were contemporaries, all reigning at the same time like they do in Revelation 17:12. However, the proponents of the literal ten kings cannot account for the fact that some of the tribes on their list that are designated to be part of the ten kings have disappeared from the stage of action. Furthermore, the proponents of the literal ten kings must admit that these ten horns no longer exist. So who, then, are the ten horns that are destroyed at the end of time in Daniel 2:44-45 and Revelation 17:12? When the Bible speaks of three literal, uprooted horns or kingdoms in Daniel 7:8, 20, and 24, the proponents of the literal ten kings claim that this proves there were ten kings because only seven have remained. However, the Bible nowhere says there remained seven horns out of the ten nor is it even so much as implied. This has simply been read into the text. If the Bible had confirmed that seven had indeed remained upon the stage of action, the interpretation would require no commentary. As correctly stated by Dr. Pfandl:

"Though many interpreters have tried to identify exactly 10 peoples and 10 kingdoms descending from them, it is best to take the number 10 as a round figure (e.g., Gen. 31:7; Num. 14:22; 1 Sam. 1:8; etc.), including a multiplicity of states in contrast to the one empire of Rome."[38]

---

[38] Gerhard Pfandl, *Daniel the Seer of Babylon*, (Hagerstown, MD: Review and Herald, 2004), 63.

Submitted are the previously quoted texts:

Genesis 31:7 "And your father hath deceived me, and changed my wages ten times; but God suffered him not to hurt me."

Numbers 14:22 "Because all those men which have seen my glory, and my miracles, which I did in Egypt and in the wilderness, and have tempted me now these ten times, and have not hearkened to my voice;"

1 Samuel 1:8 "Then said Elkanah her husband to her, Hannah, why weepest thou? and why eatest thou not? and why is thy heart grieved? *am* not I better to thee than ten sons?"

And likewise from Dr. Shea:

"It probably is preferable to take the number ten as a round number which may have fluctuated up or down at any given historical time, according to the political and military fortunes of those various powers."[39]

It becomes apparent that a literal interpretation of ten kings will not stand the test of investigation and, quite frankly, should be forthrightly discarded, for it has brought only reproach to the cause.

The following information is given to help the reader better understand the remaining texts of Revelation in their fullest sense in relation to the ten horns. In defining the "dragon" we believe all are agreed that it primarily represents Satan:

Revelation 12:9 "And the great dragon was cast out, that old serpent, called the Devil, and Satan, which deceiveth the whole world: he was cast out into the earth, and his angels were cast out with him."

However the "dragon" has a secondary application, as well:

---

[39] William Shea, *Daniel 1-7*, (Boise, ID: Pacific Press, 1996), 167.

Revelation 12:3 "And there appeared another wonder in heaven; and behold a great red dragon, having
seven heads and ten horns, and seven crowns upon his
heads."

Revelation 12:4 "And his tail drew the third part of
the stars of heaven, and did cast them to the earth: and
the dragon stood before the woman which was ready
to be delivered, for to devour her child as soon as it
was born."

Revelation 12:5 "And she brought forth a man
child, who was to rule all nations with a rod of iron:
and her child was caught up unto God, and *to* his
throne."

Certainly, the great red dragon was Satan who sought
to destroy the man-child Christ Jesus, but what kingdom
did Satan work through to accomplish this end? We are
told Satan works through "a great red dragon having
seven heads and ten horns." Notice the seven crowns are
upon his heads, meaning the heads are ruling. In
prophecy a beast represents a political power:

Daniel 7:17 "These great beasts, which are four,
are four kings, which shall arise out of the earth."

Therefore, the dragon, which is a beast, must represent political powers that are used by Satan to oppose
the cause of God. The seven heads, therefore, represent
the seven main kingdoms Satan has skillfully used
throughout human history to accomplish his greatest ob-
jectives. These "heads" rule successively, one after the
other, while the ten horns are contemporaries; they all
reign at the same time. The ruling "head" that sought to
devour the Christ child as soon as He was born was none
other than pagan Rome:

"The line of prophecy in which these symbols are
found begins with Revelation 12, with the dragon that
sought to destroy Christ at His birth. The dragon is
said to be Satan (Revelation 12:9); he it was that
moved upon Herod to put the Saviour to death. But the

chief agent of Satan in making war upon Christ and His people during the first centuries of the Christian Era was the Roman Empire, in which paganism was the prevailing religion. *Thus while the dragon, primarily, represents Satan, it is, in a secondary sense, a symbol of pagan Rome.*"[40]

It was pagan Rome and it is pagan Rome again that is represented as a "dragon" in Bible prophecy. The dragon had "seven crowns upon its heads." Crowns denote rulership, showing that the period when this particular dragon power is spoken of the heads are ruling, not the ten horns. Revelation 17:9-10 reveals that the seven heads are seven mountains that rule "successively":

> Revelation 17:9 "And here *is* the mind which hath wisdom. The seven heads are seven mountains, on which the woman sitteth."

> Revelation 17:10 "And there are seven kings: five are fallen, and one is, *and* the other is not yet come; and when he cometh, he must continue a short space."

Revelation 17:9-10 also reveals that the seven heads are seven "mountains" or "kingdoms" that rule successively:

> Jeremiah 51:25 "Behold, I   against thee, <u>O destroying mountain</u>, [Babylon] saith the LORD, which destroyest all the earth: and I will stretch out mine hand upon thee, and roll thee down from the rocks, and will make thee a <u>burnt mountain</u>."

> Daniel 2:35 "Then was the iron, the clay, the brass, the silver, and the gold, broken to pieces together, and became like the chaff of the summer threshingfloors; and the wind carried them away, that no place was found for them: and the stone that smote the image <u>became a great mountain</u>, and filled the whole earth."

---

[40] Ellen White, *The Great Controversy*, (Nampa, ID: Pacific Press, 1911), 438.

> Daniel 2:44 "And in the days of <u>these kings</u> shall the God of heaven set up a <u>kingdom</u>, which shall never be destroyed: and the <u>kingdom</u> shall not be left to other people, *but* <u>it shall break in pieces and consume all these kingdoms</u>, and it shall stand for ever."

Thus it has been shown that the seven "heads" are seven "kingdoms" that reign one after the other, whereas, the ten horns are revealed to be contemporaneous, that is, they all reign together and at the same time. The crowns on the heads indicate that when the dragon is brought into the picture at the birth of Christ in Revelation 12:2-4, one of the heads was reigning and that head or empire was Imperial or pagan Rome. When the crowns are presented to us as upon the ten horns, as pictured in Revelation 13:1, it denotes that the sea beast or the papacy is in power when the ten horns are ruling, when the Western European kingdoms have been formed and are in power. The reason we see no crowns in Revelation chapter 17 is because Revelation 17:1 informs us that the woman is under "judgment" or "punishment,"[2917] as correctly stated in the Greek. Her kingdom, "that great city," is being totally and eternally destroyed (Revelation 17:16-18). Babylon the Great no longer reigns.

3

The Three Uprooted Horns

In Daniel 8:20 a horn represents a king or kingdom:

Daniel 8:20 "The ram[352] which[834] thou sawest[7200] having[1167] *two* horns[7161] *are* the kings[4428] of Media[4074] and Persia."[6539]

In Daniel 7:8, 20 and verse 24, we then have the uprooting or demise of three literal horns or kingdoms:

Daniel 7:8 "I considered[1934, 7920] the horns,[7162] and, behold,[431] there came up[5559] among[997] them another[317] little[2192] horn,[7162] before[4481, 6925] whom there were three[8532] of[4481] the first[6933] horns[7162] plucked up by the roots:[6132] and, behold,[431] in this[1668] horn[7162] *were* eyes[5870] like the eyes[5870] of man,[606] and a mouth[6433] speaking[4449] great things."[7260]

Daniel 7:20 "And of[5922] the ten[6236] horns[7162] that[1768] *were* in his head,[7217] and *of* the other[317] which[1768] came up,[5559] and before[4481, 6925] whom three[8532] fell;[5308] even *of* that[1797] horn[7162] that had eyes,[5870] and a mouth[6433] that spoke[4449] very great things,[7260] whose look[2376] *was* more stout[7229] than[4481] his fellows."[2273]

Daniel 7:24 "And the ten[6236] horns[7162] out of[4481] this kingdom[4437] *are* ten[6236] kings[4430] *that* shall arise:[6966] and another[321] shall rise[6966] after[311] them; and he[1932] shall be diverse[8133] from[4481] the first,[6933] and he shall subdue[8214] three[8532] kings."[4430] KJV

33

The following material is taken from a thesis by Mervin C. Maxwell and establishes some Biblical and significant points about the uprooting of the three horns:

[Pg.24] "In Daniel the 1260 days are designated as "three and a half times." In Daniel 7:24-26 the statement is:

"And the ten horns out of this kingdom are ten kings that shall arise: and another shall rise after them; and he shall be diverse from the first, and he shall subdue three kings."

"And he shall speak great words against the most High, and shall wear out the saints of the most High, and think to change times and laws: [25] and they shall be given into his hand until a time and times and the dividing of time."

"And the judgment shall sit, and they shall take away his dominion, to consume and to destroy it unto the end."

Significant pointers can be gained from these verses as to the nature of the 1260 years, and a little about its dating, including:

1) The "Little Horn" is not to arise until after the Roman Empire is divided.

2) The Little Horn is to be different from the other kingdoms, and is to persecute, blaspheme, and change laws.

3) "They" are to be given into his hands for 3½ times. Apparently "they" are great words against God, the saints, and the laws.

There are some things which this passage does not teach. For instance, it does not say that the Little Horn is to have the mastery over the ten horns (or even seven of them) for the entire 3½ times. This is not even suggested. Secondly, neither this passage nor its context gives the plucking up of the three horns as necessary before the 3½ times can begin. It is true that verse 8 says that "before him three of the first horns were plucked up," but this "before" is translated from the Aramaic qodam, which means place, and not time.[41] As a matter [26] of fact, apart from the expression "after them," that is, after the ten kings, there is no indication

---

[41] "According to Young's Concordance, the Aramaic word qodam is used 31 times in the Old Testament: Three times in Ezra, and twenty seven times in Daniel. Thirty of the Old Testament: Three times in Ezra, and twenty seven times in Daniel. Thirty of these times it is translated "before," and once, "in the presence of," Daniel 2:27. In every case but two there is no question but that the word means "in the presence of." Examples of such usage include Ezra 7:19 and Daniel 6:10, 26; 7:10, 13, where the translation is "before God." Obviously this cannot mean "before God was in existence," and so must mean "in His presence." In Ezra 4:18 it is "before the people." In most other references it describes activities taking place "before" the king, and again there is no question but that the usage is in reference to location and not time.

The two cases where there might be any question are in Daniel 7. Daniel 7:7 says, "And it [the fourth beast] was diverse from all the beasts that were before it." Here time might be indicated instead of location, but verse 12, which says the lives of the beasts were prolonged, and Revelation 13, which shows them all living in composite form even after the fall of Rome, indicate that the first three beasts stayed "in the presence of " one another as they appeared in turn.

The other verse where there might be a question is, of course, verse 8, the one under discussion: "before whom there were three of the first horns plucked up by the roots." In this case the usage of qodam in 29 other instances should be conclusive, but there is further evidence. In this verse and in the parallel passage, verse 20, which contains the phrase "before whom three fell," the word qodam is coupled with the word min to form the phrase min qodam, meaning, literally, "from the East." This Aramaic idiom cannot, by any stretch of the imagination, be said to convey the sense of time. Other instances of the use of this idiom occur in Daniel 5:19 and 6:26 where reference is made to the people fearing "before" God. Since, as above, this cannot be construed to mean "before God existed," it must mean, "in His presence."

It must be concluded, therefore, that the reference to the three horns' being plucked up before the little horn gives no indication as to the timing of the 1260 days, and that any discussion based on the supposition that it does, is without value."

in Daniel 7 as to the timing of the 3½ times or 1260 days."[42]

When Mervin C. Maxwell stated the following in his footnote he was absolutely correct:

> "It must be concluded, therefore, that the reference to the three horns' being plucked up <u>before</u> the little horn gives no indication as to the timing of the 1260 days, and that any discussion based on the supposition that it does, is without value."[43]

Here is where some have read into the text that which is not there nor implied. Since the Bible does not give any definitive dating for the uprooting of the three horns, neither do we. This removes all the arguments from the opposition on that perspective. This Biblical premise should have been a clue to students of prophecy that the precise dating for the uprooting of the three horns was obviously not to be the signal event that was to indicate the commencement of the 1260, 1290, or the 1335-day/year prophecies in the book of Daniel, even though their demise had a prophetic role to play. To say otherwise reveals that we choose to sail in waters without chart or compass when the scriptures are directing our minds elsewhere. That elsewhere is emphasized in Daniel 7:25 when he shall "think to change times and laws" and then the little horn was to reign for "a time and times and the dividing of time." In Daniel 7:24 when the "little horn" (papacy) was to "subdue three kings," it did not say the papacy was to engage itself in a military conflict, for of itself it had no such army. Just the same, the little horn was to "subdue." Webster's primary definition

---

[42] Mervin C. Maxwell, *An Exegetical and Historical Examination of the Beginning and Ending of the 1260 days of Prophecy with special attention given to A. D. 538 and 1798 as Initial and Terminal Dates.* A Thesis Presented to the faculty of the Seventh-day Adventist Theological Seminary Washington, D.C. August 1951. (Andrews University, Berrien Springs, MI.), 24-26.

[43] Ibid; footnote.

for "subdue" is "to bring into subjection"[44] and, as we will see, this description is precisely the intent of the scriptures. Subdue can also mean to *suppress, hold back, check, discipline, conquer, vanquish, overcome,* or *control.* In other words, the little horn would work from behind the scenes to accomplish her means. The emphasis of the scriptures on the uprooting of the three horns prior to the fulfilling role of the little horn according to the prophecy is certainly implied but was not denied nor established on the basis of time. Although heaven could have easily specified the exact time of the downfall of these three kingdoms, it chose not to do this, so we would not misplace the central emphasis on a horizontal plane or on earthly events rather than the vertical plane or main heavenly event of the prophecy to which the scriptures are directing us. Heaven knew that the uprooting of the three horns would naturally bring the inquisitive reader to comprehend why those kingdoms were subdued or brought into subjection to the little horn, and that history would supply the exact dating for the three uprooted horns. The reason for this was emphatically established in our *A.D. 508 Source Book* as we witnessed the conflict being played out between the two separate and distinct ideologies. Those two separate and distinct ideologies, the government of God against the government of Satan, were played out between the Arians and the Catholic Church. The Arians who legally promoted religious liberty (albeit in its primitive state) refused to compel the conscience of either Catholic or Arian in religious matters which was in sharp contrast to the Catholic Church who lawfully rejected religious liberty and had no scruples in compelling all in matters of liberty of conscience. There was nothing mysterious or hidden here, for each side fully understood the other. If the Catholic Church was to regain her universal authority in the new world as she had attained under the pagan

---

[44] *Webster's New World Dictionary*-College Edition, (Cleveland and New York: The World Publishing Co. 1955), 1451.

Roman Empire when on February 28, 380,[45] the Catholic faith became the established state religion of the empire, then she must address the primary obstacle in her path. She would have to remove the concept of religious liberty from the hearts and lives of those that advocated its principles. With firsthand experience of the oppressive government of the papacy under the pagan Roman Empire, the Arians had no desire to have ambitious prelates, world-loving churchmen, and the self-important popes dictating over them again. Thus, the stage was set. Let it be remembered that in the book of Daniel the little horn is pictured as fighting vertically against Christ and His saints, stars, and the host of heaven signifying not a political, but a religious warfare. The hate and smear campaigns manifested against the Arians (as we saw in my *A.D. 508 Source Book*) by the Catholic Church was demonstrated by Saint Caesarius of Arles' commentary on Revelation when he declared in no uncertain terms the true position of the Catholic Church towards Arianism and indicated that it was the most dreaded foe of the church:

> "And all the earth wondered at and followed the beast, and they worshiped the dragon which gave power to the beast": the heretics have power without condition, *but especially the Arians.* "And they worshiped the beast, saying, who is like the beast? or who will be able to fight with it?" Therefore because the heretics delude themselves with this, that no one believes more than those, and that no one conquers the nation of those, which bases its reputation on the name of the beast: to which it was given by the devil himself, and was permitted by God, to speak great things and blasphemies; just as the Apostle says: "It is necessary that there are heresies, so that those who have been proven, may be manifest in you" I Corinthians 11:19. "And there was given to him the power to make forty-two months": the time of the very recent persecution

---

[45] Original Latin text in Mommsen, *Theodosiani libri XVI*, vol. 1-2, "De fide catholica," p. 833.

we understand in those forty-two months. "And then he opened his mouth into blasphemy against God": here it is clear that those who have withdrawn from the Catholic Church are signified;"[46]

Had we, as a church, previously understood the foundational premise correctly for the four prophetic periods of Daniel as was firmly established in chapter 1, our focus would not have been so limited to the horizontal or secondary view, which is looking for the primary fulfillment of prophecy in earthly persons, places, or things. Rightly understood, the Bible has always emphasized the primary view and application as being vertical, pointing to the true and universal issue, the government of God verses the government of Satan, the great controversy between Christ and Satan as it is depicted in every chapter of the book of Daniel. Everything else is subordinate to this central issue, the Law of God:

> Daniel 7:25 "And he shall <u>speak</u>[47]. . . . think to change times and <u>laws</u>."

Laws in the plural sense are designated here, the law of God and civil law. It was legislation that ultimately "set up" the little horn in A.D. 508[48] and it was legislation that brought down the little horn in A.D. 1798,[49] and it will be legislation that sets up or resurrects *again* the beast power in the form of the image to the beast.[50] In

---

[46] Patrologia Latina, Sancti Aurelii Augustini, *Expositio in Apocalypsim* B. Joannis, Saint Caesarius of Arles, 1841, 35: Homily X, 2436.

[47] "The "speaking" of the nation is the action of its <u>legislative</u> and <u>judicial authorities</u>." Ellen White, *Great Controversy*, (Nampa, ID: Pacific Press, 1911), 442.

[48] See my *A.D. 508 Source Book*.

[49] See my *A.D. 1798 1843 Source Book*.

[50] "When our nation shall so abjure the principles of its government as to enact a Sunday law, Protestantism will in this act join hands with popery; it will be nothing else than giving <u>life</u> [Rev. 13:15: "And he had power to give <u>life</u>. . . ."] to the tyranny which has long been eagerly watching its opportunity to spring again into active despotism. . . . If popery or its principles shall <u>again</u> be <u>legislated into power</u>, the

the final events of history, universal legislation will be the signal that brings down the little horn *again*, but this time it will be by the means of the seven last plagues.[51] We are yet to reveal in this study how legislation will play its part in the commencement of the 1260-day/year prophetic period. Simply put, the uprooting of the three horns is now placed in bold relief as its place and application in prophecy is manifest as a mile marker pointing foreword to the main event. It takes on only a secondary role, yet, nevertheless, an important role, but cannot be claimed in any sense of the meaning, in and of itself, to commence the beginning of the 1260, 1290, or the 1335-day/year prophecies.

However, the scriptures definitely affirm an uprooting or removal of three separate and distinct kingly powers or kingdoms in the life or in the presence of the papacy after A.D. 476. In an extremely significant letter, Pope Hormisdas writes to Justinian in February of 519. Amazing as it seems, the papacy singles herself out as the pope identifies the Catholic Church as the true source in rooting out her enemies, working from behind the scenes, fulfilling scripture.

> Daniel 7:8 "I considered the horns, and, behold, there came up among them another little horn, before whom there were three of the first horns plucked up by the roots: . . ."

A portion of the pope's letter to Justinian reads:

(*Cont.*)
fires of persecution will be rekindled against those who will not sacrifice conscience and the truth in deference to popular errors. This evil is on the point of realization." Ellen White, *Testimonies for the Church*, (Boise, ID: Pacific Press, 1948), 5:712.
[51] "Babylon the great is fallen, is fallen. . . . And I heard another voice from heaven, saying, Come out of her, my people, that ye be not partakers of her sins, and that ye receive not of her plagues. For her sins have reached unto heaven, and God hath remembered her iniquities." When do her sins reach unto heaven? When the law of God is finally made void by legislation." [Universally] Ellen White, *Signs of the Times*, June 12, 1893.

"The way to unity of the church is clear, the pre-
scriptions for it are known; the priests who love the
Catholic peace must not reject the Catholic confession.
For it is necessary that the falsehood not be just partly
improved but torn out by the root . . . Therefore go
forth as you have begun . . . Your sentiments as they appear in your writings to us are of the kind such that not
much exhortation is required for the execution of your
good intentions."[52]

With the church ultimately doing the rooting out,
commissioning Justinian to "go forth as you have begun"
with "the execution of your good intentions," this excerpt
requires no commentary. We will shortly view those so-
called good intentions of Justinian in his Corpus Juris
Civilis which was backed by the church when he became
the emperor in 527. Pope Hormisdas recognized what a
great interest Justinian had in the accomplishment of ecclesiastical peace and expressed his happiness about it in
letters to him and the emperor.[53] Emperor Justin appre-
ciated the organizational skill of his nephew Justinian
who was much more intellectually capable than he, and
entrusted him with the entire matter of making ecclesiastical peace between the east and western churches.
Therefore, we must look back into the history of the
church around A.D. 476 to see what three kings or kingdoms were considered by her to be the greatest threat or
challenge to her rising to worldly power and oppressive
control in the new world. Also, it must be determined
from the primary sources what kings or kingdoms, along

---

[52] "*Sacerdotes, qui catholicam pacem desiderant, professionem catholicam non recusant; . . . Animum quidem vestrum talem missa ad nos
testantur alloquia ut ad plenitudinem boni propositi non multum indi-
geatis hortatu.*"
Guenther, Otto, Epistulae Imperatorum Pontificum Aliorum, Avellana
Quae Dicitur Collectio, 2 pts. In Corpus Scriptorum Ecclesiasticorum
Latinorum, vol. 35. Prague: F. Tempsky, 1895, (ep. 57), 848. February,
519.
[53] Thiel ep. 48, 65, 77, 81, 90, 91, 95, 112. – Mansi VIII, 440, 454, 472,
482, 464, 484, 485, 518 –Baronius a. 519 and 520. Migne, Patr. lat. 63,
367—527.

with their military forces, the papacy used to achieve this objective.

Seventh-day Adventists have always recognized that there were three separate and distinct entities or kingdoms that were subdued by the little horn (papacy) of Daniel seven. However, there has been some disagreement as to the identities of those three kingdoms. The author of this study hopes to bring together a unified front that we may all move forward, united as a body and speaking with one voice. While all are agreed that the Vandals and the Ostrogoths are unquestionably two of the three kingdoms involved, it is the debate of the Heruli versus the Visigoths that has caused division among us. One side advocates the Heruli falling off the stage of action in A.D. 493 and another side advocates the demise of the Visigoths in A.D. 508. Since the Heruli are believed by some to be the first of the three Arian kingdoms to have been subdued by the little horn after A.D. 476, we will start there to see if the Heruli will withstand the test of investigation.

4

The Heruli

I have included several excerpts from the renowned historian Ferdinand Gregorovius because of his impeccable and unbiased integrity which is recognized among the academic community worldwide and the nearly unanimous agreement found among credible historians on the following era of chronological history. We begin by documenting the fall of Western Rome in A.D. 476 since it is here that the foundation has been laid according to the scriptures for the rise and existence of the ten horns that came onto the stage of action:

The Encyclopedia Britannica confirms the fall of Western Rome in A.D. 476:

> **A.D. 476** "The fall of Rome was completed in 476, when the German Chieftain Odoacer disposed the last Roman emperor of the West, Romulus Augustulus."[54]

The following historical excerpt by the world-renowned historian, Ferdinand Gregorovius, is quoted in its entirety for the purpose of documenting and establishing the fall of the Western Roman Empire in A.D. 476. This will serve the truth in its most equitable form:

"BOOK FIRST."
"FROM THE BEGINNING OF THE FIFTH

---

[54] *The New Encyclopedia Britannica*, (15th Edition, Chicago, IL. Encyclopedia Britannica, 1988), 10:154.

CENTURY TO THE FALL OF THE WESTERN EMPIRE
IN 476."[55]

Continuing from the same source:

"Orestes, however, judging it better to invest his
youthful son with the Imperial purple, cause Romulus
Augustulus to be proclaimed Emperor of the West,
Oct.31, 475. By the irony of fate, this, the last Emperor
of Rome, united in his person the names of the first
founder and the first Augustus of Rome.[56]

Only for a short time did he wear the purple, being
soon overthrown by the same rebellious mercenaries
to whom he had owned his dignity.[57] Since the time of
Alaric and Attila, the dying Empire had taken as allies
into its armies, Scyrri, Alans, Goths, and other barbarian tribes. These, with their leaders, now governed the
Empire, and weary of servitude they became naturally
masters of the country, the military power of which
had completely died away. The head of these bands at
that time was Odoacer, the son of Edecon, a Scyrrian
in the service of Attila, a man of the most adventurist
spirit, to whom as a youth, a prophecy had awarded
royal power in the future. "Go to Italy," was the command of Severin, a monk in Noricum, "go as thou art,
clad in wretched skins; soon thou wilt have great

---

[55] Ferdinand Gregorovius, Translated from the Fourth German
Edition, Mrs. Gustavus W. Hamilton , *History Of The City of Rome In
The Middle Ages*, (London, George Bell & Sons, 1900, First Published,
1894. Second Edition, Revised, 1900), xxxi.

[56] The *anon. Vales,:" Augustulus, qui ante regnum Romulus a paren-
tibus vocabatur, a patre Oreste Patricio factus est imperator."* For the
coins of the last Emperor with the inscription, *D.N.Romulus Augustus
P. F. Aug*, see cohen, vol.VIII. The Greeks corrupted the name
Romulus into Momyllus, and, on account of his youth, that of
Augustus was likewise transformed into Augustulus. The name of
Romulus had been that of his maternal grandfather. Sievers, *Studien*,
p.523.

[57] Procopius, *De bello Goth.*, i. I, at the beginning.

power to confer great wealth."[58] After an adventurous
and heroic career, [249] passed chiefly amid the din of
battle (he had distinguished himself under Ricimer in
the war against Anthemius), Odoacer had become the
foremost leader in the motley company of mercenaries. These homeless warriors, Rugians, Heruli, Scyrri,
and Turcilingians, persuaded by him that it would be
more to their advantage to become settled masters of
this beautiful land of Italy than to wander in the pay of
miserable emperors, impatiently demanded from
Orestes the third part of the soil of Italy. On his refusal
to comply, they rose in indignant rebellion and ranged
themselves under the standard of Odoacer. Originally
ambitious to become as powerful in the State as
Ricimer had been, Odoacer ended by far surpassing
his predecessor. Having been proclaimed King by his
motley army, he immediately proceeded to Ticinum or
Pavia, where Orestes had stationed himself. The town
was stormed and Orestes beheaded soon after at
Piacenza, while the last Emperor of Rome, Romulus
Augustulus, fell at Ravenna into the hands of the first
real King of German descent who reigned in Italy.

Odoacer assumed the title of King, and at once
obliged the abject Senant in Rome to satisfy him in the
dignity. He refrained, however, from adopting the purple diadem. His elevation took place in the third year
of Zeno the Isaurian, the ninth year of Pope [250]
Simplicius, the second of the consulate of Basiliscus
and the first of Armatus, on Aug. 23, 476 A.D.[59] The

---

[58] The *Anon. Val.* Relates this in his life of S. Severinus. *Vade ad
Italiam, vade vilissimis nunc pellibus coopertus, sed multis cito
plurima largiturus.* The name, which is, strictly speaking, Odovacar,
signifies "guardian of property" (Pallman, ii. 168). He was an ordinary freeman of low birth, and was held to have been a Rugian or
Scyrrian. The remarkable *Fragm. Johannis Antiocheni* says: . . . .

[59] Cassiodor., *Chron.: nomenque regis Odoacer adsumpsit, cum tamen
nec purpura, nec regalibus uterur insignibus; Theoph., Chronogr.,
pp.102 and 103; Incert, Chron.: Basilisco II. Et Armato coss. Levatus
est Odoacer rex X. Kal. Sept. Item eo anno occisus est paullus frater ejus
in Ravenna prid Non. Sept.*

fortunate barbarian did not, however, entertain the
idea of setting himself up as Emperor of the West, or
even of making Italy an independent Teutonic kingdom
apart from the Imperium. The majesty of a single and
indivisible Empire, the centre of which Constantinople now was, still survived as a political principle recognized by the barbarians with respect. Odoacer
merely desired to be lawful ruler in Italy, the last
province which remained to the Empire in the West,
and founded here no national, but only a barbarian,
military monarchy, without foundation and without
stability.[60] To his soldiers he gave the third part of the
soil to Italy, and, to avoid all appearance of usurpation,
forced Augustulus to a formal resignation before the
Senate, and the Senate to the declaration that the
Western Empire was extinct. The last political act of
the Senatorial Curia excites a melancholy sympathy: it
sent to the Emperor Zeno at Constantinople ambassadors, who, in the name of the Imperial Senate and
people declared that Rome no longer required an inde-
pend-[251]ent Emperor, that a single Emperor was sufficient for both East and West. They had chosen, they
said, as protector of Italy, Odoacer, a man experienced
alike in the arts of war and peace, and they entreated
Zeno to bestow the dignity of Patrician and the government of Italy on the man of their choice. The deplor-
able condition in which Rome found herself lessens the
ignominy of this declaration; Imperial rule had become impossible, and afflicted people recognized that
the dominion of a German patrician, under the supremacy of Imperial power still existing in the East,
was preferable to the continual change of powerless
puppet emperors.

Zeno, himself s barbarian from Isauria, received at
the same time an earnest application for aid from the
dethroned Nepos, who desired his restoration as lawful Emperor of the West. Zeno replied to the Senators

---

[60] He was not, however, King of Italy. Pallman justly terms him a King
of Mercenaries—a German King, and Felix Dahn speaks of his followers not as a race or people, but as an army of henchmen—"Lands-
knechtsregimenter" (*Die Könige der Germanen*).

that, of the two emperors he had sent to Rome, one had been banished and the other put to death; that as the former was still living they must again receive him, and that it rested with Nepos to confer the Patriciate on Odoacer. Zeno, nevertheless, that his client, Nepos, had no longer any hopes of regaining the throne, and that he must accept what was an already an accomplished fact. The Emperor of the East received the diadem and crown jewels of the Western Empire committed to his keeping, and deposited them in his place. The usurper, who had presumed to snatch for himself the sovereignty of Italy, he endured for just so long a time as he himself was powerless to remove him. In his letters to Odoacer, Zeno merely bestows on him [252] the title of "Patrician of the Romans." Abandoning Nepos, he resigned Rome and Italy to the rule of the German leader, under his Imperial authority.[61] Thus was the country received again as a province into the universal Empire, the division between East and West again removed, and the whole united under one Emperor, who now had his residence in Constantin-ople. The ancient unity of the Empire, as it had existed in the time of Constantine, was restored, but Rome and the West were given over to the Germans, and the ancient Latin Polity of Europe expired.

The extinction of the Roman Empire, from which the Germans had already snatched one province after another, only set the seal to the inward decay of the Latin race and the ancient Roman traditions. Even the Christian religion, which had everywhere replaced the old faith in the gods, no longer awoke any life in

---

[61] On account of this Embassy is given in the Excerpt of the lost history of the Malchus in Photius *(Corp. Scriptor. Hist. Byz., ed. Bonn, i. 235,236).*The Excerpts of Candidus pass it over in three words *(ibid.,* p. 476). Such are the scanty crumbs concerning this memorable event which have fallen to us from the table of Photius. The *Anon. Vales* is silent. As all readers are aware, the last Roam Emperor, the beautiful boy Romulus Augustulus ended his unhappy life in Castellum Lucullanum, near Naples. Nepos was murdered at Salona, on May 9, 480.

the people. The Gallic bishop Salvian casts a glance
over the moral condition of these effete but now
Christianized nations, and pronounces them all sunk
in indolence and vice; only in the Goths, Vandals, and
Franks, who had established themselves as conquerors
in the Roman provinces, does he find purity of morals,
vigor, and the energy of youth. [253] "These," said he,
"wax daily, we wane; they advance, we decay; they
bloom, we wither—and shall we therefore be surprised
if God gives all our provinces to the barbarians, in
order that through their virtues these lands may be purified from the crimes of the Romans?" The great name
of Roman, ay, evens the title which was once the
proudest among men, namely "Roman citizen," had already become contemptible.[62]

The Empire, dying of the decrepitude of age, was
finally destroyed by the greatest conflict of races
recorded in history. Upon its ruins Teutonism established itself, bringing fresh blood and spirit into the
Latin race, and reconstituting the Western world
through assertion of individual freedom. The overthrow of the Roman Empire was in reality one of the
greatest benefits which mankind ever received.
Through it Europe became reinvigorated, and from
out of the chaos of barbarism a many sided organism
arose. The process of development was, however, slow
and attended by terrible struggles. For Rome herself,
the extinction of the Imperial power was followed by
momentous consequences: now sinking into the position of provincial town, her buildings fell into ever
deeper decay, and her last political and civil life died
out. No longer dominated by the Emperor of the West,

---

[62] Salvian, De vero judicio, v.32, p.53: *Itaque nomen civium Romanorum aliquando non solum magna aestimatum, sed magno empium,
nunc ultro repudiator ac fugitur; nec vile tantum, sed etiam abom-
inabile pene habetur.* Further, lib.vii., and his lamentations at the end
of lib.vi.: *vendunt nobis hostes lucis usuram, tota admodum salus nostra commercium est. O infelicitates nostrae, ad quid devenimus!—quid
potset esse nobis vel abjectius, vel miseries!*

the Papacy gained ascendency, and [254] the Church of Rome grew mighty amid decay. It assumed the place of the Empire, and, already a firm and powerful institution when the Empire fell, remained unshaken by the fate of the ancient world. It filled, for the time; the void caused by the disappearance of the Empire, and formed the bridge between antiquity and the modern world. Admitting the Germans who had destroyed the Empire into the civic rights of the Roman Church, it sought in them to prepare the elements of the new life in which it was to take the ruling place , until, a long and extraordinary process, it became possible to restore the Western Empire under a Germanized Roman form. Amid the terrible conflicts, through dark and dreary centuries, was accomplished the metamorphosis which is alike the grandest drama of history and the noteworthy triumph of the ever-advancing, ever-developing Genius of Man."[63]

With the fall of Western Rome complete, the prophetic stage was then set for the rise of multiple nations, the ten symbolic horns, to emerge upon the New World. The Pope now had to appeal to the Byzantine Emperor of the East. This was problematic at times for he had to contend with Odoacer, an Arian who had been Patrician and was now King of Italy, but who retained Roman law because the Heruli had not for themselves a valid legal code of law:

"The death of Pope Simplicius in 483 gave rise to a point of controversy destined in the course of time to develop into a question of the highest importance. The Bishops of Rome had hitherto been nominated by the assembled congregations, or churches of the city, that is to say, by the people of all classes. The nomination ac-

---

[63] Ferdinand Gregorovius, Translated from the Fourth German Edition, Mrs. Gusta-vus W. Hamilton , *History Of The City of Rome In The Middle Ages*, (London, George Bell & Sons, 1900, First Published, 1894. Second Edition, Revised, 1900), 1:248-254.

complished, the returns of the election were laid before
the Emperor, and not until after their validity had been
examined into by an official, did the Emperor confirm
the election of the bishop, his subordinate. Odoacer now
claimed this right of ratification. He was Patrician and
King, and filled the place of the Western Roman
Emperor. He did not, however, belong to the Catholic
Church, but instead, like all of German race at this period, was a follower of Arianism, the form of faith which
most readily adapted itself to the untutored German intellect. Odoacer sent to Rome as his plenipotentiary,
Cecina Basilius, Prefect of the Praetorium, his chief official, with authority to enforce the royal claim on the
Senate and people and to inquire into the election.
Before the clergy and laity assembled in the mausoleum
of the Emperor Honorius in S. Peter's, Cecina Basilius
laid a decree, to which Simplicius must already have
given his assent. This decree ordained that no Papal
election henceforward could take place without the co-
operation of the royal plenipotentiary. The conclave
yielded to the will of the King, whose justice was recognized alike by [262] Arians and Catholics. The Arians
still, however, retained undisturbed possession of all
their churches both in Rome and elsewhere. A Roman
of the renowned family of the Anicii was now elected
Pope as Felix III.[64] [A.D. 483-492]

Forbearance towards the Church, as towards all
the State institutions, was for the German conqueror a
necessity of self-preservation. His followers did not
form a nation in Italy, only a mixed swarm of warlike
adventurers, whose rude barbarism placed an impass-
able chasm between them and Roman civilization. The
rule of Odoacer was consequently nothing more than
the rule of a military camp, and although endowed

---

[64] Pope Symmachus refers to this Synod *in. Mausoleo quod est apud b.
Petrum ape* ; A. Thiel, *Ep. Rom. Pont. Genuinae*, Braunsberg, 1868, i.
685. It is, moreover, difficult to decide whether Odoacer issued this
decision as a decree intended to apply to future occasions, or only to
that in question. Dahn, *Dahn, Könige der Germanen*, iii. Abt.
p. 203, holds the latter view, while Staudenmaier, *Gesth. der Bischofs-
wahlen*, p. 63, maintains the former.

with the highest dignity of the Empire, he remained in
Ravenna a foreigner, dreaded and hated, and powerless
to bequeath the Italian crown to his descendants.[65]

Even though Odoacer had been proclaimed King by
his motley army, his followers did not form a nation in
Italy that was viewed as such by the populace of the day.
They simply saw them as a hoard of homeless warriors
or mercenaries (though Procopius has informed us that
from time to time they did have a king). Odoacer's military camp or coup consisting of the Heruli, Rugians,
Scyrri, and Turcilingians was, thereby, established but
detested and hated by all:

> "He was not, however, King of Italy. Pallman justly
> terms him a King of Mercenaries—a German King,
> and Felix Dahn speaks of *his followers not as a race or
> people, but as* an *army of henchmen*—"Landsknechts-
> regimenter" (*Die Könige der Ger-manen*)."[66]

While it is true that history confirms Odoacer as an
Arian, it is also true that history and credible historians
the world over recognize Odoacer's motley army as pagans, heathen mercenaries of a military camp. They were
not Arians and neither were they of any one race or
people, nor were they considered to be a nation by the
populace of the day. With the Heruli (Eruli) becoming
gradually superior to the Rugians, Scyrri, and Turcilingians, we, then, naturally ask who and what type of people they were. Procopius, a Byzantine scholar-historian
and of the orthodox faith, was an eye witness to many of
the events of the early 6th century, and he answers this
question succinctly:

---

[65] Ferdinand Gregorovius, Translated from the Fourth German
Edition, Mrs. Gustavus W. Hamilton , *History Of The City of Rome In
The Middle Ages*, (London, George Bell & Sons, 1900, First Published,
1894. Second Edition, Revised, 1900), 1:261-2.
[66] Ibid., 1:250, footnote.

"The Eruli, or Heruli, were one of the wildest and most corrupt of the barbarian tribes. They came from beyond the Danube."[67]

"Now as to who in the world the Eruli are, and how they entered into alliance with the Romans, I shall forthwith explain.[68] They used to dwell beyond the Ister [69] River from of old, worshipping a great host of gods, whom it seemed to them holy and appease even by human sacrifices. And they observed many customs which were not in accord with those of other men. For they were not permitted to live either when they grew old or when they fell sick, but as soon as one of them was overtaken by old age or by sickness, it became necessary for him to ask his relatives to remove him from the world as quickly as possible. And these relatives would pile up a quantity of wood to a great height and lay the man on top of the wood, and then they would send one of the Eruli, but not a relative of the man, to his side with a dagger; for it was not lawful for a kinsman to be his slayer. And when the slayer of the relative had returned, they would straightaway burn the whole pile of wood, beginning at the edges. And after the fire had ceased, they would immediately collect the bones and bury them in the earth. And when a man of the Eruli died, it was necessary for his wife, if she laid claim to virtue and wished to leave a fair name behind her, to die not long afterward beside the tomb of her husband with a rope. And if she did not do this, the result was that she was in ill repute thereafter and an offence to the relatives of her husband. Such were the customs observed by the Eruli in ancient times."[70]

[67] Procopius. *History of the Wars.* Translated by H. B. Dewing. Bks. 1–8. In Loeb Classical Library, edited by Jeffrey Henderson. Cambridge, MA: Harvard Univ. Press, 2000–2001, IV. iv. 32 (footnote).

[68] Cf. Book IV.iv.30

[69] Modern Danube.

[70] Procopius. *History of the Wars.* Translated by H. B. Dewing. Bks. 1–8. In Loeb Classical Library, edited by Jeffrey Henderson. Cambridge, MA: Harvard Univ. Press, 2000–2001, VI. Xiii. 16-xiv. 1-7.

"And they [Heruli] mate in an unholy manner, especially men with asses, and they are the basest of all men and utterly abandoned rascals."[71]

Procopius now reveals their conduct and rule amongst the populace:

"But as time went on they [The Heruli] became superior to all the barbarians who dwelt about them both in power and in numbers, and, as was natural, they attacked and vanquished them severally and kept plundering their possessions by force. And finally they made the Lombards, who were Christians, together with several other nations, subject and tributary to themselves, though the barbarians of that region were not accustomed to that sort of thing; but the Eruli were led to take this course by love of money and lawless spirit."[72]

The conduct of the Heruli was a threat to everyone, Catholic, Arian, and even the pagans themselves. Therefore, it brought upon them the contempt of all classes of people and faiths. In light of these events, Theodoric the Great petitioned the Eastern Roman Emperor Zeno, reminding him of the "tyranny" (unlawful rule) of the city of Rome by Turcilingi and Rugii. Jordanes, a 6th century Roman bureaucrat turned historian who wrote the only remaining classical work dealing with the early history of the Goths, gives us the record of that account between Theodoric the Great and the Eastern Roman Emperor Zeno:

LVII
[289] "When the Emperor Zeno heard that Theodoric had been appointed king over his own people, he received the news with pleasure and invited him to come and visit him in the city, appointing an escort of

[71] Ibid., VI. xiv. 35-38.
[72] Procopius. *History of the Wars.* Translated by H. B. Dewing. Bks. 1–8. In Loeb Classical Library, edited by Jeffrey Henderson. Cambridge, MA: Harvard Univ. Press, 2000–2001, VI. xiv. 8-11

honor. Receiving Theodoric with all due respect, he placed him among the princes of his palace. After some time Zeno increased his dignity by adopting him as his son-at-arms and gave him a triumph in the city at his expense. Theodoric was made Consul Ordinary also, which is well known to be the supreme good and highest honor in the world. Nor was this all, for Zeno set up before the royal palace an equestrian statue to the glory of this great man. [290] Now while Theodoric was in alliance by treaty with the Empire of Zeno and was himself enjoying every comfort in the city, he heard that his tribe, dwelling as we have said in Illyricum, was not altogether satisfied or content. So he chose rather to seek a living by his own exertions, after the manner customary to his race, rather than to enjoy the advantages of the Roman Empire in luxurious ease while his tribe lived in want. After pondering these matters, he said to the Emperor: "Though I lack nothing in serving your Empire, yet if Your Piety deem it worthy, be pleased to hear the desire of my heart." [291] And when as usual he had been granted permission to speak freely, he said: "The western country, long ago governed by the rule of your ancestors and predecessors, and that city which was the head and mistress of the world,—wherefore is it now shaken by the tyranny of the Torcilingi and the Rugi? Send me there with my race. Thus if you but say the word, you may be freed from the burden of expense here, and, if by the Lord's help I shall conquer, the fame of Your Piety shall be glorious there. For it is better that I, your servant and your son, should rule that kingdom, receiving it as a gift from you if I conquer, than that one whom you do not recognize should oppress your Senate with his tyrannical yoke and a part of the republic with slavery. For if I prevail, I shall retain it as your grant and gift; if I am conquered, Your Piety will lose nothing—nay, as I have said, it will save the expense I now entail." [292] Although the Emperor was grieved that he should go, yet when he heard this he granted what Theodoric asked, for he was unwilling to cause him sorrow. He sent him forth enriched by great gifts and commended to his charge the Senate and the Roman People. Therefore Theodoric departed from the royal city and returned to his own people. In company with the whole tribe of the Goths, who gave him their unanimous consent, he set out for Hesperia. He went in straight march through Sirmium to the places bordering on Pannonia and, advancing into the territory of Venetia as far as the bridge of the Sontius, encamped there. [293] When he had halted there for some time to rest the bodies of his men and pack-animals, Odoacer sent an armed force against him, which he met on the plains of Verona and destroyed with great slaughter. Then he broke camp and advanced through Italy with greater boldness. Crossing the river Po, he pitched camp near the royal city of Ravenna, about the third milestone from the city in the place called Pineta. When Odoacer saw this, he fortified himself within the city. He frequently harassed the army of the Goths at night, sallying forth stealthily with his men, and this not once or twice, but often; and thus he struggled for almost three whole years. [294] But he labored in vain, for all Italy at last called Theodoric its lord and the Empire obeyed his nod. But Odoacer, with his few adherents and the Romans who were present, suffered daily from war and famine in Ravenna. Since he accomplished nothing, he sent an embassy and begged for mercy. [295] Theodoric first granted it and afterwards deprived him of his life. It was in the third year after his entrance into Italy, as we have said, that Theodoric, by advice of the Emperor Zeno, laid aside the garb of a private citizen and the dress of his race and assumed a costume with a royal mantle, as he had now become the ruler over both Goths and Romans. He sent an embassy to Lodoin, king of the Franks, and asked for his daughter Audefleda in marriage. [296] Lodoin freely and gladly gave her, and also his sons Celdebert and Heldebert and Thiudebert, believing that by this alliance a league would be formed and that they would be associated with the race of the Goths. But that union was of no avail for peace and harmony, for they fought fiercely with each other again and

again for the lands of the Goths; but never did the Goths
yield to the Franks while Theodoric lived."[73]

The statement of Theodoric the Great to Emperor
Zeno, "Send me there with my race" cements the fact
that the Arians formed no part of Odoacer's henchmen.
Another critical point is that the little horn or the papacy
can in no wise be said to have had a part in subduing
Odoacer and his military camp, for this was an act of
Zeno on behalf of Theodoric alone. Equally significant is
the fact that, though this campaign was against the heathen or pagans, this was a political warfare, not a religious one. Our understanding is to be further enriched
from the following which shows that the Emperor Zeno
had his own motives for agreeing to dispatch Theodoric
to the west:

> "The Byzantine Emperor regarded him [Odoacer]
> as a usurper, and only awaited the first opportunity to
> set him aside. For this undertaking there was at hand a
> yet greater tribal leader of German race, and an entire
> people who had forsaken their devastated homes on
> the slopes of the Haemus, to descend upon the fertile
> plains of Italy. These were the warlike Ostrogoths,
> ruled at that time by Theodoric. The Emperor Zeno,
> fearing that in his repeated incursions across the fron-
> tiers of the Eastern [263] Empire the Gothic King
> might prepare for Byzantium the fate which Italy had
> suffered at the hands of Odoacer, constituted Theo-
> doric his ally, bestowing on the barbarian the titles of
> Consul and Patrician. In order to remove him from the
> East, the Emperor exhorted him to turn the thirst of

---

[73] Jordanes, *The Origins and Deeds of the Goths*, LVII. 289-296, trans.
by Charles C. Mierow. It has been said that Jordanes was asked by a
friend to write this book as a summary of a multi-volume history of
the Goths (now lost) by the statesman Cassiodorus. Jordanes was selected chiefly for his interest in history (he was working on a history
of Rome), his ability to write succinctly, and because of his own
Gothic background. He had been a high-level *notarius*, or secretary,
of a small client state on the Roman frontier in Moesia, modern
northern Bulgaria. As for the dating of this work he mentions the
great plague of 546 as having occurred "nine years ago" (*Getica* 104.)

his people for spoil and adventure towards the West and to snatch, the land of Italy from the "tyrant" Odoacer. By virtue of a formal treaty Zeno made over to him and his people the investiture of this province of the Empire. Theodoric accordingly led his entire tribe across the Alps in 488, and appeared in formidable power on the banks of the Isonzo, in the summer of 489. The Goths of Theodoric had been more or less imbued with the influences of the civilizations both of East and West, and although judged by the standard of Latin culture, they may have been deemed barbarians, they were not altogether barbarians, such as the followers of Alaric had been. They formed moreover a nation which presented to the enervated and effeminate Italians the unusual spectacle of heroic manhood. It was in short the conviction of their own superiority as free men to which the Goths owed the subjugation of the ancient, world.[74]

The struggle of the two military leaders for the possession of the beautiful and unhappy country was [264] long and fierce. Defeated on the Isonzo and afterwards at Verona, Odoacer in despair threw himself on his last stronghold, Ravenna. The isolated assertion of a chronicler that, after the defeat at Verona he retreated to Rome, there to entrench himself, and that out of revenge for his rejection by the Romans he laid waste the Campagna, is very doubtful. The Roman Senate, whose adhesion had been gained by the Byzantine Emperor, had already arrived at a secret understanding with Theodoric, and, after Odoacer had been driven to bay at Ravenna, had openly declared in favor of the Gothic King. As early as the year 490 Theodoric, therefore, was able to send the Patrician Festus, the head of the Senate, to Zeno to request the royal mantle.[75]

---

[74] The probable number of Theodoric's followers remains unknown. Gibbon estimates it at a million. Later investigators, such as Kopke and Dahn, are content with from 200,000 to 250,000, with about 60,000 fighting men. But is it possible that the Ostrogoths can have found accommodation in Pavia side by side with the former inhabitants? (Sartorius, *Regierung der Ostgothen*, p. 15.)

[75] Anon. Valesii, 53: Fausto et Longino Coss., i.e., A.D. 490.

For three years Odoacer made a gallant resistance at Ravenna. At length, reduced by want, he opened the gates to Theodoric (March 5, 493). A few days later the victor faithlessly broke the treaty he had made with his valiant enemy, stabbing Odoacer with his own hand, and causing all his followers to be slain. Without waiting for the ratification of Anastasius, who, on the death of Zeno (April 9, 491) had succeeded to the Imperial throne, Theodoric had already adopted the title and insignia of King of Italy. Not until 498 did he receive recognition, the Emperor then surrendering all the jewels of the Imperial palace previously sent by Odoacer to Constantinople. Theodoric was by right of his people King of the Goths; by that of conquest, the election of his followers and the allegiance of the conquered [265] also King of Italy; by the surrender of the insignia of Empire, he now received the Imperial ratification of this right-the right, that is to say, to govern Italy as it had been previously governed by the Emperors of the West.[76]

But while the Byzantine Emperor had only commissioned Theodoric to rescue the prefecture of Italy from the possession of a usurper, the Goth was himself little better than a usurper in his eyes. The new conqueror, on his side, recognized the legitimate authority of the Emperor, professing subjection to Anastasius, although at the same time regarding himself as nothing less than ruler in a country, the third part of which he had bestowed on his soldiers. He also fixed his residence at Ravenna, thence resolved to govern, according to Roman institutions, Rome, Italy, and perhaps the West. The project was, however, one, which threatened danger, owing to the fact that Theodoric professed the Arian faith. The people whom he had led

---

[76] Anon. Vales., 64: Facta pace cum Anastasio imperatore per Festum de praesumptione regni, et omnia ornamenta palatii, quae Odoacher Constantinopolim transmiserat, remittit. Dahn, Die Konige der Germanem, ii. 162, justly lays stress on this surrender of the insignia of the Western Empire, by which the views held by Belisalius, Justinian and Procopius regarding Theodoric's usnrpation are deprived of all legal ground.

into Italy were a heretic people, and in Rome he found himself opposed by the already powerful bishop, the recognized head of the Church in the West."[77]

Because Theodoric and his followers professed the Arian faith, they had been branded as heretics since the council of Nicea in A.D 325. This became a major obstacle for the papacy, one with which she would have to contend. Theodoric naturally found himself already at odds with the powerful bishop of Rome. However, the long, fierce battle finally ended on March 5, 493, when Odoacer threw open the gates to his victor, Theodoric the Great, King of the Ostrogoths. This established the Ostrogoths as the very first barbarian race to found a colony upon the soil of Italy:

> "The Goths [Ostrogoths] established themselves permanently in Italy, which now, for the first time, suffered an entire barbarian race to found a colony upon her soil, and henceforward had no choice but to admit an infusion of German principles into her Latin nationality."[78]

While it has been assumed by some that the Heruli were fully uprooted in A.D. 493 by Theodoric the Great, that was simply not the case. Latest academic scholarship has recognized that the final overthrow of the remaining Heruli was in A.D. 508 by the Lombards:

> "In the oriental theater of operations, in 508, Anastasius had pushed the Lombards against Rodulf, the adoptive son of Theodoric and the king of the continental Herules who lived in what is now Slovakia. Without the support of the master of Ravenna, the Herules, who fought nude, arms in hand, in order to better unchain their murderous violence, were crushed (*Procope*, VI, 14). A good number of them came back to

---

[77] Gregorovius, Ferdinand. History of the City of Rome in the Middle Ages, vol. 1. Translated from the 4th German ed. London: George Bell, 1900, 262-265.
[78] Ibid., 266.

their motherland, what is now Sweden, and others fused with the Ostrogoths."[79]

The New Encyclopedia Britannica declares:

> "Their kingdom [Heruli] on the middle Danube, founded in the late 5th century, fell to the Lombards early in the 6th century."[80]

According to Troels Brandt, Andreas Schwarcz (2005) dates Cassiodorus' letter to Theodoric's Herulian "son in arms" to early A.D. 509. He arrives at this from the order of the letters of Cassiodorus. As stated before, historians have recognized that Procopius probably mixed up the time of the defeat of Odoacer with the defeat of Hrodolphus—both being Herulian defeats. The battle most likely took place in A.D. 508. The historical accounts from the primary sources regarding this battle reveal that it was political and do not provide any substance for the involvement of the little horn. For those who fought against the Heruli, it was never about religion, rather it was always about further restraining the heathens from plundering their possessions, lands, and women. From this point in time, the Heruli fused and splintered off into various tribes, regions and militaries of various kingdoms. Some of these small remaining bands of Heruli mercenaries were described by Procopius as having joined Justinian's army, as well.[81] The Heruli, as we have witnessed, were unable to withstand the test of time and neither have they been able to withstand the test of investigation.

---

[79] Rouche, Michel. *Clovis*. (Fayard, France 1996), 323.

[80] The New Encyclopedia Britannica, (15th Edition, Chicago, IL. Encyclopedia Britannica, 1988), 5:893.

[81] Procopius. *History of the Wars*. Translated by H. B. Dewing. Bks. 1–8. In Loeb Classical Library, edited by Jeffrey Henderson. Cambridge, MA: Harvard Univ. Press, 2000–2001, VI. xiv. 33-37.

5

The Visigoths

Some have erroneously concluded that the Visigoths were pagans[82] and that, therefore, the conflict in the West was over paganism. In fact, though, the Visigoths were Arian Christians. Similarly, a few decades later, the issue in the East between the Vandals and Ostrogoths (also Arian Christians) and Justinian was not about paganism, nor was it solely a political conflict. It was a religious war, as well, that would ultimately decide the dominance of the Catholic or Arian faith in Eastern Europe.

With the Heruli forever dismissed as one of the uprooted horns of Daniel 7:8, 20, and 24, and the fact that Theodoric the Great, King of the Ostrogoths, reigned in Italy virtually unobstructed until his death in 526 (there was a small episode in 507-8 and a skirmish with the pope and the eastern Emperor Justin in 524), we are forced to look outside of Italy for the fulfillment of an uprooted horn or horns, if there was to be such before that time. In our quest for truthful answers in that which we seek, we are fortunate to have the following primary document:

". . . . There were many Gothic nations in earlier times, just as also at the present, but the greatest and

---

[82] *The American Heritage College Dictionary*, 3rd ed., 1997, s.v. "pagan." "One who is not a Christian . . . , One who has no religion . . . , Professing no religion; heathen."

most important of all are the Goths, Vandals, Visigoths and Gepaedes. In ancient times, however, they were named Sauromatae and Melan-chlaeni;[83]and there were some too who called the nations Getic. All these, while they are distinguished from one another by their names, as has been said, do not differ in anything else at all. For they all have white bodies and fair hair, and are tall and handsome to look upon, and they use the same laws and practice a common religion. For they are all of the Arian faith, and have one language called Gothic; and, as it seems to me, they all came originally from one tribe, and were distinguished later by the names of those who led each group."[84]

While there was a difference between the Goths and the Ostrogoths, it must be understood that when Procopius is referring to the Goths it is in reference to the Ostrogoths. This is confirmed in his books, *History of the Wars*. However, Procopius informed us of a very important point that must not be overlooked when he wrote of these Arian kingdoms:

"They use the same laws and practice a common religion. For they are all of the Arian faith." For they "do not differ in anything else at all." [85]

From the pen of Procopius himself, we have the actual viewpoint of someone then living as to who was considered to be the chief armaments of opposition to the Catholic faith because they were of the Arian faith.

Since Procopius introduced us to the Gepaedes, we will comment briefly as to their background even though the Gepaedes play no part in the prophetic picture and their primary sources are scarce. According to the sources available, the Gepaedes or Gepids were an East

---

[83] "Black—Coats"
[84] Procopius. *History of the Wars*. Translated by H. B. Dewing. Bks. 1–8. In Loeb Classical Library, edited by Jeffrey Henderson. Cambridge, MA: Harvard Univ. Press, 2000–2001, III. ii. 1-8.
[85] Ibid., III. ii. 1-8.

Germanic Gothic tribe most famous in history for defeating the Huns after the death of Attila. The Gepids territory was composed of parts of modern day Romania, Hungary and Serbia. As early as A.D. 260 they, together with the Goths, invaded what was then the Roman Empire province of Dacia. They later settled on the eastern bank of the Tisza River. They became vassals of the Hunnic Empire, forming the army's right-flank. After Attila's death, they joined the Ostrogoths in breaking up the empire for which they had previously fought. Next, after quarreling with their allies, they settled in the Carpathian Mountains and, thereby, distanced themselves from them. Tombs have been excavated dating back to the sixth century containing ceramics, bronze articles and armor. They are believed by some to have been conquered by the Byzantine-Lombard alliance in 567, while others claim they were overthrown by the Avars.

With that information, we are left with three chief armaments of opposition to the Catholic faith. Given in their chronological order we will establish and document that the Visigoths, Vandals, and the Ostrogoths comprised the three uprooted horns of Bible prophecy. When the Lombards defeated the Heruli in A.D. 508, it did not affect Eastern Rome. There was nothing in Eastern Rome, in and of itself, that demanded the subduing of a foreign power or kingdom, for everything was still largely under the emperor's control. Except for the Acacius schism between the east and western orthodox churches and the Henotikon, an edict issued by the Emperor Zeno, the church was mainly biding her time there. Therefore, we need not look to eastern Rome until the time of Justinian, and he did not take the throne until 527. Theodoric the Great in Italy, although considered a heretic, did not infringe upon the rights of the people regardless of race or faith.

Theodoric was loved by both Arians and Romans and there was no king in the entire west at that time that would have had the military might to overthrow him. With everything running quite smoothly (as we witnessed in my *A.D. 508 Source Book*), Theodoric's early reign was recognized by historians as the "golden age for the

church."[86] Under his rule, as stated earlier, was largely
peace and quiet after 493 except for around 507-8 and
near the end of his reign in 523-526. The latter skirmish
will be reviewed shortly. Therefore, in our search, Italy in
western Rome merited nothing either and we must again
look elsewhere for our first uprooted horn. This brings us
to Gaul, the last territory of Christendom in western
Rome. Procopius unveils how the Visigoths came into
dominance of this entire territory:

> ". . . . But when Odoacer changed the government
> into a tyranny, then, since the tyrant yielded to them, *the
> Visigoths took possession of all Gaul as far as the alps*
> which mark the boundary between Gaul and Liguria."[87]

As Procopius has rightly informed us, the Visigoths
were one of the main Arian kingdoms in opposition to
the principles or government of the Catholic Church.
Gregory of Tours confirms that the Visigoths embraced
the principles of religious liberty. The Visigoth Agilan
once admonished Gregory of Tours declaring:

> "You must not blaspheme against a faith which you
> yourself do not accept. You notice that we who do not
> believe the things which you believe nevertheless do
> not blaspheme against them. It is no crime for one set
> of people to believe in one doctrine and another set of
> people to believe in another. . ." "Legem, quam non
> colis, blaspheme noli; nos vero quae creditis etsi non
> credimus, non tamen blasphemamus, quia non deputur
> crimini, si et illa et illa colantur. Sic enim vulgate ser-
> mon dicimus, non esse noxium, si inter gentilium aras
> st Dei ecclesiam quis transiens utraque veneriyur."[88]

[86] Amory, Patrick. *People and Identity in Ostrogothic Italy, 489–554.*
Cambridge: Cambridge Univ. Press, 2003, 203.
[87] Procopius. *History of the Wars.* Translated by H. B. Dewing. Bks.
1–8. In Loeb Classical Library, edited by Jeffrey Henderson.
Cambridge, MA: Harvard Univ. Press, 2000–2001, V. xii. 20-21.
[88] Thorpe, L. Trans. Gregory of Tours - The History of the Franks
(Harmondsworth, 1974), 309-10.

The Catholic Church now had two powerful "heretical" Arian tribes largely in control of all of Gaul and Italy with a mutual ideology diametrically opposed to the government of the papacy. The church Council of Agde was held Sept. 10, 506, at Agde in Languedoc, France under the authority of Caesarius of Arles and was attended by thirty-five bishops. It should be noted that even up to the year 506 the Catholics had to administer a proclamation of tolerance of West Gothic Arianism. This was done only because the Catholic Church did not as yet have a civil force in the west to enforce her dogmas, much less one to subdue her enemies:

"The Council of Agde was a proclamation of tolerance of West Gothic Arianism for the Roman Catholic subjects, to whom a codification of their law had been presented a few months prior in the Lex Romana [law code]. In the opening section the synodical acts emphasized the authority of the king, who granted the Catholic bishops the authorization to convene the synodical assembly, and in the conclusion he was thanked for that following thanks to God. At the top of the resolutions, demonstratively emphasizing Catholic continuity, the doctrine was stated that the canons and statutes of the fathers should be read aloud.[89] *Thereby the Arian problem was implicitly side-stepped.* Notably, the conversion of Jews and convivium with them was brought up, *yet not a word about the Arians.*[90] In Epao,

---

[89] A decretal statement of Innocent I (JK. 293 c. I, no. 2, 4) was also included verbatim in the canon (c. 9).

[90] An indirect, indeed acknowledging reference to them is argued by Hauck, Kirchengeschichte Deutschlands 3.4 I, p. 117 note 1 (corroborating von Schubert, Geschichte der christlichen Kirche im Frühmittelalter. 1921, p. 25) in c. 42: *Ac ne id fortasse videatur omissum, quod maxime fidem catholicae religionis infestat, quod aliquanti clerici sive laici student auguriis* etc. However, *maxime* here undoubtedly does not mean "mostly," "especially," but rather "at the most." A praise "even indirectly" of the Arians from the mouth of the Catholic synod would be unthinkable.

[The church council of September 517] on the other hand, this very topic was at the center of interest. Not only with Jews but also with heretics, convivium was prohibited[91], and for lapsi, the baptized Catholics who "crossed into damnable heresy," a period of penance limited to two years per the old canon was prescribed. Also forbidden was the further use of Arian churches, with the exception of those that had formerly been Catholic."[92]

On the surface it looked bleak, but behind the scenes the Catholic Church was working to achieve her means. The following letter, addressed to Clovis in 481 from the Bishop St. Remi, is part of a collection of letters called Austrasicae contained in a single manuscript from the beginning of the 9th century. The letters from this manuscript were collected at Metz at the end of the 6th century. Numbering 48, they are the work of the most important people of the period and are addressed to very high dignitaries such as bishops, kings, queens, emperors, and

---

[91] c. 15 Epaon, cf. with c. 40 Agath. (The canons 60 and 67 of Agde, which dealt with heretics, are later additions; cf. Hefele, Conciliengeschichte. II, p 650; French translation Leclercq II, p. 980).
[92] c. 32. In a separate opinion (ep. 7, I. c. p. 35 ff.) Avitus had already previously treated this question in depth. Here, the Catholic disdain of the heretics, otherwise carefully hidden from the landed proprietary power of the kingdom, expressed itself freely. The worldly wisdom of Avitus was also evidenced by his advice, not to turn the heretics into martyrs through absorbing them into the Arian churches, and not to pro-voke other Arian kings to retaliatory measures. Thus reads his summarizing judgment: *Dices forsitan haereticos, si eis potestas datur, altaria nostra temerare. Verum est, nec refello. Saeviunt quidem, cum possent, foedis unguibus alienarum aedium pervasores. Sed vim intendere, loca pervadere, altaria commutare non pertinent ad columbam...Quocirca non quid statuam, sed quid optem, breviter indicabo. Haeretici cultus loca pervadi nollem, cuperem praetermitti in morem ergastulorum, quae usu careant. Semper optandum est, non ut mutata transeant, sed infrequentata torpescant. Salubri populorum correctione desertis maneat aeterna viduitas, nec unquam recipiatur a nostris, quod conversionis studio repudiator a propriis.*
Erich Caspar, *Geschicthe des Papsttums*, [*History of the Papacy*] 1933, 2:4-5.

high officials. However, we want to center our attention on the oldest document that we possess on Clovis that is from that collection, translated from the Latin. In it, St. Remi salutes Clovis who just took over the administration of the Second Belgium and urges him to govern well. This was not a military victory but a political achievement. This letter also establishes that the prestige of the kingdom of the Franks began with Clovis with the working of St. Remi behind the scenes:

> **To the seigneur illustrious for his merits, the King Clovis, Bishop Remi**
> "A big rumor has come to us, you have taken up the administration of the Second Belgium. This is not new as you will have started by being that which your parents always were. First you must see to it that the judgment of God does not abandon you there where your merit comes by way of your activity from your humility to this very high summit. For, as we say vulgarly, it is with actions that we identify the man. You must appoint yourself advisors that will be able to adorn your renown. Your gift must be pure and honest. Your will have to consult your bishops and always rely on their advice. For if you get along well with them, your province will only be consolidated by this. Give courage to the citizens, relieve the distressed, favor the widows, nourish the orphans; rather than enlighten them, may they all love you and respect you. May justice be spoken by your mouth without expecting anything from the poor and foreigners so that you will not want to accept gifts or anything else from them. May your court be open to all so that none return from it sad. You possess certain paternal riches with which you will liberate the prisoners and deliver them from the yoke of servitude. If anyone is admitted to your presence, may he not feel like a stranger. Joke with the young, deliberate with the old, and if you want to rule, judge nobly."[93]

---

[93] *Epistolae Austrasicae*, Corpvs Christianorvm, Series Latina Vol. CXVII, Tvrnholti, 1957, 2, 408-409.

A second letter from St. Remi to Clovis from the same manuscript reveals St. Remi trying to console King Clovis on the death of his sister Albochlede. This takes us behind the scenes and reveals the very close relationship between Clovis and the Catholic Church:

To the seigneur illustrious for his merits, the King Clovis, Remi bishop

"The announcement of the death of your sister of glorious memory Albochlede saddens me even more because of the sadness you feel. But we can console ourselves because she that has gone from this light must that much more be conserved in your memory than she was mourned. In effect, she lived such a life that we believe that she was taken by the Lord, she who, chosen by God, has gone to heaven. She lives for your faith and if the chosen has the desire to see him, Christ satisfied her because she received the benediction of the virgins. She that was consecrated should not be mourned because she shines under the gaze of God in virginal splendor, to know him of the crown with which she was covered and that she received as a gauge of her virginity. May she be absent, so that she may be mourned by the faithful, she that deserved to be the good odor of Christ so that thanks to him, whom she pleased, she may bring help to those that ask for it. My lord {king}, cast off sadness from your heart; govern the kingdom in a more penetrating manner, in a spirit justly mastered, making bolder decisions thanks to the zeal of serenity. Comfort your limbs thanks to a joyous heart. The torpor of bitterness shaken off, you will consecrate your waking hours to the salvation {of all} with more acuity. May the kingdom remain in your hands to be administered and, with the help of God, to prosper. You are the head of the people and you carry the government. May those that are used to seeing you thanks to you in happiness not perceive you stricken with the sourness of mourning. Be yourself the consoler of your soul by maintaining in yourself the innate providence that is found in it, so that sadness does not smother the clarity of your mind. As for her actual death,

of she that is now joined with the chorus of virgins, as
we should believe it, the king rejoices of it in the sky.
In saluting your glory I also recommend to you the
priest Maccolus who is part of my entourage and that I
am sending to you. I beg you to deign to pardon me, I should have sent
him to meet you and I made the decision to entrust
him with words of exhortation. Nonetheless if you
order by way of the carrier of these letters that I come,
after having disregarded the hardness of winter, neglected the cold, overcome the painful route, I will
strive to, with the help of God, come before you."[94]

The efforts from the papacy were soon to bear fruit
and in Clovis the church was to find a refuge. Clovis pre-
pares for war against the Arian Visigoth King Alaric II in
507/8:

". . . The Franks were heavily recruited into the
Roman army and a segment known as the Salians was
settled in what is now the Netherlands. In the early 6th
C., the Franks were united politically by Clovis
(Chlodovechus, 481_ -511), who extended Frankish
rule over the whole of Roman Gaul with the exception
of Septimania and Provence. Clovis also converted to
Orthodox [Catholic] Christianity, the first barbarian king
to do so. This conversion and his victory over the
VISIGOTHS (508) contributed to a Byz. perception
of the Franks as potential allies against the Arian
Gothic kingdoms and later the Lombards in Italy. Merovingian kings from Clovis onward were frequently honored by Constantinople with the titles
consul and patrikios."[95]

"To these last year's also belong the few contemporary pieces of evidence on Clovis' church policy. . . . The

---

[94] *Epistolae Austrasicae*, Corpvs Christianorvm, Series Latina Vol.
CXVII, Tvrnholti, 1957, 1, 407-408.
[95] *The Oxford Dictionary of Byzantium*, s.v. "Franks" (New York:
Oxford University Press, 1991), 2:803.

earliest piece of Merovingian ecclesiastical legislation
was in many ways the manifestation of the ideals of
Remigius; in a letter written after Vouille [Vougle], Clovis
announced to his bishops that en route for the battle he
had promulgated an edict protecting widows, clerics and
those whom the church wished to defend."[96]

We submit the entire just quoted letter from Clovis to
the bishops, translated from the Latin:

Letter from Clovis to the Bishops
****

"King Clovis to the saint seigneurs and to the bishops very dignified by the apostolic see.

The news having been announced concerning that
which was done and ordered to all our army, before we
entered the homeland of the Goths, this could not have
escaped Your Beatitude.

Firstly, we order, in that which concerns the service of all the churches, that nobody should try to take
away in any way either saint nuns [saintes moniales in
French] or the widows of which we know that they
were dedicated to the service of the Lord; that it may
be the same for the clerics and the children of the
aforementioned, both of clerics and of widows of
which we know that they reside with them in their
homes; the same, for the slaves of churches for whom
it will be proven by the oaths of bishops that they were
taken from the churches, the order to follow is to exercise no harm or violence towards them. This is why we
order, so that all this may be well known, that whoever
among the aforementioned will have suffered the violence of captivity, either in the churches or outside of
them, be totally and immediately given back. For the
other lay prisoners that will have been taken outside of
peace and that this be proven, we will not refuse letters

---

[96] Ian N. Wood, *Revue Belge de Philologie Et D'Histoire*, (Brussels:
n.p., 1985), 63:264. See also *Chlodowici Regis ad episcopos epistula*,
Capitularia Merowingica, ed. A. Boretius, *Monumenta Germaniae
Historica, Capitularia Regum Francorum, I* (Hannover, 1883), 1-2.

written upon your decision for whom you will desire it. In effect, for those that will have been seized in our peace whether clerics or laymen, if you make it known to be true by letters signed with your seals, may they may be sent to us in any way and you will learn that the orders issued by us will confirm it. Thus our people demand that, for all those that you judge worthy of your letters, you will not hesitate to say under oath in the name of God and with your benediction that this thing is true that needed to be proved, since the variations and falsifications of many were discovered to the point that, as it is written: "the just perish with the impious."

Pray for me, saint seigneurs and very dignified fathers by the apostolic see."[97]

That is the only authentic document that has come to us from Clovis which is from a manuscript of the monastery of Corbie dating from the 6th -7th centuries. The battle between Clovis and the Visigoths was a religious war:

"It is evident, from the language of Gregory of Tours, that this conflict between the Franks and Visigoths was regarded by the orthodox party of his own preceding ages as a religious war, on which, humanly speaking, the prevalence of the Catholic or the Arian creed in Western Europe depended."[98]

"Clovis fought his last campaign, against the Visigoths in 507, [508] as a Catholic."[99]

---

[97] Alfredvs Boretivs, Monvmenta Germaniae Historica, Rervm Germanicarvm Medii Aevi, Capitvlaria Regvm Francorvm, (Hannoverae, 1883), 1:1-2. [*Chlodowici Regis ad episcopos epistula, Capitularia Merowingica*, ed. A. Boretius, *Monumenta Germaniae Historica, Capitularia Regum Francorum, I* (Hannover, 1883), 1-2.]
[98] Walter C. Perry, *The Franks* (London: Longman, Brown, Green, Longmans, and Roberts, 1857), 85. Perry quotes from Gregory of Tours' *The History of the Franks*, trans. O. M. Dalton (Oxford: Clarendon Press, 1927), 2:36-43. The authority on Clovis, Gregory lived from A.D. 538 to 594.
[99] J. M. Wallace-Hadrill, *The Long Haired Kings* (New York: Barnes and Noble, 1962), 173.

"It was a religious war that Clovis declared against them. The war against the Visigoths was the big event of the reign of Clovis. Reconciled with Gondebaud, he made him an ally, and after having beaten the Visigoths at Vouille where their king Alaric was killed, he pursued them without stopping."[100]

"Chlodowech [Clovis] already had not held back on gifts to the church.[101] It is not improbable that he had granted the bishops the necessary possessions to improve poorer churches' facilities.[102] After the Goth War he conferred the former Arian chapels upon the Catholic Church, doubtless along with the Arian church's possessions.[103] He also began the freeing of individual churches and ecclesiastical persons from the burdens of state.[104] Chrodechilde [Clovis' wife] did not remain in his shadow; Gregory of Tours is full of her praise: she richly gave churches, monasteries, and other holy places; one could have held her not for a queen but for a maiden of God."[105]

"Then, from the 22nd of June, 508 (Variae, I, 42), Theodoric, liberated from imperial attacks on the Italian coasts, thanks to the retreat of the fleet that believed to have attained its goal—that is to help Alaric

[100] On the war of Clovis against the Visigoths, cf. EWIG, Die Fränkische Reichsbildung, 258-260; LOT F., Naissance de la France, 28-32; ROUCHÉ M., L'Aquitaine des Wisigoths aux Arabes, naissance d'une nation (418-781), Paris, 1978; ZÖLLNER, op. cit., 67.
Pontal, Odette. Histoire des Conciles Mérovingiens.N.p.: Éditions du Cerf, 1989, 38.
[101] Cf. Chapter 1 p. 120 note 1.
[102] This conjecture is guided by the way in which the first Synod of Orléans can. 5 speaks of the king's gifts, still to be made: De oblationibus vel agris, quos domnus noster rex ecclesiis suo munere conferre dignatus est vel adhuc non habentibus deo sibi inspirante contulerit.
[103] Con. Aurel. I (a. 511) can. 10.
[104] Cf. Con. Aurel. I (a. 511) can. 5, where the subject is gifts: ipsorum agrorum vel clericorum immunitate concessa.
[105] Hist. Franc. III, 18; cf. IV 1.
Albert Hauck, Kirchengeschichte Deutschlands, [Church History of Germany] Bd. I 3rd and 4th edition, 1904, 1:136.

II—hurried to rally his troops. Lead by Duke Ibba, they entered Provence.

These events verified one more time the principle of *lex gothica*, this law that confounded ethnic belonging and Arian belief. As Gregory of Tours said: "they call, in effect, the men of our religion Romans" (G.M., 24 and 78-79).) This confusion between Roman political status and Catholic faith shows to what extent the conflict was insoluble. *It could only be separated through the disappearance of one of the two religions, the one that mixed the State and the Church.*[106]

Professor Rouche just placed his finger on the central contentious issue between the Catholic Church and the Arian Christians: religious liberty. The religion that did not have the "arms" of Clovis backing it was destined to be nothing but a memory of history. And that was exactly what happened to the Visigoths as nearly all of Gaul was now under the jurisdiction of Catholic Clovis except for two provinces that were under the rule of Theodore the Great. Here is illustrated the very reason why heaven did not provide definitive dating for the uprooting of the three horns. It is indisputable that there was a war between Catholic Clovis and the Arian King Alaric II. And it goes without argument that Gaul changed hands from Arian jurisdiction to that of Catholic jurisdiction. However, all the Visigoths from other provinces, including Spain, were not uprooted at all during this time. In fact, these peoples existed for many more years thereafter until the "Visigothic monarchy adopted Catholicism in 587."[107] By the introduction of the 8th century they had faded into oblivion. This fact and principle will be reinforced and repeated when we contend with the Ostrogoths, for that is the whole point. The emphasis of the scriptures was not focused on the end of a race because all who would renounce their former faith and succumb to Catholicism could live out their lives in peace. This is

---

[106] Rouche, Michel. *Clovis*. Fayard, France, 1996, 322.
[107] Scott, S. P., trans., ed. *The Visigothic Code (Forum Judicum)*. Boston: Boston Book, 1910, xxxix.

confirmed by a letter sent from Pope Vigilius (537-555) to
Bishop Menna on October 15, 540:

Letter V. of Pope Vigilius to Menna.

Mansi states: "He is congratulating him that he has
embraced four holy universal synods with heretics
having been condemned: that those repenting from the
heresy ought to be received. . . ."[108]

We begin with Pope Vigilius's letter:

[38] "Although I have advised with a universal sermon, insofar as I have been able and believed to expe-
dite with God helping, for our lord son and very serene
and very Christian emperor concerning the ecclesiastic reasons of my insinuation; nevertheless I have
judged it necessary also to direct writings through the
person of our very Christian brother patrician Dominicus to your dearness: know that I have supported for
them with great exultation and joy, because you help to
protect inviolably the very holy synods of Nicaea,
Constantinople, Ephesus, and Chalcedon, in which the
foundations of orthodox and apostolic faith are shown
. . . . [39] **(Concerning heretics who repent.)** Reserving
this only, just as it is fitting for apostolic moderation,
through everything, that if anyone either of these or of
whatever ones are erring as if doing penitence with the
truth of the Catholic faith recognized wanted to revert,
and condemned the universal depravity of the heresy
in which he was rolled up by a contemptible error, and
of the scripture also by a profession of his errors and
accomplices, and following the precepts of apostolic
doctrine he spoke anthemas to him, who either does
not follow the four synods mentioned above in the case
of faith, or does not confess in all things the venerable
laws of my predecessor Leon, of blessed memory, and
does not follow in all strength and all purity of mind,
then he is handled under the apostolic and canonic sat-

---

[108] Mansi, Joannes Dominicus. *Sacrorum Conciliorum: Nova, et Amplissima Collectio*, bk. 9, facs. ed. Paris: Welter, 1902, 9:38.

isfaction of our communion (which it is fitting that I deny to no penitent), [40] just as I said above, in all ways: because our redeemer did not come to destroy anyone, but to save all through his own piety. "And by the hand of the lord pope." With God helping through the grace of himself Vigilius the bishop of the holy Catholic church of the city of Rome has recognized, and signed these pages of the letter written above, with himself aiding, which I have spoken with God helping. "And with another hand the subscription of Flavius Dominicus patricius." I, Flavius Dominicus a very famous official of the domestics, exconsul and patrician, rereading, conferring, and agreeing, have signed these pages made by the most blessed an apostolic pope Vigilus in the case of faith for the our lord the very pious and very Christian leader Justinianus, but also for Menna a very blessed man bishop of the city-state Constantinople, I relegating, conferring, and agreeing have signed, on the 15 day of the Kalends of October, when Justinus a very famous man is consul. **(In the year of the lord 540.)**"[109]

The real emphasis of the scriptures was the removal of Arian jurisdiction from the three main and distinct Arian kingdoms as stated by Procopius and having it replaced with Catholic jurisdiction. As long as that Arian principle of religious liberty (which was diametrically opposed to the government of the Catholic Church) was still in place and upheld judicially by those Arian powers and enforced by civil means, the scriptures could not yet be fulfilled:

Daniel 7:24 ". . . . And he shall subdue three kings"

Unfortunately, there has been a misreading of the Bible here. Simply put, the uprooting of a race is when the nationality of those peoples no longer exists. The uprooting of a kingdom occurs when its legislative branch

[109] Mansi, Joannes Dominicus. *Sacrorum Conciliorum: Nova, et Amplissima Collectio*, bk. 9, facs. ed. Paris: Welter, 1902, 9:38-40. [Bold wording is found along the margins.]

no longer functions and its means of civil enforcement ceases to exist. *The Billings Gazette* fully illustrates this universally accepted and understood principle.[110] By setting up Catholic legislation as supreme in a previously held Arian territorial jurisdiction, that kingdom was "plucked up by the roots." That legal basis under Clovis was fully documented in our *A.D. 508 Source Book.* Nevertheless, we will briefly recap to reinforce our point:

> "The sources of Roman law, however, which included the Hermogenian, Gregorian and Theodosian codes, the Theodosian Novels and the writings of the jurists, and interpretations of law now unknown were too voluminous, their language was not sufficiently clear for popular use, and custom had also made changes in their interpretation. These facts and the opportunity to conciliate his Catholic subjects, who had suffered persecution under Euric, and who, it was feared, might support the Franks in the conflict with that nation which seemed imminent, led Alaric II to undertake a compilation of Roman law for use in purely Roman litigation. This was the *Lex Romana Visigothorum*, generally known as the *Breviary of Alaric*. It is the work of a commission of provincial Roman lawyers and bishops. It was approved by a

---

[110] 1939: Russia invades Poland
"Soviet Russia was reported to have sent her mobilized Red army surging across the frontier into eastern Poland early Sunday along a 600-mile line of invasion," reported the Albuquerque Journal on September 17, 1939. Russia officially proclaimed neutrality while invading the already-overcome country.
"The government was understood unofficially to have sent a note Saturday night to the Polish ambassador here saying that the red army would enter the Polish Ukraine and White Russia at six a.m. today [...] from Polotzk to Kamanetz-Podolsk," explained The Ogden Standard-Examiner on September 17, 1939. "Copies of this note were said also to have been sent simultaneously to all diplomatic representatives here saying the action was taken because Poland no longer exists. It was said to have declared there no longer is a Polish government because its whereabouts are unknown." *The Billings Gazette*, September 17, 1939.

council of bishops and nobles and was then published in 506 with the command that in the future no other source of law should be used by Roman subjects. In its legislation and interpretations of law, which were derived from existing glosses, we have the Roman law of the fifth and early sixth centuries as it was applied in the courts. A review of its provisions relating to the church and clergy will illustrate their position in an age when the civilizations of German and Roman were blending and ecclesiastical aims were coming to dominate both. The political conditions under which the Breviary was compiled prevented any extensive reproduction of the imperial edicts against heresy. Only two of these in the Theodosian code were included, one in which Honorius ordered the 'one and true Catholic faith' to be observed in Africa, the other his confirmation of the legislation of Theodosius, while the Novels of Theodosius II and Valentinian III, enacted when heresy was no longer a political problem, were allowed to remain unaltered."[111]

It was Alaric II, the Arian Christian King, that undertook the compilation of *the Lex Romana Visigothorum* law code, commonly called *"Breviaricum Alaricianum,"* in part to "conciliate his Catholic subjects" since bishops participated in its formulation and in its approval. But with Alaric II and his army put out of the way and replaced with Catholic Clovis and his military forces, there was no longer a need to just "conciliate his [Alaric II] Catholic subjects." As the Arians were now legally and methodically being driven out of Gaul, the following legislation now applied to them, as well, when and where it could be enforced:

"TITLE 11: RELIGION (DE RELIGIONE)

1. Emperors Arcadius and Honorius Augustuses to Apollo-dorus, Proconsul of Africa.

---

[111] William K. Boyd, *The Ecclesiastical Edicts of the Theodosian Code* (New York: Columbia University Press, 1905; reprint, Clark, New Jersey: Lawbook Exchange, 2005), 109-11.

Whenever there is an action involving matters of religion, the bishops must conduct such action. But all other cases which belong to the judges ordinary and to the usage of the secular law must be heard in accordance with the laws.

Given on the thirteenth day before the kalends of September at Padua in the year of the consulship of the Most Noble Theodorus.–August 20, 399.

[Interpretation:] This law does not need any interpretation.

2. Emperors Arcadius, Honorius, and Theodosius Augustuses to Diotimus, Proconsul of Africa.

It is Our will that the edict regarding unity which Our Clemency dispatched throughout the districts of Africa shall be posted, throughout various regions, in order that all men may know that the one and true Catholic faith in Almighty God, as confessed by right belief, shall be preserved.

Given on the third day before the nones of March at Revenna in the year of the second consulship of Stilicho and the consulship of Anthemius.—March 5, 405.

3. Emperors Honorius and Theodosius Augustuses to Their dear friend, Marcellinus, Greetings.

We abolish the new superstition, and We command that those regulations in regard to the Catholic law shall be preserved unimpaired and inviolate as they were formerly ordained by antiquity or established by the religious authority of Our Fathers or confirmed by Our Serenity.

Given on the day before the ides of October at Revenna in the year of the consulship of the Most Noble Varanes.—October 14, 410."[112]

Clyde Pharr lists the *Breviary of Alaric* law codes in his footnotes for title 11 on pg. 476, 600. The following

---

[112] Clyde Pharr, *The Theodosian Code and Novels and the Sirmondian Constitutions* (Clark, New Jersey: Lawbook Exchange, 2001), 476. Clyde Pharr lists the *Breviary of Alaric* law codes in his footnotes for title 11 on pg. 476. See also pg. 600.

quote is taken directly from the *Lex Romana Visigothorum*. Also called the *Breviary of Alaric*, this is the most
complete work of this law code to date which was originally issued in 506 in Latin. The original is supplied for
those who would appreciate the documentation:

"TITULUS V. [a]) DE RELIGIONE. 1. [b]) Impp.
Arcadius et Honorius AA. Apollodoro Proconsuli
Africae. Quoties de religione agitur, episcopos convenit
agitare; ceteras vero *causas* , quae ad ordinarios cogn-
itores vel ad usum publici iuris pertinent, legibus
oportet audiri. Dat. XIII. Kal. Sept. Patavio, Theodoro
V. C. Cos. Haec Lex interpretatione non indiget. (2.) [c])
Imppp. Arcadius, Honorius et Theodosius AAA.
Diotimo Proconsuli Africae. Edictum, quod de unitate
per Africanas regiones clementia nostra direxit, per di-
versas provincias proponi volumus, ut omnibus in-
notescat, Dei omnipotentis unam et veram fidem
catholicam, quam recta credulitas confitetur, esse reti-
nendam. Dat. III. Non. Mart. Ravenna, Stilicone II. et
Anthemio Coss. (3.) [d]) Impp. Honorius et Theodosius
AA. Marcellino suo salutem. Ea, quae circa catholicam
legem vel olim ordinavit antiquitas, vel parentum nos-
trorum auctoritas religiosa constituit, vet nostra seren-
itas roboravit, novella superstitione summota, integra
et inviolata custodiri praecipimus. Dat. prid. Id. Oct.
Ravenna, Varane V. C. Cos. Haec Lex interpretatione
non indiget [e]). EXPLICIT CODICIS THEODOSIANI
LIBER DECIMUS SEXTUS."[113]

For this same work in German, see Max Conrat
(Cohn), *Breviarium Alaricianum* (1903, 1963). See also
Theodor Mommsen, Theodosiani, for a good reference to
the *Breviary* codes in Latin.

Also included in the *Lex Romana Visigothorum* law
code were the Novels of Theodosius II and Valentinian
III which were enacted against heretics. When heresy
was no longer a political problem, they were allowed to

---

[113] Gustavus Haenel, *Lex Romana Visigothorum* (Teubner: (Lipsiae)
1849, 1962), 252.

remain unaltered, but later were enforced against the Arians in Gaul, as well:

"DE IUDAEIS, SAMARITANIS, HAERETICIS ET PAGANIS."
[Concerning Jews, Samaritans, Heretics and Pagans]

Novellarum of Theodosius II. Tit. III. (a)

(b) *The August Emperors Theodosius and Valentinianus to the Very pious Pope Florentius.*

[256] "Among other concerns, which public love has brought to us by vigilant knowledge, we understand that the special care of the imperial majesty is the dragnet to ferret out true religion; if we have been able to keep the worship of it, we open the way of prosperity to human undertakings. And this is what by the use of an experienced long lifetime, we have decreed to establish by the decision of a pious mind all the way up to posterity by the law of eternity with a ceremony of sanctity. ~1. Indeed who when he has been seized by such a mind, has been condemned by such cruelty of new fierceness, that, when he sees the heaven of divine art end determine the limits of time for the empire by incredible swiftness under its own spaces, when {he sees} the motion of stars, the moderating of life by convenience, the earth endowed with harvests, the liquid sea and the vastness of an immense work enclosed by the boundaries of nature, he does not seek the author of so great a mystery, so great a building? We know what the Jews, blinded to their senses, Samaritans, pagans and the rest of the heretical omens dare {or: that they are bold}. If we try to call these back to the sanity of an excellent mind by a healing law, they themselves will offer the blame of severity, they who do not leave the place of forgiveness with an obstinate expiation of a harsh forehead. ~2. On account of which since, by the old opinion, no treatment should be applied to hopeless diseases, at last tell me, in order that the fatal sects not spread into life, when they are heedless of our lifetime, just as by indiscrete confession rather will-

ingly, we sanction with this (c) law to prevail for every age, that no Jew, no Samaritan invariable from neither law approach to honors and political offices, extend to no one the administration of civil obedience, nor even enjoy the office of a defender. Indeed we believe that it is wrong

---

Sich. Has "Tit. II." Cod. 19 has "Tit. I." It is missing in codices 23, 24, where in fact the rest of the Novellas have been marked with the right number, that this has been omitted either by design, or has fallen out in the codex, from which 23, 24 descend, it would be necessary.

The whole novella with the interpretation is in codices 1, 2, 4-11, 14-16. Everything except the interpr. Is missing in cod. 33, which indeed, since the title also is omitted, is consistent with the earlier Nov.; but since the followings of the Novellas received in Br. A. keep themselves correctly, the copyist seems to have fallen in error. The inscr. and text are missing in codd. 21, 22. 25; the text and subscr. in codd. 27, 28; the subscr. and interpr. In cod. 26; the text alone in codd. 12, 29-32, 34-38, 40; part of the text is omitted in cod. 39; the interpr. alone in cod. 19; the text alone and a bit of the interpretation remain in codd. 42, 44, 45. Can. 73 of the Council of Meldense. Cod. Barberin. P. 11, 9, p. 197 {107?}. See note *c*. Concerning cod. 17 see below note *d* and *e*.

Here Inc. c. 73 Council of Meld. are cited? and a fragment of the cod. Barber, which is ended with the word "he brought over" Sphi 4.

Epit. Aeg.

Tit. III. Concerning Jews, Samaritans, Heretics and Pagans (a).

In cod. 48 all in red.

[257] **Epit. Suppl. Lat. 215.**

Tit. III. Concerning Jews, Samaritans, Heretics and Pagans

Epit. Guelph.

III. Concerning Jews. Samaritans, Heirs. and Pagans.

{symbols} (a)

Confer? Th. II, 1, 10.

Epit. Lugd.

III. Concerning the Jews.

Epit. Monachi.

III. Concerning the Jews, Samaritans, Heretics and Pagans.

Epit. S. Gall.

III. (a) Concerning the Jews Samaritans, Heirs and (b) Pagans.

66 *II.* See above at the beginning of the Novell. note *h*.

65 omits "and."

[258] that worshipers who are unfriendly to Roman laws and their majesty also are governed by the pretense (d) of the stealthy jurisdiction of our laws, and have the power of judging or pronouncing what they wish, when they have been fortified with the authority of an acquired honor, against Christians and often even the priests of the sacred religion, just as if gloating over our faith: ~3. When the [ancestors] prevent that also by an equal consideration of reason, that not any synagogue should rise into a new building, even when they granted permission of supporting, things which [synagogues] threaten immediate ruin. ~4. We have added to these things, that whosoever has led a slave or native unwillingly or by a persuasive beating from the worship of the Christian religion into a wicked sect or rite, should be punished (e) by the loss of his property by his head. ~5. In order therefore that anyone who has either received fillets, or has constructed a synagogue, should not have power when these honors have been acquired, he should know that he has labored by the profit of the Catholic Church. Indeed the one who has sneaked in to honors, should be held, as before, of

an extreme condition, even if he has deserved an honorary worthiness. And the one who has begun the building of a synagogue, not with the desire of repairing it, should be cheated out of his own attempts with the forfeiture of five hundred pounds of gold. Moreover he should determine his own goods proscribed, since he is about to be designated soon to the penalty of blood, if he has attacked the faith of another by a perverse doctrine. ~6. And since it is fitting that imperial majesty be embraced by all that provision, so that public utility is harmed among no one, the ward members of all the citystates, and the cohortalinos as well, since they are obligated to their own orders by onerous duties yea indeed of military service or by the diverse duties of property and personal responsibilities, of whatever sect they are, we decree should inhere so that we do not seem to have granted a benefit to humans who should be execrated by the contumelious area of immunity, when we wish to condemn them by the authority of this constitution. ~7. With this exception preserved, that the servants of the above mentioned sects follow the opinions of no judge in only private businesses, and not preside over the guard of a prison, lest Christians, as it is customary to happen, sometimes allow another prison to be concealed by the hatreds of the guards, uncertain, or seem obstructed by law. ~8. Hence our clemency understands, that we ought to obtain the vigil of the pagans also and of the gentile cruelty, who, by natural insanity and pertinacious license, disagreeing with the path of true religion, refuse to practice the wicked rites of sacrifices and the errors of destructive superstition with hidden as it were solitudes, unless their crimes are made public for the injury of the celestial majesty and the contempt of our time by a kind of profession, those whom a thousand terrors of promulgated laws do not restrain, nor by the penalty of a threatened exile; so that, if they are not able to be changed, at least they would learn to abstain from the mass of crimes and from the filth of sacrifices. But truly this boldness of fury is wronged; our patience is struck by those attempts of the wicked, so that, if he wishes to be forgotten, he is

not able to pretend. Although the love of religion therefore is never able to be secure, although the pagan de-
mentia of all supplications demands acerbities,
nevertheless mindful of the leniency inborn in us, we
decree with a beam-like order, that, whoever has been
caught in whatever place in sacrifice with polluted and
contaminated minds, our anger may rise against the
blood, against the fortunes of him. Indeed it is proper
that we give this better victim, with the intact altar of
Christianity protected. Or do we carry for a longer
time, that the alternations of times be changed by an
irate temper of heaven? This exacerbated treachery of
the pagans does not know how to protect the balances
of nature. For whence has the spring perjured the accustomed grace? Whence has time abandoned the
farmer who has been laboring in hope of ears of grains
with a poor harvest? Whence has the intemperate fe-
rocity of winter harmed the richness of the lands with
the injury of sterility with penetrating frost? Unless
that which has been decreed crosses to the revenge of
impiety by the nature of its own law. Lest we are forced
to sustain this afterwards, by pacific punishment, as
we said, the venerable majesty of the heavenly divine
will must be held pious.

~9 . It remains, that the things which have been
brought against the Manichaeans, who have always
been offensive by God, and the things against the
Eunomians, the originators of the heretical silliness,
and the things against the Montanistas, the Cataphry-
gans, the Photinians, the Priscillianists, the Ascodrogans,
the Hydroparastatans, the Borboritans, the Ophitans
with innumerable constitutions, with sloth ceasing,
should be entrusted to swift execution, Florentius,
most dear and most loving father.

~10. Therefore may your illustrious and magnificent authority, to which it is agreeable, that obedience
adhere to both the divine, as well as the principal commands, see to it that the things which we have decreed
by the insatiable honor of the catholic religion, when
the edicts of your excellence have been solemnly proposed, arrive into the notice of all. It should also in-

struct to become known to the moderators of the provinces also, so that they also make known both to all the citystates and the provinces with their equal solicitude, the things which we sanction necessarily. *Dated on the first day of the Kalends of Febr. At Constantinople, when Theodosius the August XVI is. Consul and the one who has been announced. By the same copy to the illustrious man the Most Pious Pope of Illyricus.*

Interpretation. This law especially orders, that no Jew, no Samaritan should be able to approach to any honor of the military or administration, nor to receive the office of defender by any reason, nor be guards of a prison: so that by chance under the appearance (f) of whatever office those, written above, who are enemies of our law do not dare to bother Christians or even priests under any occasion with injuries, nor presume either to condemn or to judge with our laws, anyone. Also they should not dare to build any synagogue. For if they have done so, they should know, that this building will be used for a Catholic Church, and that the makers of the building should be punished by five hundred pounds. But they should know that it has been granted to them, that they ought to repair the ruins of their synagogues. This especially is also contained in this law, that no Jew should dare to transfer a slave or native Christian by any kind of persuasion into his own law. But if it should happen, when his resources have been lost, he should be punished by death. Concerning the rest in truth this law condemns the sects, which are contained by name inserted in this law.

d) The words "cover/pretense—although the love of religion therefore" in Sphi 8 in cod. 17 have been transposed to c. 3 concerning the Episcopal judgment and are consistent with the words "of all the priests" in c. 3 Siromond. Then they are equal to the final words of c. 3 Siromn, and then Nov. Th. tit. 1., next Nov. Th. tit. II., and finally Nov. Th. tit. III. Concerning the Jews all the way up to the words of Section 4 "of fortunes with his head," by which the words of the first Novella cod. 17 are ended.

e) The word "must be punished" (Section 4) is the first one of the quaternion XXII. Codex 17a, as, at that place where the quaternion XXI. Cod. 17 is ended, at that place it continues into cod. 17d.

f) This and the following are in can. 73 of the Council of Meldense.

Epit. Aeg.

[Interpretation]

It is not permitted that a Jew or Samaritan conduct any kind of army, nor become for any reason a defender, nor be a guard of a prison, nor build a new synagogue, nor should those written above, who are enemies of our law, presume either to condemn or to sentence anyone by our laws, for if they have done so, they should be punished by five hundred pounds of gold. Nor should they presume to transfer a Christian slave or native into their own law. But if he has, he should be punished (b) by death after his property has been taken.

Aeg. has "they have—they should be punished." 54 omits {the last two sentences:} "Nor should . . . aken."

Epit. Suppl. Lat. 215.

It is not permitted that a Jew or Samaritan conduct any kind of army, nor become for any reason a defender, nor be a guard of a prison, nor build a new synagogue, but a presumer of the same kind of buildings should be fined (a) five hundred pounds of gold, nor should he presume to transfer a Christian slave or native by any kind of occasion into his own correct things (b). But if he has, he should be punished (b) after his property has been taken. This must be condemned also concerning the remaining sects.

Read "of the building—should be fined."

Read "sects."

[259] **Epit. Guelph.**

[Interpretation]

It is not permitted to these to approach any honor for the military (b), nor should they presume to build a synagogues by/for Jews. They should be forced to pay five hundred pounds of gold. For they were willing to transfer into their own laws (c). By death he should be punished with property.

b) Sp.has "permitted..military {better spelling} or of a synagogue."
Sp. has "to transfer by law he should be punished {better spelling} by death."

Epit. Lugd.

That no Jew, finally no Samaritan ought to approach to any honor of the army or of administration, nor undertake the duty of defendor, nor the guarding of a prison, nor by our laws, ought any who are enemies of our law, to condemn or sentence anyone; nor to build a synagogue, unless only to repair an old one. A Jew who has persuaded a slave or native in his own law, is punished by death when his property is first taken away (a) and the rest.

Read {variant spelling of} "taken away."

Epit. Monachi.

No Jew, nor Samaritan may become for the army or the honor of administration either a defender or a guard of a prison, lest they should be able to impose injuries on Christians or (a) also on priests under any occasion, nor should those, who are contrary to our laws, presume to judge any. They should consider (b) to construct no synagogue. But if he have, a catholic church should be constructed in the same place and the authors of this building should be punished by five hundred pounds of gold: and this only should only be for them an agreement, that they ought to repair the ruins of their synagogues.. No Jew should dare to transfer a Christian by any kind of persuasion into his own law. But if he has, he should punished by death when his property has been removed. Our anger should rise with indeed pagans, heretics, Manichaenas, Eunomians, Montanissts, Photinians and all heretics (c) into their fortunes and into blood. It is necessary indeed that we give this victim, in order that we keep intact the better altar of Christianity. *Dated on the first day of Kal. of Febr. when Theodosius the August XVI. Is Consul.*

63 has "a Christian or"
Read "they should dare."
The remaining words are taken from the law itself. See Section 8, 9.

Subscript. is omitted in cod. 62.
Epit. S. Gall.
Given by Emp. Theods. II (c) on the kal. of feb.
Intrp. No Christian should presume to send for a Jew I
Samaritan neither a judge nor an agent (d) nor ought a
Jew to judge cases of Christians in any manner but if
someone has done so, he should presume to send him
an agent. He should pay 50 pounds of gold; Similarly
no Jew (g) should presume to lead not (i) a Christian
slave to his (h) own law lest if he has done this he
should be punished by death.
65 has "Theodosius—XII."
65 has "by judge nor agent."   61   has   "by   an
agent."
65, 67 have "Jews" and 61 has "none."
65, 67 have "by an agent."
66 has "jews." 67 has "Christian."
66 has "by his own law." 67 has "by his own."
66 omits "not."[114]

With Clovis' Merovingian dynasty coming into power
and ascending to the Catholic faith, Theodore the Great,
the Arian King of the Ostrogoths, decreed between the
years 507-511 a most remarkable decree. This decree
was honored by the Arians but was diametrically opposed to the principles and government of the Catholic
Church:

The Letters of Cassiodorus

507 A.D.—511 A.D
Book II—27.

King Theodoric to all the Jews living in Genoa

"The Jews are permitted to roof in the old walls of
their synagogue, but they are not to enlarge it beyond
its old borders, nor to add any kind of ornament, under

114 Gustavus Haenel, *Lex Romana Visigothorum*, "DE IUDAEIS,
SAMARITANIS, HAERETICIS ET PAGANIS" (Teubner: (Lipsiae)
1849, 1962), 256-259.

pain of the Kings sharp displeasure; and this leave it granted on the understanding that it does not conflict with the thirty years 'Statute of Limitations.'

'Why do ye desire what ye ought to shun? In truth we give the permission which you craved, but we suitably blame the desire on your wandering minds. *We cannot order a religion, because no one is forced to believe against his will.*"[115]

While the Arian Christians of the West and East were not at all free from some entanglements of church and state as we know and understand today, nevertheless, they never crossed the red line by resorting to force in religious matters against the will of an individual whether he be of the Arian or Catholic faith. This could hardly be said of the Catholic Church. It is here, in the issue of religious liberty that the war between two completely different ideologies climaxes in 538. This has been the best kept secret of the Dark Ages. Theodore Mommsen dates Theodore the Great's Book II, 27, law code between 507-511, and no one disputes the dating of his letters of Cassiodorus. When Clovis overthrew the Visigoths at Vougle in A.D. 508, religious intolerance reared her ugly head. This came about slowly at first but, nevertheless, methodically. Hereby, it has been demonstrated from the primary and judicial sources that this was a religious war and that the Visigoths were the first of the three horns to be "plucked up by the roots."

[115] Cassiodorus, Magnus Aurelius, Hodgkin, Thomas, *The Letters of Cassiodorus*. London: Henry Frowde, 1886, 185-6.

6

The Vandals

The fall of the Vandal kingdom transpired under the rule of the Byzantine Emperor of the East, Justinian I. Justinian came to the throne in August of A.D. 527, but it would not be until the years 533-4 that we would see the demise of the second horn or kingdom subdued, the Arian Vandal kingdom of Africa.

"On April 1, 527 the emperor named him a co-regent. The collective government granted only four months. Justin died and left complete sovereignty to Justinian. . . . he turned his attentions to the execution of far-fetched plans for the government. "It seemed that he wanted to fulfill greater things than he was able. Centralization and uniformity were his solution. *One* state, *one* law, *one church should rule the world*; an absolute authority should reign in them, and he himself should be this authority."[116] To restore Roman world-empire within its old borders, to elevate it to olds previous power, to win back its earlier glory, was the goal of Justinian's external politics. He had attained this goal. His wars brought him the fame of a *restitutor urbis et orbis* and the title of "a ruler of the Alemanni, Goths, Franks, Germanics, Anten, Alani, and Vandals in Africa.[117]

---

[116] Ad. Schmidt. l.c. p. 12.
[117] Nov. (17) XXI ed. C.E. Zachariae a Lingenthal. Lipsiae 1881. pars I. p. 137; Byzant. Ztschr. 3 (1894). p. 21—23.—Georgii Cyprii descrip-

Justinian dreamed of a universal empire. To him this Roman world disappeared by the heretical Germanic kingdoms. He proclaimed himself the legitimate inheritor and wished to reconstitute it in his integrity. These imperial rights that all his predecessors had carefully reserved, he aspired to increase to their fullest extent. To accomplish this, Justinian fully understood what he must do and so also did the Catholic Church. Working from behind the scenes, the Catholic Church set out to accomplish her primary objective, the overthrow of the Arian Vandal kingdom:

"John the Cappadocian, the Pretorian Prefect, a man of the greatest daring and the cleverest of all men of his time. For this John, while all the others were bewailing in silence the fortune which was upon them, came before the emperor and spoke as follows: "O Emperor, the good faith which thou dost shew in dealing with thy subjects enables us to speak frankly regarding anything which will be of advantage to thy government, even though what is said and done may not be agreeable to thee. For thus does thy wisdom temper thy authority with justice, in that thou dost not consider that man only as loyal to thy cause who serves thee under any and all conditions, nor art thou angry with the man who speaks against thee, but by weighing

---

(*Cont.*)
tion orbis Romani ed. H. Gelzer. Lipsiae 1890. Cf. Byzant. Ztschr. 1. (1892) p. 601 ff.—L'Illyricum ecclésiastique par L. Duchesne in Byzant. Ztschr. 1 (1892) p. 531 ss.—G. H. Bruckner, An Justinianus imp. recte usurpaverit titulos Germanici e Alemannici. Jenae 1709.— F. G. Grebel-Leyser, *Defensio Justiniani contra obtrectatores.* Vitenbergae 1748. p. 12 ss: The Roman emperors attached such titles to themselves when they had achieved a victory over a people, even if they had not brought said people into their power. Justinian did not name himself *pater patriae*, and much less *pontifex maximus*, as had Constantine and his direct successors, but he did likely call himself *servus dei*, l.c. p. 15.
    Knecht, August. *Die Religions-Politik: Kaiser Justinians I: Eine kirchenges-chichtliche Studie.* (Dissert. Würzberg, 1896), 7-8. [Andreas Gobel, *The Religious Politics of Emperor Justinian I*, Wurzberg, 1896.]

all things by pure reason alone, thou hast often shewn
that it involves us in no danger to oppose thy purposes.
Led by these considerations, O Emperor, I have come
to offer this advice, knowing that, though I shall give
perhaps offence at the moment, if it so chance, yet in
the future the loyalty which I bear you will be made
clear, and that for this I shall be able to shew thee as a
witness. For if, through not hearkening to my words,
thou shalt carry out the war against the Vandals, it will
come about, if the struggle is prolonged for thee, that
my advice will win renown. For if thou hast confidence
that thou wilt conquer the enemy, it is not at all unrea-
sonable that thou shouldst sacrifice the lives of men
and expend a vast amount of treasure, and undergo the
difficulties of the struggle; for victory, coming at the
end, covers up all the calamities of war. But if in reality
these things lie on the knees of God, and if it behooves
us, taking example from what has happened in the
past, to fear the outcome of war, on what grounds is it
not better to love a state of quiet rather than the dangers of mortal strife? Thou art purposing to make an
expedition against Carthage, to which, if one goes by
land, the journey is one of a hundred and forty days,
and if one goes by water, he is forced to cross the
whole open sea and go to its very end. So that he who
brings thee news of what will happen in the camp must
needs reach thee a year after the event. And one might
add that if thou art victorious over thy enemy, thou
couldst not take possession of Libya while Sicily and
Italy lie in the hands of others; and at the same time, if
any reverse befall thee, O Emperor, the treaty having
already been broken by thee, thou wilt bring-the danger upon our own land. In fact, putting all in a word, it
will not be possible for thee to reap the fruits of victory,
and at the same time any reversal of fortune will bring
harm to what is well established. It is before an enterprise that wise planning is useful. For when men have
failed, repentance is of no avail, but before disaster
comes there is no danger in altering plans. Therefore it
will be of advantage above all else to make fitting use
of the decisive moment." Thus spoke John; and the
Emperor Justinian hearkening to his words, checked

his eager desire for the war. *But one of the priests whom they call bishops, who had come from the East, said that he wished to have a word with the emperor. And when he met Justinian, he said that God had visited him in a dream, and bidden him go to the emperor and rebuke him, because, after undertaking the task of protecting the Christians in Libya from tyrants, he had for no good reason become afraid. "And yet," He had said, "I will myself join with him in waging war and make him lord of Libya." When the emperor heard this, he was no longer able to restrain his purpose, and he began to collect the army and the ships, and to make ready supplies of weapons and of food, and he announced to Belisarius that he should he in readiness, because he was very soon to act as general in Libya."*[118]

As revealed in his Corpus Juris Civilis, Justinian trusted in divine protection, considering every ensemble as the restorer of the rights of the empire and the champion of God. He waited only for his opportunity to translate into action his ambitious dreams, and thanks to the church he found his pretext to strike:

"However, this was a grave day, when June 22 of the year 533 the expedition put to sail in order to leave Constantinople. The emperor himself, the windows of the palace, presided over the ceremony; the patriarch of Byzance, surrounded by his clergy, descended on the port in order to call the celestial benediction on the combatants of the pious enterprise, and bless the chief and the soldiers that departed for this sort of crusade."[119]

The following is the account of the war with the Vandals by Diehl that I have summarized:

---

[118] Procopius. *History of the Wars.* Translated by H. B. Dewing. Bks. 1–8. In Loeb Classical Library, edited by Jeffrey Henderson. Cambridge, MA: Harvard Univ. Press, 2000–2001, III. X. 7-24.

[119] Procopius, De *Bello. Vandalico*, ed. De la Byzantine de Bonn. 362. Diehl, Charles. *L'Afrique Byzantine: Histoire de la Domination Byzantine en Afrique (533–709)*, (Paris, New York, 1896), 1:15. [*History of the Byzantine Domination in Africa*]

[21] "The Battle of Ad Decimum took place on September 13, 533 between the armies of the Vandals, commanded by King Gelimer and Justinian's general Belisarius and in one day Belisarius proved the victor. . . . [22] This victory of Ad Decimum opened the route from Carthage for the Byzantine army. . . . [23] The fall of the Vandal capital was an event of the utmost significance. It gave the Byzantine army the point of support that it had lacked until then, an excellent base of operations for further military initiatives. . . . [24] Patiently, the Byzantine general waited for his hour; finally it came around the [25] middle of December, around three months after the day of Ad Decimum, he decided to march to the enemy. [December 13, 533] at Ticameron. Gelimer and his people were established at Ticameron. . . . [26] by the end of the winter Gelimer being forced to his last asylum, touched above all by the deprivations without number he yielded to his destiny and put himself in the hands of Belisarius, depending on the promise that his life would be saved and he would have honorable treatment (March 534). The emperor's representative promised with willingness all that the overthrown king demanded. [According to Procopius the promise was made good and Gelimer lived to be an old man in ancient Galatia with his family, now modern Turkey. Procopius continues, "However, Gelimer was by no means enrolled among the patricians, since he was unwilling to change from the Arian faith of Arius."[120]]

. . . . [34] Since the month of December 533, upon the news of the taking of Carthage, Justinian proclaimed in magnificent terms that "all of Libya is reunited to the empire[121]." In April 534, after the victory of Ticameron, he pompously declared that "God, by his graciousness just placed in his hands Africa and all its

---

[120] Procopius. *History of the Wars.* Translated by H. B. Dewing. Bks. 1–8. In Loeb Classical Library, edited by Jeffrey Henderson. Cambridge, MA: Harvard Univ. Press, 2000–2001, IV. ix, 11-16.
[121] *De Confect Digest.* 23; *Codex Just.* I, 17, 2, 1 and 24.

provinces,"[122] and almost amazed himself by the unexpected rapidity of the conquest, he pervaded in actions of grace and gave thanks to Providence to have chosen, "him, the most humble of his servants" to be the avenger of the Church and the liberator of the people."[123]

This was truly a victory for Justinian over the Arian Vandals as the following primary edict issued in 534 will verify:

TITLE XXVII.

CONCERNING THE OFFICE OF PRAETORIAN PREFECT OF AFRICA, AND THE CONDITION OF ALL THE PROVINCES OF HIS JURISDICTION.
In the Name of Our Lord Jesus Christ.

1. *The Emperor Cæsar-Flavius-Justinianus, Alemannicus, Gothicus, Germanicus, Francicus, Anticus, Alanicus, Vandalicus, Africanus, pious, fortunate, illustrious, victor and triumpher, ever Augustus, to Archelaus, Prætorian Prefect of Africa.*

"Our mind cannot conceive nor Our tongue express the thanks and the praise which We should manifest to Our Lord Jesus Christ; for We have previously received many benefits from God, and acknowledge that We have obtained many favors from Him, for which We admit that We have done nothing to render Us worthy; and now what Almighty God has deemed proper to manifest by Our agency for His own praise, and the glory of His Name, exceeds by far all the wonderful occurrences which have taken place during this century; as Africa through Our efforts has received her freedom within a short time, after having for ninety

---

[122] Krueger, Paulus, *Corpus Iurus Civilis, Codex Iustinianus*, (Berlin: Apud Wiedmannos, 1959), *Codex*, I. 27, 1, 7.
[123] Krueger, Paulus, *Corpus Iurus Civilis, Codex Iustinianus*, (Berlin: Apud Wiedmannos, 1959), *Codex*, I. 27, 1, 1, 5. Diehl, Charles. *L'Afrique Byzantine: Histoire de la Domination Byzantine en Afrique (533–709)*, (Paris, New York, 1896), 1:21-26, 34. [*History of the Byzantine Domination in Africa*]

years previously been held in captivity by the Vandals, who are at the same time enemies of both the soul and the body, since by rebaptism they have brought to their perfidious belief such souls as were not able to endure the tortures and punishments inflicted upon them, and the bodies of the latter, illustrious by birth, were subjected to their barbaric yoke, by the exercise of the greatest severity; and some of the Holy Churches of God were profaned with their perfidy, and others were turned into stables. We saw venerable men who with difficulty related their sufferings, whose tongues had been cut out by the roots; and others who, after having endured various cruelties, and having been dispersed through different provinces, passed their lives in exile. In what terms, and with what labor could We give proper thanks to God, who rendered Me, the most humble of His servants, worthy to avenge the wrongs of His Church, and to rescue the people of so many provinces from the bond of servitude?

Our predecessors did not deserve this favor of God, as they were not only not permitted to liberate Africa, but even saw Rome itself captured by the Vandals, and all the Imperial insignia taken from thence to Africa. Now, however, God, in his mercy, has not only delivered Africa and all her provinces into Our hands, but the Imperial insignia as well, which, having been removed at the capture of Rome, He has restored to us.

Therefore after Divinity has conferred upon Us so many benefits, We implored the mercy of our Lord God, to keep firm and unimpaired the provinces which He deigned to restore to Us, and that He would enable Us to govern them according to His will and pleasure; so that all Africa might experience the mercy of the Almighty, and its inhabitants might realize from what a severe captivity and barbaric [131] yoke they had been released, and with what freedom they were entitled to remain under Our most fortunate Empire.

With the intercession of the Holy, Glorious, and Immortal Virgin Mary, the Mother of God, We implore and pray that God will, in His Name, through Us the most humble of His servants, restore everything which has been taken from Our Empire, and will render Us worthy of serving Him.

(1) With the assistance of God, and for the happiness of the State, We order by this divine law that all Africa, which God in His mercy has conferred upon Us, shall enjoy perfect order and have a prefecture of its own; so that, like that of the Orient and of Illyria, Africa, by Our indulgence, may be adorned with the highest praetorian dignity, whose seat We direct to be at Carthage, and that its name be joined with those of the other prefectures, in the preamble of public documents; and We now decree that Your Excellency shall govern it.

(2) From the aforesaid city, with the aid of God, seven provinces with their judges shall be controlled, of which Tingi, Carthage, Bysatium, and Tripoli, formerly under the jurisdiction of Proconsuls, shall have consular rulers; while the others, that is to say, Numidia, Mauritania, and Sardinia shall, with the aid of God, be subject to Governors.

(3) We decree that three hundred and ninety-six persons, distributed among the different bureaus and military departments, shall be attached to your office, as well as to that of all other succeeding Praetorian Prefects of Africa. We also decree that fifty subordinates shall be attached to the office of each of the provinces presided over by consular rulers, or Governors.

(4) The notice appended hereto specifies the emoluments to which You yourself, as well as the said consular rulers and Governors, and each of their employees, shall be entitled from the Public Treasury.

(5) We desire then that all Our judges shall, in accordance with the will and fear of God, and Our choice and direction, endeavor to discharge their duties in such a way that no one may be actuated by cupidity, commit violence himself, or allow other judges or their subordinates, or any persons associated with them to do so. For We shall have reason to rejoice if We should have, throughout the provinces, with the assistance of God, officials free from reproach; and We especially provide for the interests of those tributary to the African jurisdiction, who, with God's assistance, can now perceive the light of freedom after so long a cap-

tivity. Therefore, We order that all violence and avarice shall cease, and that justice and truth shall prevail among all Our tributaries, so that God will be pleased, and Our subjects themselves can more rapidly be relieved and prosper, as do the others of Our Empire.

(6) We order the tax designated *sportulæ* to be collected not only by the illustrious Praetorian Prefect of Africa, but also by the other judges, in the way provided for by Our laws, which should be obeyed [132] throughout all Our Empire, and that no one shall presume at any time or in any way to increase the amount of said tax.

(7) We have thought it best to prescribe by the present law that judges shall not be obliged to incur great outlay for their letters or commissions, either in Our court, or in the offices of the Praetorian Prefect of Africa; because if they are not burdened with expense they will have no reason to oppress Our African subjects. Therefore, We order that the judges of the African jurisdiction, civil and military, shall not, in Our court, be charged more than six *solidi* for their commissions, and the letters authorizing their promotion; and that, in the office of the prefecture, they shall not be obliged to pay more than twelve *solidi*.

If any judge should exceed the amount of the above-mentioned tax, he shall be required to pay a fine of thirty pounds of gold, and he will not only be liable to this fine, but also to the punishment of death. For if anyone should dare to violate Our commands, and should not, with the fear of God, hasten to observe them, he will run the risk of losing his office, and his property, as well as of undergoing the extreme penalty.

(8) The notice above referred to, and which We, with the assistance of God have drawn up, is as follows.[124] . . . .

We have by this Divine Constitution fixed these sums to meet the expenses of the civil magistrates of

---

[124] I have omitted the long schedule of amounts to be paid by the numerous subordinate officials and attaches of the Prefecture of Africa, for the reason that the information it contains could not possibly be of any value to the modern reader.—ED.

Africa and their subordinates, not only those attached to the different departments of the prefecture itself but also to other tribunals. Your Excellency shall see that they are paid and carried into effect beginning with the *Kalends* of September of the thirteenth coming indiction, and you are hereby directed to give notice of this in public edicts addressed to all persons.

We order, by the present Divine Constitution, that these regulations, promulgated by you, shall be established for all time; and with the assistance of God, by Our decree, We have also formulated them with reference to military judges and their subordinate officials, and the remainder of Our army.

2. *The Same to Belisarius, General of the Army of the East.*

In all Our designs and undertakings, We proceed in the name of Our Lord Jesus Christ, from whom We have received the rights of empire, through whom We have established a lasting peace with the Persians, and with His aid, We have defeated the most inveterate enemies and powerful tyrants, and have surmounted the greatest difficulties; and also, by means of His aid, it has been granted Us to defend Africa, and bring it under Our control. Likewise, with His assistance, We trust that it will be governed properly under Our direction, and firmly protected; wherefore, We have already, by the grace of God, appointed judges of civil administration, and established offi- [133] ces in each of the provinces of Africa, assigning to them such emoluments as each should receive; and, committing Our soul to His Divine power, We are now about to make a disposition of the various armies and their leaders.

(1) We order that the commander of the army of the Province of Tripoli shall have his headquarters in the city of Leptis Magna. The military commander of the Province of Byzacene shall alternately reside at Capsal, and the other Leptis. The military commander of the Province of Numidia shall reside in the city of Constantine. The military commander of the Province of Mauritania shall have his headquarters in the city of Caesarea.

(2) We also order you to station at the point opposite Spain, which is called Septa,[125] a considerable
body of troops with their tribune, who must be a pru-
dent man, and one who is devoted to Our Empire, who
can always guard the strait, and give information of
everything that occurs in Spain, Gaul, or the country
of the Franks, to his commander, in order that he may
communicate the information to you; and you shall
cause to be prepared for service in the strait as many
swift vessels as you may deem expedient.

(3) We order Your Excellency to appoint a military
commander in Sardinia, and provide as many soldiers
as may be necessary to guard the places in his jurisdiction, who shall be stationed near the mountains where
the people of Barbary are known to reside.

(4) Let those men to whose care the defence of the
provinces has been entrusted be vigilant and protect
our subjects from being injured by incursions of the
enemy, and be ready to implore the aid of God, by day
and by night, and exert all their efforts to extend the
boundaries of the provinces of Africa to that point
where the Roman Empire had its limits before the invasion of the Vandals and the Moors, and where the
ancient guards were posted; as is shown by the forts
and defences; and, moreover, let them, by all means,
hasten to inclose and fortify those cities which formerly were situated near the fortifications which were
erected when those regions were under Roman domination, when with God's assistance the enemy was ex-
pelled from the said provinces. And, let them dispatch

---

[125] *Septa*, the modern Ceuta, derived its name from the seven *(septem)*
hills, upon which, like Rome, it was constructed. The promontory
nearest the sea was, in ancient times, one of the far-famed Pillars of
Hercules, so called by the Phoenician navigators. Ceuta, of great historical interest, was one of the earliest cities founded by human enterprise, its traditions far transcending in antiquity those of venerable
Damascus. From its harbor, the Moorish army of Tarik, early in the
seventh century, embarked for the conquest of the Spanish Peninsula,
whose success led to the establishment of the most opulent, culti-
vated, and magnificent of mediæval empires. It is now a Spanish
penal colony.—ED.

officers and soldiers to those points where their boundaries were situated at a time when all the provinces of
Africa formed a part of the Roman Empire, as, with the
aid of God, through whose favor they have been restored to Us, We hope speedily to be successful.

In order that these provinces may be preserved in
security and peace, within their ancient limits, through
the vigilant efforts of our [134] most devoted soldiers,
and may remain intact under the care of Our illustrious generals, it is proper that guards should always be
stationed at the boundaries of each province; in order
that no opportunity may be afforded to the enemy to
invade or lay waste those places which are possessed
by Our subjects.

(5) Your Excellency must determine, arrange, and
report to Us, the number of soldiers, either infantry or
cavalry, which it is necessary to post at the boundary
for the purpose of guarding provinces and cities, so
that if We consider the provision which you have made
to be sufficient, We may confirm it; but if We think that
something more should be done, We can increase the
number.

(6) What the general is required to do with reference to himself and the men under his command, and
what his duty is is set forth in the following notice.

(7) Therefore, as has already been stated, while the
officers and soldiers are taking their positions in the
places or towns to which We have ordered them to go,
in accordance with Our disposition of them; then, with
the aid of God and by Our efforts they can be stationed
in those portions of Our dominions whose former
boundaries were defined, when the above-mentioned
provinces constituted an integral part of the flourishing Roman Empire.

(8) In order to maintain the boundaries it seemed
necessary to Us that other soldiers, in addition to those
in the camps, should be posted along them, who could
defend the camps and cities situated there, as well as
cultivate the soil; so that, other inhabitants of the
provinces, seeing them there, might betake themselves
to those places. We have made a list of the number of
soldiers to be appointed to guard the frontiers, to en-

able Your Excellency, in accordance with the said list which We send to you, to make provision for their distribution through the camps and other places; so that, if you should find suitable detachments in the provinces, or where a military force was formerly stationed, you can fix the number of frontier guards for each boundary; and if any trouble should arise, these soldiers can, with their leaders, and without the aid of those in the camps, defend the points where they have been distributed; and neither they themselves nor their officers should extend the boundaries; and all this must be done in such a way that the aforesaid frontier guards may not be subjected to any expense by their officers and the latter may not fraudulently convert any of their pay to their own use.

(9) We desire that these rules shall not only be observed by soldiers appointed to guard the frontier, but also by those who are stationed in camp; and We order that every commander, and the tribunes of said soldiers shall constantly subject them to military exercises, and not permit them to wander about, so that, if necessity should arise, they can offer resistance to the enemy. And no general or tribune shall venture to give them leave of absence, lest while they attempt to earn money for themselves, they may leave Our provinces unprotected; for if any of the above-mentioned officers or their subordinates, or the tribunes, should unlawfully attempt to withhold any pay from the sol- [135] diers, or to acquire any profit from their emoluments, We order that they shall not only be condemned to publicly repay fourfold the amount appropriated, but shall also be deprived of their offices; for the generals and tribunes should expect a greater remuneration from Our liberality, in accordance with their services, than any profit they could acquire in the manner above stated; as the soldiers are appointed for the defense of the provinces, and We certainly furnish sufficient pay to their generals and other officers, and always make provision for their promotion to higher rank, and more important positions, in proportion to their efficiency.

(10) After it may have pleased God for all the boundaries to be restored to their ancient condition,

and properly defined; and whenever necessity may arise, the generals, in their turn, when the case requires it, can, with the assistance of God, contribute by their vigilance and care to preserve the provinces or their frontiers unimpaired.

(11) As We order Our judges and soldiers to be bold and fierce towards the enemy; so We desire them to be gentle and kind towards Our subjects, and to cause them no damage or injury. If, however, any soldier should dare to inflict any wrong upon one of Our tributaries, he shall be punished in a manner worthy of the commander, the tribune, and the Emperor, so that Our tributaries may be secure from injustice.

(12) But if they should be interrogated before Our judges in any legal proceeding, We order the bailiffs not to receive any more *sportulae*,[126] than are prescribed by Our laws, under penalty of suffering the punishment prescribed by the said laws for their violation.

(13) Therefore when, with the aid of God, Our African provinces have been placed at Our disposition

---

[126] Judgment with costs was not specifically asked for in the early ages of Roman jurisprudence, since all legal expenses being considered to be included in the decision as a matter of course, it would have been superfluous to mention them. The practice of the tribunals was, in this respect, afterwards changed, and the costs were taxed by the court, after the successful party to the suit had solemnly made oath as to the amount court, after the successful party to the suit had solemnly made oath as to the amount which should be paid. If he demanded a larger sum than was equitable, he lost his case; but in time, an assessment of triple damages was substituted for this penalty.

Various provisions were, at intervals, made by law, regulating the payment of costs. The plaintiff was obliged to file a bond to proceed within sixty days, or pay double the expense which might be subsequently incurred. If the judge failed to tax the costs, he was individually liable for them. As the amount available for this purpose was ascertained by computing a certain percentage of the value of the property in controversy, unscrupulous litigants were in the habit of claiming more in their pleadings than they were entitled to, and where this was proved, heavy damages could be collected. When evidence of bad faith existed, the judge was authorized to impose a fine of one-tenth the amount for which suit was brought, for the benefit of the Public Treasury.

by your grandeur, and their boundaries re-established,
and all Africa restored to its former condition; [136]
and these matters have been disposed of and effected
by you with Divine assistance; and you have reported
to Us the establishment of all the dioceses of Africa,
that is, how many, and what soldiers have been stationed in certain places or towns, and what frontier
guards have been posted in what places, and to what
branch of the service they belong; We order that you
shall then return to Our presence.

(14) In the meantime, however, if Your Excellency
should ascertain that certain cities or castles situated
near the boundaries are of too great extent to be properly defended, you will take measures to have such fortifications constructed as can be well garrisoned with a
small number of men.

(*Cont.*)

Sportulae were the fees payable to the various court officials for
the service of summons, and other duties.

The name comes from the baskets in which presents of provisions
and other articles formerly bestowed by patrons upon their clients
were contained, and which, in time, became applicable to the gifts
themselves. These were originally donated by way of compensation
for the public attendance of his followers upon a patron. As was natural, what was at first gratuitous was afterwards exacted as a right,
and became subject to great abuse. Crowds of greedy clients, many of
whom were wealthy, flocked to the palaces of the Roman nobles, and
were given great quantities of food which, kept warm by means of
heated vessels, was transported through the streets on the heads of
their perspiring slaves. Juvenal refers to this custom, as follows:

"*Nonne vides quanto celebretur sportula fume? Centum convivce; se-
quitur sua quemque culina, Corbula vix ferret vasa ingentia, tot res
Impostas capiti, quot recto vertice portat Servulus infelix.*" (Juvenal,
Satiræ, III, 249.)

Money eventually took the place of other property in the bestowal
of the *sportulæ* and the term, through its original association with the
legal representative of the *cliens* in the tribunals, was employed to
designate one species of costs incurred in litigation. The sum fixed by
custom was a hundred *quadrantes*, equal to between five and six dol-
lars. This fee, when paid to members of the Roman bar, evoked the
sarcasm of the satirist.

"*Sed nee causidico possis impune negare Nec si te rhetor grammati-
cusve rogent: Balnea post decimam lasso, centumque petuntur Quadrantes.*" (Martial, *Epig.* X, 90.) —ED.

(15) When Your Excellency, having disposed of all these matters, has been ordered to return to Us, the commanders of each boundary, whenever it becomes necessary to make any new arrangements with reference to cities or camps, and they have need of money to pay the troops, or for provisions, shall notify the Illustrious Prefect of Africa, so that he may immediately do whatever is requisite, in order that no injury may result to the province through delay.

(16) The said illustrious Praetorian Prefect of Africa, and the commanders of the army, must frequently report to Us what they have effected, and what remains to be accomplished, as well as everything which is taking place there; in order that We may approve what has been properly done, and that what is suitable to do hereafter may be carried out in accordance with Our wishes.

(17) We also decree that the judges appointed to preside over the frontiers of Africa shall not pay to anyone, no matter what his rank or dignity, in Our Most Sacred Palace in the Praetorian Prefecture of Africa, any more than the amounts contained in the notice hereto annexed. For if anyone should unlawfully take or accept any more than [137] is specified in the said notice, he shall pay thirty pounds of gold by way of fine, and, in addition, run the risk of Our resentment; and no person, no matter what his rank or dignity may be, shall receive anything from the said judges, with the exception of those whose names are included in the notice hereto attached.

(18) For this purpose We (with the assistance of God) order that every military commander and his subordinates shall, in accordance with the notice hereto annexed, receive their pay from the tributes of the Province of Africa, from the *Kalends* of next September, of the thirteenth most fortunate indiction.

(19) This notice, God willing, shall be sent to the military commanders and their offices established in Africa, to secure their support and payment each year."[127] . . . .

---

[127] The prescribed list of fees which follows, has, like the former one, been omitted for the same reason.—ED.

Scott, S. P., trans., ed. *The Civil Law* [of Justinian] (Union, NJ: Law-book Exchange, 2001), Codex I. XXVII, 12:130-137.

In light of the legal benefits reaped by the church, it will hereby be shown that this victory over the Arian Vandals was truly a victory for the Catholic Church, as well:

"The Catholic clergy. . . . exalted with happiness, and the bishops reunited in 534 to the council of Carthage expressed in enthusiastic terms the goodness to be newly submitted to the orthodox empire.[128] It was easy to look after these sentiments of devotion, in order to do it, the piety of Justinian found itself in agreement with his interest. Also he made up for its liberalities in the African Church[129] since 534,[130] a edict ordered to restore to the religious establishments of all the diocese of Africa the domains that had been to them unjustly taken, to repute them in the possession of the edifices of the cult, to make render them the vases and the sacred ornaments of which they had been dispossessed, and authorized to them to claim in justice all the well usurped on them by particulars.[131] At the same time, all the privileges accorded by the Code of the metropolitan churches were conferred to the bishop of Carthage,[132] all the churches of his diocese must enjoy the right of asylum, all legitimately receive bequests and donations.[133] But above all the emperor applied himself to satisfy the long rancor and the profound hatefulness that the Catholic clergy [40] against his persecutors: all the dissidents, Arians, Jews, Donatistes and pagans, were treated with the last rigor. Not only were their preachers chased from their churches, and it was forbidden for them to administer the sacraments, but still their adherents were excluded from all public charges, and even conversion

---

[128] Labbe, *Sacrosancta Concilia*, IV, 1755.
[129] *Nov.* 37, *praef*; Schoell, Rudolfus, *Corpus Iurus Civilis, Novellae*, (Berlin: Apud Wiedmannos, 1959), 3:244-5.
[130] Ibid., 3:244-5.
[131] Ibid., 3:244-5.
[132] Ibid., 3:244-5.
[133] Ibid., 3:244-5.

was scarcely open to them the access of the magistrates,[134] the exercise of all heretic cults was carefully proscribed; the Arian temples, the synagogues were transformed into Catholic churches; secret meetings were even forbidden, "anticipated that it is absurd to permit the impious the accomplishment of sacred ceremonies."[135] Thus Justinian proved to god his recognition, and showed that he knew "to avenge the offenses of the church." Also, when taking the pious traditions of elsewhere, the bishops of the Preconsulary, of Byzacene and Numidie reunited in 534, in the number of 120, and a grave council in Carthage,[136] they could express to the pope Agapet the joy almost without mixing that caused them the reestablishment of imperial authority,[137] and in their name the Sovereign Pontiff congratulated the emperor with zeal that he deployed "for the growth of the Catholic people" and of the piety that made, everywhere where one heard empire, to prosper immediately the kingdom of God.[138]

The Roman populations were not treated with less favor. Not only did Justinian want the capital of reconquored Africa, endowed with "imperial privileges,"[139] took in his honor the name of Carthago Justiniana, but he accorded to these victims of the Vandal tyranny the most effective satisfactions. A pragmatic sanction of 534 authorized the Africans to take back, during the length of five years, [41] all the lands that had been unjustly taken from them, making amends of this sort of long ago plundering, ordered by Genseric.[140]

. . . . [48] On the other hand, the religious intolerance carried its effects: despite the ardor of his piety,

---

[134] Ibid., 5, 6, 7, 3:244-5. See also Procopius, De *Bello. Vandalico*, ed. De la Byzantine de Bonn. 471.

[135] Ibid., 8, 3:244-5.

[136] Labbe, *Sacrosancta Concilia*, IV, 1755, 1784-5.

[137] Ibid., 1755-6.

[138] Ibid., 1793.

[139] *Nov.* 37, 9, Schoell, Rudolfus, *Corpus Iurus Civilis, Novellae,* (Berlin: Apud Wiedmannos, 1959), 3:244-5.

[140] *Nov.* 36, *praef.* and 5, Schoell, Rudolfus, *Corpus Iurus Civilis, Novellae,* (Berlin: Apud Wiedmannos, 1959), 3: 243-4.

the emperor had understood that some concessions
had to be made and that the interest commanded to
treat with management the Arian priests, whose influence was very strong. Justinian was therefore inclined
to conserve in their control and dignity the members of
the heretical clergy that returned to the orthodoxy.[141]
But this political indulgence seemed intolerable to the
African bishops, the council of Carthage protested, the
pope blamed the emperor of admitting a compromise
as condemnable,[142] and it was necessary to pass by his
will. The result was graver than was thought, the ex-
communicated Arian priests were to the Byzantine authority an irreconcilable opposition, and like they
counted still, in the country and until the army,[143] a
somewhat large number of adherents, this was a new
cause of trouble and of disorganization added to those
that paralyzed the defense. . . .[50] "While Belisarius triumphed in Constantinople, and spread out to the daz-
zling eyes of the populace of the capital the seats of gold,
gems, precious vases and dishes, magnificent clothes,
sumptuous vehicles, all the treasures that 100 years of
pillaging had accumulated in Carthage,[144] while the
pride and piety of Justinian glorified itself to see reconquored the whole ensemble of vases of Solomon and the
ornaments of the empire,[145] while in the imperial
palace, on the walls of the vestibule of Chalce, one made
represent, in brilliant mosaic murals, the episodes of the
conquest of Africa, the towns submitted and Gelimer rendered humble homage to Justinian and Theodora. . . ."[146]

---

[141] Labbe, *Sacrosancta Concilia*, IV, 1793-4; Morcelli, *Africana Chris-
tiana*, III, 284.
[142] Ibid., 1756, 1791-2, 1793-4.
[143] Procopius, De *Bello. Vandalico*, ed. De la Byzantine de Bonn. 471-
2.
[144] Ibid., 445-447.
[145] Ibid., 445-6.
[146] Procopius, *Aedificiis*, De la Byzantine de Bonn. 204. Corippus,
Johannis, *In lauden Justini*,ed. Partsch (Mon. Germ. Hist., Auct. Antiq.,
III, 2. I, 285-7. Diehl, Charles. *L'Afrique Byzantine: Histoire de la
Domination Byzantine en Afrique (533–709)*, (Paris, New York, 1896),
1: 39-41, 48, 50. [History of the Byzantine Domination in Africa]

The following referenced documents of Justinian's
Novels, numbers 36. January 1, 535 and 37., August 1,
535, quoted by Diehl are hereby submitted. However, the
work of S.P. Scott is heavily abridged, so we provide the
work of Schoell-Kroll, translated from the Latin:

NOVEL
XXXVI.

THAT THOSE WHO ARE IN AFRICA WHO ARE SEEKING FOR THEMSELVES PROPERTY UP TO A CERTAIN LEVEL OUGHT TO CLAIM IT WITHIN FIVE YEARS.

The same to A. Salomon pp. of Africa.

"We approve to limit our actions by certain boundaries since we believe that every infinite and perversely
excessive thing is with merit both uncivil and incom-
plete. Recently therefore in our Africa, which god has
subjugated to the Roman domination by our vigils, we
have promulgated a holy pragmatic sanction, that
everyone should be able to get back from the unjust
withholders and to claim for themselves all the things
which they have lost now in the times of the Vandals,
and we have established a term of five years within
which it is allowed to do this. We wish this sanction to
remain in its own strength also, but with a certain control and certain definition, so that it is not permitted to
Africans when so much extended agedness has slipped
away and old nations have almost been deleted to re-
suscitate old misrepresentations and to bring troubles
in turn on themselves and to wage wars in the midst of
such great internal peace.

Therefore through this law we decree, if anyone al-
leges that property belongs either to himself or to his
father or to his grandfather and that it is detained unjustly against our laws by others, that it is possible to
recover this property, if of course proofs which were
known to the law before have been offered, either by
reciting legitimate documents or by producing suitable
witnesses whose seriousness is acceptable to the judges,
namely if the contest pertaining to the trial has been

impelled: and that this determination of ours is extended only to the fathers and grandfathers, but not to another former degree.

2. And we sanction this namely for each gender, so that that of his which each male or woman should show has belonged to his or her either father or mother or grandfather or grandmother, this he may remove from unjust detainers, if further requisition thoroughly ceases, lest anyone when introducing his great-grandfather or great-great-grandfather or great-great-great-grandfather, or great-grandmother or great-great-grandmother or great-great-great-grandmother should bring a heap of false accusation on the poor later generations. And we direct this to be observed also in a line lying crosswise, so that it may be continued only up to the third degree, that is for brothers and sisters, for paternal uncles and aunts, and maternal uncles and aunts, but not for other higher degrees of blood relationship on the father's side or of relatives.

3. And if anyone is ready to report a question of this kind, he should offer proofs of this kind not otherwise, but for the judgment of your loftiness or of the governors of provinces and islands when a strict judgment has been announced, and not from one part nor in other provinces or in this very flourishing city, but only in the African diocese, when his adversaries are present, [244] and then he should deserve the aid of our divine power and of our constitution.

4. We grant in no way that from one part the proofs concerning the trustworthiness of a family should be offered, and if anyone has shown deeds of this kind as if done in this.

5. But the requisition of property according to the preferred method among your loftiness or governors of provinces we wish to happen within the defined time for our sanction, that is in the space of five years, with the year which has already been accomplished to be computed from the publication of the earlier pragmatic sanction into the period of five years, so that the petitioner has the remaining space of four years for the investigation of this kind, namely if the computation of

the time exceeds legitimate exceptions. For in no way do we allow the limits of the four year period of this kind to go beyond, lest the completion of the investigations become immortal.

6. Therefore the things which my eternity has sanctioned for the security of Africa, your loftiness should hurry to make known to all the citizens of Africa through your edicts published in every African district, so that all may hasten to observe this which they know is necessary to be observed in the completed years. Concerning the rest, if any such occasion has emerged, we assign all successions and temporal directions to proceed thus just as the most holy laws assign in all the lands included in our world, and that all the degrees both of descending ones and of the ascending ones and of those coming from each side and the temporal courses should be intact, just as the general laws of our divine power have handed them down to all."[147]

"Given on the calends of Jan. when CP Belisarius v. c. is consul." (535)

NOVEL
XXXVII

CONCERNING THE AFRICAN CHURCH.

The same to A. Salomon pp. of Africa.

"We hasten day and night to alleviate the Venerated Church of our Carthago Justinian and all the other sacrosanct churches of the African diocese by imperial kindnesses, so that, after our republics, which were snatched through the protection of God from tyrants, have been united, they might also feel our liberalities.

1. Since therefore the very holy man priest Reparatus of our same Justinian Carthage, who is discerned to be in charge of the reverend council of the very holy churches of all Africa, together with other

---

[147] Schoell, Rudolfus, *Corpus Iurus Civilis, Novellae*, (Berlin: Apud Wiedmannos, 1959), 3:243-4.

very reverend bishops of the same province with their own letters which were brought through Theodore the deacon a religious man and relating to an answer of the same venerable church of the city of Carthago Justinian supplicated our majesty to take possession firmly of the possessions of the churches of all of the African tract which were taken from them by an indeed tyrannical time, which were returned to them, after the victories bestowed by us with a heavenly protection against the Vandals through the pious disposition of our divine will, with the payment of tributes preserved in whatever place in which it had been manifestly arranged, according to the direction of the law which was already promulgated on top of this reason, to agree to the requests of those we have influenced with an inclined and willing spirit.

2. Therefore we command your loftiness to dispose by your precepts, that the venerable churches both of our Carthago Justinian as well as of all the cities of the African diocese should firmly possess the possessions mentioned above, according as it has been specified by the sound reason of tributes, and without any shaking, and they should be seized by absolutely no one.

3. If it has been proved however that these other possessions as decorations either of the home or of the churches were detained among any either Arians or pagans or some other persons, that these things also wholly without any delay are snatched and assigned to the sacrosanct churches of orthodox faith, with no fullness of time to be granted to those who detain the same things unjustly, but they should be forced to make restitution of this property when every stratagem has been discredited, because we do not allow the very sacred vases or ornaments of the venerable churches or other possessions to be kept among pagans or other persons; and the law which was brought to us before is sufficient and has made the decree by the prominent part of this kind abundantly.

4. The prerogatives also of our other constitution, which we made for ecclesiastic property and possessions, we believe the venerable churches of Africa also possess, and according to its [245] direction we give

permission to them of recovering their own property and possessions which have been seized by a certain person throughout the province. In order that they are able to claim whatever pertaining to this property was taken or will have been by unjust detainers.

5. It will be of concern to your loftiness, as far as neither for the Arians nor for the Donatists nor for the Jews nor for others who are known to worship the orthodox religion very little that any communion be given absolutely to the ecclesiastic rites, but they are to be excluded from any kind of blaspheming of the sacred and temples, and absolutely no permission should be granted to them to ordain either bishops or clerics or to baptize certain persons and to draw to their insanity, because sects of this kind not only by us, but also by earlier laws were condemned and are worshiped by the very wicked as well as defiled men.

6. But that all heretics according to our laws which we have imposed by public acts are removed, and the heretics are granted to do absolutely nothing public nor to undergo any administration for any kind of campaigning, lest heretics seem to be appointed to rule over the orthodox, when it is enough for them to live, not also to claim any authority for themselves, and from this to affect with certain detriments orthodox humans and the very correct worship of the omnipotent God.

7. We grant however that in no way indeed the rebaptized may have an army. But their penitence, if they preferred to come to the orthodox faith with a very pure mind, we have not rejected, but we give them permission of doing this, because even for an omnipotent God nothing is so acceptable as the penitence of sinners. We deny moreover to Jews to have Christian slaves, because it is warned both by earlier laws and it is dear to us to protect the unimpaired one, so that neither should they have slaves of an orthodox religion nor, if they receive by chance catechumens, should they dare to circumcise them.

8. But we do not grant that their synagogues stand, but we wish them to be reformed for the image of churches. Indeed we allow neither Jews nor pagans nor

Donatists nor Arians nor any other heretics either to have caves or to do certain things as if for an ecclesiastic rite, since it is absurd enough to allow sacred rites to be conducted by impious humans.

9. Furthermore we remit all the privileges of the sacrosanct church of our Carthago Justiniana which the metropolitan cities and their priests are recognized to have, which also even when separated from sacrosanct churches in his first book are recognized to offer their honor by our Codex: so that the city which we regarded should be decorated by the name of our divine will bloom while decorated also with imperial privileges.

10. You may also take refuge, those who are eager to flock together at the venerable churches and their boundaries and to look out for their own safety, [that] it is permitted to absolutely no one to take from these with sacrilegious hands, but that they get possession of the reverences owed to the venerable places, unless they are murderers or raptors of maidens or violators of the Christian faith: indeed who does not confess that those who do such evil deeds are worthy of no privileges? Since it is not possible that the sacrosanct church both assist evil humans and to offer its help to injured humans.

11. If however anything besides of the sacrosanct church of the often called Carthago Justinian has been forgotten either by other venerable churches of the African diocese by a certain persona for his own safety of mind or will have been by whatever legitimate way either in possessions or in any other kinds, we also commend that this remains firmly among these same venerable churches, that it should be taken by the wicked hands of no one, when humans who hurry enough to do acts so laudable as well as acceptable to God and pious offerings and the kindness of the heavenly God should be returned.

12. Therefore [learning] all these things which we have dedicated for the honor of the sacrosanct churches of the whole African diocese through the most pious present law which will be valid forever, which we have regarded to be consecrated to the om-

nipotent God, your loftiness, learning this, will hasten
to protect as firm and unimpaired and by displaying all
the edicts everywhere by which it is accustomed to
make known, that our commands which have the reason of the highest piety should be preserved un muti-
lated in every way; by punishing the thoughtless ones
of these by the penalty of ten pounds of gold, and by af-
flicting with other very serious indignation of our divine will all who have tried or complied to violate our
arrangement in whatever way or time."[148]
"Given on the calends of August CP. when Belisarius v. c. is consul" (535)

From Novel 37. 9. we see Justinian's authority implemented in the former Vandal province to, first and foremost, bring honor to his *"Codex"* so "the name of our
divine will bloom while decorated also with imperial
privileges." This was standard protocol for Justinian
when he claimed legal jurisdiction of a newly conquered
territory, and will prove to be extremely significant when
it is understood what is contained in the Codex of
Justinian's law code. The subsequent excerpt is taken
from a letter by Justinian that he wrote to Pope John II
on March 15, 533. This documents the ecclesiastical
"voice" behind the code of Justinian:

"For we do not suffer anything which has reference
to the state of the Church, even though what causes the
difficulty may be clear and free from doubt, to be discussed without being brought to the notice of Your
Holiness, because you are the head of all the Holy
Churches, for We shall exert Ourselves in every way (as
has already been stated), to increase the honor and authority of your See."[149]

"We shall exert Ourselves in every way" is legally confirmed by the legislative support from the state that the

[148] Schoell, Rudolfus, *Corpus Iurus Civilis, Novellae,* (Berlin: Apud
Wiedmannos, 1959), 37. 9. 3:244-5.
[149] Scott, S. P., trans., ed. *The Civil Law* [of Justinian] (Union, NJ:
Lawbook Exchange, 2001), Codex I. 1.4, 12:12.

church canons received. Codex I.3.44 of Justinian's law codes, for example, was implemented on October 18, A.D. 530, thereby giving total authority to the canons of the synods.

> "Whatever the holy canons prohibit, these also we by our own laws forbid."[150]

This codex alone was sufficient to elevate the laws of the church to equality with the laws of the state. Having been accorded this political backing, church canons had to be obeyed by all. This serves as the only explanation as to why the papacy claims that Justinian's Corpus Juris Civilis is the basis of all Roman Catholic canon law:

> "So the immortal 'Corpus Juris Civilis' was produced. . . . It would be difficult to exaggerate the importance of this 'Corpus.' It is the basis of all canon law . . ."[151]

The following letters are given in their entirety except for the footnotes from Guenther largely detailing misspellings that were in the Latin. This first letter was sent from Pope Agapitus I (who reigned 535-536) to Emperor Justinian on October 15, 535. With the defeat of the Arian Vandals now history, the pope praises Justinian for their demise, ranking the victory as an answer to the prayers of the church and the uplifting of the Catholic faith as the papacy continues to work from behind the scenes, subduing her enemies:

---

[150] Paul Krueger, *Corpus Iuris Civilis, Codex Iustinianus*, I.3.44 (decreed Oct.18, A.D. 530) (Berolini Apud Weidmannos, 1888), 2:30. See also Asterios Gerostergios, *Justinian The Great The Emperor And Saint* (Belmont, MA: Institute for Byzantine and Modern Greek Studies), 163-4.
[151] *Catholic Encyclopedia*, s.v. "Justinian I" (New York: Appleton, 1910), 8:579.

(88). Agapitus to Justinian Augustus

Bishop Agapitus to Justinianus Augustus. October 15, 535

[333] "Although I was obligated in many ways concerning the first fruits of my priesthood to bear thanks with gifts of divine piety, nevertheless, venerable emperor, with discourses of your serenity received through the venerable presbyter Heraclius our son, which very full with the fertility of eternal fruit you appointed, the joys in the lord of my prayers have been doubled, because you place the earthly kingdoms after the advancements of your felicity [334] have been joined by you under the proposal of such a glorious mind, in order that you seek carefully the heavenly at the same time. The records of this matter are not disputed when the light shines by your oracles, which you directed, of the Catholic profession in such a way, that it begins to brighten also with blessed works. If indeed that belief in our God is full and firm, which the fertility of spiritual fruits recommends at the same time, just as the vessel of election announces saying Gal. 5:6 in Jesus Christ neither circumcision prevails to some degree nor foreskin but faith, which works through love. What indeed greater work of your faith was able to exist, than that you have elevated with so great pledges the apostolic seat of charity and munificence, so that you passed through even the desires themselves of the ones hoping? And indeed this once established in you always flourished, just as I also have proved, through the grace of God, in order that the quantity of your power shows the merit of things granted and you extended to these advancements the moments of power which were gained, in order that kindness inborn to you either preceded or conquered the prayers of the ones asking. From here there is, what all the way up to the traces of the crown of the emperor and beyond now continuously your tranquility is proud boasts of by fortunate successes nor will it ever be cheated out of by celestial supports, because it has been written Rom. 8:28 for those highly esteeming God all things work for

the good. Whence I also have made the most pious elo-
quences of your generosity with the devotion of the rejoicing church, just as you have instructed, to be close
to the writings by the divine offices, in order that they
are said repeatedly up for the gazes of supernal
majesty by always tireless prayers and in order that
there may be sempiternal commemoration for the purpose of obtaining your retributions by you. And therefore, most kind lord son, paying back homage of very
rich greeting reverently I embrace you with the folds of
spiritual charity hoping, that from my devotion, as
much as there is in [335] me there is, in these things,
which you instruct for the sake of the unity of the ecclesiastic peace, you promise more for you, which are
Catholic things, according to this, which the apostle
says Rom. 1:15 thus what is in me, is visible also for
you, nor in someone of them, in whom we are able to
obey lawfully, should you believe that we resist by the
exhortations of your kindness, because, just as the
teacher of nations has asserted II Cor. 10:15, I have
hope with your faith growing that it is magnified in you
according to my example. And therefore I exhibit immense thanks to my God, which you burn with such
great ardor of Catholic charity for the multiplication of
the people, that, wherever your rule is propagated; the
sempiternal kingdom may soon begin soon to advance.
Persisting rather strongly in the benevolence of the interest of which in rejoicing in them, whom you signify
wish to avoid the Arian faithlessness you believe that I
am able to deflect the censure of the paternal tradition,
namely in order that they persist in these honors, in
which they were among the heretics, and are encouraged to others. Wherefore indeed you desire this good
and distinguished with the greatest praise thing, that
everyone join the sheepfold of the lord through true
faith; but it is not right for me to receive those, who do
not strive to enter correctly, with the blessed apostle
Paul warning II Cor. 6:3 giving to no one any offense,
so that our ministry is not criticized. However how
great an offense of the paternal laws, if they are received in such a way, is run into—may it never happen—lest anything affect your piety on the side, I have

believed the rules themselves should also be fastened, which had especially advised, lest some one of such who has been reconciled either should be honored by the advancements of ecclesiastic order or desire to get possession of honors further, which it is not now responsible that he doubts that he has acquired guiltily: from which your piety was able to believe better, if by any method it should be fitting to infringe upon such proven and synodal laws of the apostolic seat, when the opinion of the apostle declares Gal. 2:18 if however [336] the same things which I have destroyed, I build again, I myself decree that I am a transgressor. And therefore secure with the voice of the apostle himself I make a confession Gal. 5:10, because I trust in you and in the Lord that you believe no other thing; indeed, just as the teacher has asserted the same thing Rom. 15:14. I am certain also concerning you, because you are filled with goodness, full of all knowledge, so that you are able to warn in turn. If therefore these, concerning whom you have given evidence, hasten to come to the correct faith, they should not decline to follow the rules of our faith with the Lord saying Matt. 16:24 if any wishes to come after me, he should refuse his very self and he should follow me. Because if they are still encouraged by criticizing ambitions of honor and are afraid to suffer losses of human glory for the gain of the sacred faith, they themselves pronounce that they do not yet depart from the vices and error and that they wish more that we join with their excesses. Concerning such therefore the apostle says Gal. 4:17 they however emulate you not well but wish to exclude you, in order that you emulate them. Since these things are so, by your holy interest, by which you wish the Catholic Church to be amplified, you would believe not at all from this, if such are not received in the clergy, I have been intent with the apostle forewarning Rom. 3:8 why indeed? If certain ones of them did not believe, has their incredulity made void the faith of God? Let it be absent! for although by a similar interest of charity for the multiplication of the faithful that blessed Peter the doorkeeper of the celestial kingdom was drawn, who in order to gain more Jews, had de-

scended from the doctrine and the regular path in not
refusing all Judaism, nevertheless that younger Paul
conquered in the lord reported to him to have met saying Gal. 2:14 but when I saw, that they approach not
rightly to the truth of the gospel. I said to Peter in front
of all 'if you. Although you are Jewish, live like the
Gentiles, how [337] do you force the nations to Juda-
ize? Therefore you were able to know when you were
pondering these things through everything with God
sitting next to your heart that I was not inquiring the
occasion of excuse but to make known those things,
which I am not able to transcend for the reason of my
duty, humbly to you with the apostle saying II Cor. 13:8
indeed I have no power against the truth but for the
truth. Whence both concerning the person of the bishop
Stephanus at the same time also the reason you should
not believe that I am impelled by the interest of defense
of someone (may it be absent from the Christian minds
of any, so that they either refute the innocence or ab-
solve the crime in any person), but the universal
things, which have been arranged by the apostolic seat
above this part, have flowed always by that interest,
which you also desire for the rule of the blessed Peter
to be held onto through all things, so that of course not
in these, who had demanded a hearing of his seat,
there does not appear a reverence of the one himself
which has been rejected by the opinion of another. And
therefore, because your kindness granted beneficially
to offer, so that all business is reviewed by my legates, I
entrust this work to these, whom I direct without
delay, with God the author, in such a way however, so
that our religious man Achilles already now by my association ought to be glad for the sake of your order;
but in truth concerning performing gladly the priesthood, since the universal things, which our legates
knew about, had been brought to me by their very full
report, when the rules of the holy canons were examined, which you instruct to be protected, they will be
believed to have to be followed more firmly. Because
however, your kindness granted to excuse the person of
my brother and co bishop Epiphanius, because in the
consecration of the previously mentioned Achilles your

order had appeared more important than his ordination, I believe, also because he himself knew he was blamed by right, who except for in addition to other things, which [338] he left behind, was scarcely able to excuse this certainly, because he did not suggest to the so very pious and very kind prince, who was defending also the privileges of the blessed Peter, II Tim. 4:2 either opportunely or not importunely, what was required in this part of the apostolic seat of reverence. Concerning which business at the same time but concerning also the Justinian city-state aware of your glorious birth and also concerning the duties of my seat which must be imposed, I make known what happened to be considered more fully by the sovereignty of blessed Peter, whom you esteem, which was preserved and the affection of your piety, through those legates, whom I directed to you quickly with God propitious. It remains that, just as unceasingly I entreat earnestly from blessed Peter, I rejoice concerning the safety and prosperity of your rule always."[152]

(89). Copy of a very pious little book of our lord Justinian the emperor which he gave to Agapitus the pope at Constantinople concerning faith. March 16, 536

Copy of a little book of our very pious master Justinianus the emperor which he gave to Agapitus the pope of Constantin-ople concerning faith.

"IN THE NAME OF OUR LORD GOD JESUS CHRIST THE EMPEROR CAESAR FLAVIUS JUSTINIANUS ALAMANNICUS GOTHICUS FRANCICUS GERMANICUS ANTICUS ALANICUS VANDALICUS AFRICANUS LOYAL BLESSED FAMOUS VICTOR AND TRIUMPHATOR ALWAYS AUGUSTUS TO AGAPITUS THE MOST HOLY AND MOST BLESSED ARCHBISHOP OF THE KINDLY CITY OF ROME AND PATRIARCH."

---

[152] Guenther, Otto, Epistulae Imperatorum Pontificum Aliorum, Avellana Quae Dicitur Collectio, 2 pts. In Corpus Scriptorum Ecclesiasticorum Latinorum, vol. 35. Prague: F. Tempsky, 1895, (ep. 88), 333-338 October 15, 535.

"The first safety is to protect the rule of the correct
faith and to deviate not at all from the tradition of the
fathers, because the opinion of our lord Jesus Christ is
not able to be overlooked, when he says Matt.
16:18 you are Peter and over this rock I will build my church.
These things, which were said, are proven by the results of things. Because the Catholic religion is always
protected inviolably in the apostolic seat. [339]
Therefore concerning this faith, since I desire that the
decrees of the fathers not fall and I follow them in all
things, that is the three hundred eighteen holy fathers,
who were gathered in Nicaea and put forth the holy
mathema or symbol of faith, and the one hundred fifty
holy fathers, who convened in the city-state of
Constantinople and elucidated and made known that
holy mathema itself, and the holy fathers, who were
gathered in the Ephesus the first synod, and the holy
fathers, who convened in Chalcedon, and following the
dogmas which are contained in each of them concerning faith, through which every heresy is removed when
it attacks the holy and apostolic church, and proving
through all things and embracing all the letters of Leon
of blessed memory, which he wrote about the Christian
faith, and confessing that the one and the same Christ
the lord son born of one in two natures that is in divinity and humanity must be recognized inseparably in-
commutably indistinctly, with a difference of natures
never endured on account of unity and with a more
safe/sound propriety of each nature, and joining into
one person and substance meeting and not separated
and divided into two persons but one and the same son
born of one parent God the word the lord Jesus Christ,
just as the prophets before and Jesus Christ himself
taught us about him and handed down to us the symbol of the holy fathers: I anathematize every heretic,
who beyond these things, which were said, has understood and does understand, especially Nestorius the
heretic of the city-state Constantinople formerly a
bishop who has been condemned in the synod of
Ephesus by the pope Caelestinus of blessed memory of
the city of Rome and by holy Cyrillus the priest of the
city-state Alexandria; and with him I anathematize

Eutychis and Dioscorus formerly a bishop of the city-state of Alexandria who has been condemned in the sacred synod of Chalcedon, which embracing I follow, joining to these [340] Timothy the murderer given the name Helurus and his disciple and follower in all things Peter of Alexandria, similarly condemning. I reject moreover both Acacius formerly a bishop of the city of Constantinople who has been made a co heretic and follower of these and besides also those who persist in the communion of them and in participation. Indeed who of them embraces communion, and follows a similar opinion of them in condemnation. In a similar way I also condemn Peter of Antioch with his followers and all the writings above. Wherefore, just as I have said before, following the apostolic seat in all things, which have been established by it, I preach and I profess that those things are protected resolutely and that I compel, that according to the tenor of that little book all bishops should bring it about, that indeed the most holy patriarchs produce to your sanctity, and others truly of the metropolitan patriarch so that they bring about for their own metropolitans, as far as to what extent our holy Catholic Church holds its firmness through everything. And in another hand: May the divinity protect you through many years, holy and very religious father."[153]

(91). Agapitus to Justinian Augustus. March 18, 536.

[* This letter of Agapitus without the two letters of Justinianus which were inserted here, are nearly entirely extant. . . .]

A letter of Justinianus was given to Agapetus on the day 14 March 536

[344] "In the name of our lord god Jesus Christ the emperor Caesar Fl. Justinianus Alamannicus Gothicus

---

[153] Guenther, Otto, Epistulae Imperatorum Pontificum Aliorum, Avellana Quae Dicitur Collectio, 2 pts. In Corpus Scriptorum Ecclesiasticorum Latinorum, vol. 35. Prague: F. Tempsky, 1895, (ep. 89), 338-340, March 16, 536.

Francicus Germanicus Anticus Alanicus Uandalicus
Africanus Pious Fortunate Famous Victor and Triumphator Always Augustus to Agapitus the most holy
and most blessed archbishop of the kindly city of Rome
and patriarch. Before the time in this royal city of mine
a sickly struggle concerning the case of faith of certain
people existed, which I repressed with an edict introduced, rejecting properly. And because it is of my interest to refer to the judgment of your apostolic seat
the emerging cases of this kind, of the same faith,
which I have considered must be followed, I have
directed the direction of my letter inserted for your
predecessor of blessed memory John through the venerable bishops Hypatius and Demetrius with a legation
having been sent; which on behalf of the wholeness of
faith your predecessor mentioned above when he received with willing joy has supported with the assent
of himself and of the whole Roman church. The tenor
of my letter is of this kind":

[* {25} see in letter 84, p. 322, l. 6 through p. 325, l.
11.

The letter of Justinianus given to John on June 6, 533,
was inserted also into letter 84, where I have combined
various readings with the codices of Justinianus and the
collection of Anselm Lucensis. Here I have considered it
enough to have recorded the writing of codex V. Then on
p. 347, l. 20, the letter continues]:

"On account of which I ask your holiness, that you
uphold the mentioned letter with your authority and
that you consider Cyrus or ones resembling him as foreign from communion, until they comply with the
statutes of your holiness. COPY OF SUBSCRIPTION: May
the divinity protect you through many years, holy and
very religious father. Given on the first day of the Ides
of March at Constantinople after the consulship of
Belisarius a famous man. . . . Therefore should anyone
have presumed to speak against this confession, as it
was mentioned earlier, and to this faith, he would have
known himself alien from the Catholic communion.

Given on the 15th of the Kalends of April. at Constantinople after the consulship of Belisarius a famous
man."[154]

With the church accepting nothing short of complete
submission, it has been demonstrated from the primary
and judicial sources that this was, indeed, a religious war
and that the Vandals were the second of the three horns
to be "plucked up by the roots."

---

[154] Guenther, Otto, Epistulae Imperatorum Pontificum Aliorum, Avellana Quae Dicitur Collectio, 2 pts. In Corpus Scriptorum Ecclesiasticorum Latinorum, vol. 35. Prague: F. Tempsky, 1895, (ep. 91), 344,
347 March 14, 536.

7

The Ostrogoths

"The victory over the Vandals gave motivation for the raids against Rome and Italy, where for five decades Germanic tribes had roamed city and countryside. The Ostrogoths had primary control at the time. Justinian demanded from them the delivery of the foothills of Lilybäum to Sicily, to which he could lay claim, since it had become Vandal imperial property as the dowry of the wife of Thrasamund, the Gothic princess Amala-frida. During the negotiations for this, the Gothic king's widow, Amalasuntha, fell victim to a political murder (April 535). Her cousin Theodahad, whom she had elevated to the kingship with the intent of securing her throne, was blamed for the murder by public opinion. Justinian took advantage of the excitement of the people. Under the pretence of vendetta, he had troops immediately prepared to sail to Italy."[155]

"Conquered Africa furnished Justinian with an admirable base of operations to carry out the efforts of his ambition for Italy. The circumstances, as in Africa, were going to promptly offer an excellent pretext for intervening in the peninsula."[156]

---

[155] Knecht, August. *Die Religions-Politik: Kaiser Justinians I: Eine kirchengeschicht-liche Studie.* (Dissert. Würzberg, 1896), 9. [Andreas Gobel, *The Religious Politics of Emperor Justinian I*, Wurzburg, 1896.]
[156] Diehl, Charles. Justinien et la Civilization Byzantine au Vie Siècle. Paris: Ernest Leroux, 1901, 181.

Historians are agreed that Justinian was looking for a pretext in order to strike against the Ostrogoths. Admittedly, they had done no wrong, but the stage was set. To understand this injustice and the true motivating nature of Justinian's pretext, we must go back to the year 523. Under the reign of the eastern Emperor Justin and Pope John I, we have a demonstration of the two ideologies or governments at war against the government of the Arians. Under the reign of the Ostrogoths leader, Theodoric the Great, the nature of the warfare will be shown to be that of *religious liberty*:

"John, Fifty-Second Bishop of Rome
[Justin, Theodoric, King of Italy]

[324] "[Year of Christ 523.] Hormisdas was succeeded by John, surnamed Cateline, ordained on the 13th of August, after a vacancy of seven days. He was a native of Tuscany, the son of one Constantius, and presbyter of the Roman Church;[157] which is all we know of him before his election. His pontificate was short and unhappy; and the calamities that befell him were owing to the indiscreet zeal of the emperor Justin. For that prince, not satisfied with having put an end to the schism, undertook, in the next place, to clear his dominions from heretics, as he styled them, of all denominations. He began with the Manichees, who, taking advantage of the general confusion that reigned in the church, during the late disputes between the Eutychian and orthodox parties, had perverted, unobserved, great numbers of both to their impious tenets. Against them therefore the emperor issued an edict, in the sixth year of his reign that is, in 523, commanding them to be put to death without mercy, wherever they should be discovered, and convicted.[158] This edict was attended with no bad consequences; the Manichees being universally abhorred and detested, on account of the execrable principles, and immoral practices of that famous

---

[157] *Cod. Just.leg.12*
[158] Evargr. Lib. Pont.

sect. But the zeal of Justin, savoring not a little of enthusiasm, did not suffer him to stop here. The following year, 524, he enacted another edict, ordering the
Arians, who were very numerous in the east, to deliver
up all their churches to the catholic bishops, and the
catholic bishops to consecrate them anew. The Arians
had been allowed, by the emperors, the free and open
exercise of their religion; had contented themselves
with worshiping God in their own way, without ever
attempting to bring over any, either orthodox or
Eutychian, to their persuasion; were as good subjects
as the best of the Catholics; and, on all occasions, had
served, with as much zeal and fidelity as they, their
prince and their country. Being therefore conscious to
themselves, that they had given no occasion to such an
edict, nor offence to their fellow- subjects, or their sovereign, they often and warmly remonstrated against
the treatment which they so undeservedly met with.
But the emperor was not to be moved, and the
Catholics were already in possession of most of their
churches. In this distress, none of their friends at court
daring to speak a word in their favor, they resolved to
recur to King Theodoric, whom they all knew to be a
zealous Arian, though, by a principle of toleration, he
no less favored his Catholic, than he did his Arian subjects. He was the only prince in the world whose inter-
position and good offices they thought would be of
some weight with the emperor; and to him they privately dispatched some of their chief men, with letters,
in the name of all, to acquaint him with the evils,
which they so [325] unjustly suffered, and the far
greater evils, which they had reason to apprehend, unless, touched with compassion, he interposed in their
behalf, and espoused their cause as his own, since the
holy religion, which was common to both, and for
which they suffered, made it his own. The king received the deputies in the most obliging manner, assured them of his good offices, and wrote, without
delay, most pressing letters to the emperor, and all the
great men at court, in their favor. But no kind of regard was paid to his letters; the persecution continued,
and the Arians were everywhere driven from their

churches, and in some places, by the over-zealous Catholic's, out of the cities. This Theodoric could not brook; and resolved to resent it in a proper manner. The first thing that occurred to him, was to retaliate on the Catholics in the west all the severities that were practiced on the Arians in the east. But as he was a prince of most humane disposition, and besides an enemy, by principle, to all persecution, he could not prevail upon himself to proceed to such extremities, till all other means he could think of had proved ineffectual. He thought of many; weighed and examined many; and at last fixed upon one, which he apprehended could not fail of the wished for success. He knew what weight the advice and counsels of the pope had with the emperor; how much the emperor deferred to the judgment of the bishop of Rome, in all matters of religion and conscience; and therefore did not doubt but the persecution would soon be at an end, could the pope, by any means, be prevailed upon to espouse the cause of the persecuted Arians, and, disapproving the measures which the emperor was pursuing, employ his counsel and authority to divert him from them.

The king was sensible, that it was only by menaces, by force, and compulsion, that the pope could be brought to act such a part; and resolved, accordingly, to employ them at once, that no room might be left for delays and excuses. Having therefore sent for him to Ravenna, he complained to him, with great warmth, of the unchristian spirit and proceedings of the emperor; remonstrated against the violence's that were daily practiced on the Catholics in the east, meaning the Arians, which he hoped no Christian bishop would ever countenance or approve; strove to convince the pope of the injustice of the late edict; and, comparing the happy situation of the heretics, meaning the Catholics in his dominions, with the unhappy condition of the Catholics in those of the emperor, he added; "But I must let you know, that I am determined not to sit as an idle spectator on such an occasion. I am, you know, and I have often declared it, an enemy to all kind of persecution; I have suffered not only the inhab-

itants of Italy, but even my Goths, to embrace and profess, undisturbed, which of the two religions they
thought the most pleasing to God; and, in the distribution of my favors, have hitherto made no distinction
between catholic and heretic. But if the emperor does
not change his measures, I must change mine. Men of
other religions the emperor may treat as he pleases,
though every man has a right to serve his Creator in
the manner in which he thinks the most acceptable to
him. But as for those, who profess the same holy religion which I profess, and believe to be the only true religion, I think myself bound to employ the power
which it has pleased God to put into my hands, for
their defense and protection. If the emperor therefore
does not think fit to revoke the edict, which he has
lately issued against those of my persuasion, it is my
firm resolution to issue the like edict against those of
his; and to see it everywhere executed with the same
rigor. Those who do not profess the faith of Nicea, are
heretics to him; and those who do, are heretics to me.
Whatever can excuse and justify his severity to the former, will excuse and justify mine to the latter. But the
emperor," continued the king, "has none about him,
who dare freely and openly speak what they think, or
to whom he would hearken, if they did. But the great
veneration, which he professes for your see, leaves no
room to doubt, but he would hearken to you. I will
therefore have you to repair forthwith to Constantinople, and there to remonstrate, both in my name
and your own, against the violent measures, in which
that court has so rashly engaged. It is in your power to
divert the emperor from them; and till you have, nay,
till the Catholics are restored to the free exercise of
their religion, and to all the churches, from which they
have been driven, you must not think of returning to
Italy."[159]

An anonymous writer, who flourished at this time,
adds, that Theodoric likewise insisted on the emperors
allowing those to return to the Catholic faith (the

---

[159] Theoph. ad ann. 524. Marcell. in chron.

Arian), whom he had by any kind of violence obliged to abjure it; that the pope promised to do all that lay in his power to procure the revocation of the edict, and the restitution of the churches; but as for those who had already changed their religion, he assured the king, that the emperor would, upon no consideration whatever, suffer them to change it anew; and that, as to himself, he could not, in conscience, take upon him to suggest it, nor would he be charged with such a commission. The king, says the anonymous writer, was greatly provoked at this speech, and, in the transport of his passion, ordered the pope to be immediately conveyed on board a vessel, and the vessel to put to sea.[160] However that be, certain it is, that the pope undertook the embassy, not out of any [326] kindness to the Arians, with which he has been by some unjustly reproached, but to divert the storm that threatened the Catholics in the kings dominions. With him were joined, in the same commission, five other bishops, and four senators, all men of first rank. A most splendid embassy.

On his arrival at Constantinople, he was received with the most extraordinary marks of honor, by persons of all condition and ranks. The nobility and clergy went out to meet him; and he made his entry amidst the loud acclamation of numberless crowds, that flocked form all parts, to see the first bishop of the Catholic Church; who had never before been seen in the east. The emperor, says the anonymous writer, quoted above, met him, among the rest, and could not have honored St. Peter himself more that he did him. The bibliothecarian adds, that Justin bowed down to the very ground before the vicar of the blessed Peter, and, coveting the honor of being crowned by him, received at his hands the imperial diadem.[161]

---

[160] Anonym. Val.p.59. The pope received with extraordinary marks of honor at Constantinople; - [Year of Christ, 525.] An instance of his pride. The emperor revokes the edict against the Arians. The pope nevertheless imprisoned by the king on his return to Ravenna.. Several conjectures concerning the motives of the king's indignation. The most probable conjecture.

[161] Anast. in Joann.

I will not quarrel with the bibliothecarian about the bow, but that the emperor, though now in the eighth year of his reign, had not yet been crowned, is highly improbable; and if he was crowned before, it is no less improbable, that he should now desire to be crowned anew. The patriarch invited the pope to perform divine service in the great church, together with him. But he would neither accept the invitation, nor even see the patriarch, till he agreed not only to yield him the first place, but to seat him on a kind of throne himself. It is observable, that the pope alleged no other reason, why he should be allowed this mark of distinction, than because he was bishop of Rome, or of the first city, "quia Romanus esset pontifex.[162]

The patriarch indulged him in everything he required, and they celebrated Easter together, with extraordinary pomp and solemnity. Authors observe, that the pope officiated in the Latin tongue, according to the rites of the Latin church; and admitted all to his communion but Timotheus, the Eutychian patriarch of Alexandria, who happened to be then at Constantinople.[163] As to the subject of the embassy, all authors agree, that the emperor, yielding to the reasons alleged by the pope, and the other ambassadors, revoked his edict, restored to the Arians all their churches, and allowed them the same liberty of conscience which they had enjoyed before the edict was issued.[164]

The ambassadors therefore, taking leave of the emperor, set out from Constantinople on their return to Ravenna, in the latter end of this, or the beginning of the following year. On their arrival they were immediately introduced to the king, who was so far from being satisfied with the account they gave him of their embassy, that, on the contrary, he expressed against them to be conveyed from the palace to the public jail.[165] What could provoke, to so great a degree, a prince of

---

[162] Theoph. ubi supra.
[163] Theoph. Marcell. in Chron. Niceph. Calist.
[164] Theoph. Ibid. Marcell. Chron. Auct. Miscell.1. 15. Ad Ann. 6. Just. Chron. Vet. Pontif. Anonym. Vales & c.
[165] Idem Auct.

Theodoric's moderation and temper, none of the many contemporary historians have thought fit to let us know; none even of those who relate to this very event. Their silence has left room for conjectures of the moderns; and many have been offered, some favorable to the pope, and some quite otherwise, according to the disposition and bias of the different writers. Baronius would make us believe, that the pope, in imitation of the famous Regulus, sacrificed himself on this occasion, advising the emperor by no means to grant what he was sent to demand in the king's name. But he therein contradicts all the contemporary writers to a man;[166] and besides, makes the pope a mad enthusiast, instead of a second Regulus. The Roman hero only sacrificed himself, whereas the pope could not sacrifice himself without sacrificing, at the same time, the far greater part of the innocent Catholics in the west, who were either subject to King Theodoric, or to other Arian princes, in alliance with him. A protestant writer of some note[167] is of opinion, that the pope, swelled and elated with the extraordinary honors paid him at Constantinople, assumed, on his return, such airs of authority as the king could not bear in a vassal. But thus, the writer only accounts for the severe treatment the pope met with, and it is certain, that the other ambassadors, bishops as well as senators, were treated with no less severity than he. Others arraign them all of high treason; and truly the chief men of Rome were suspected, at this very time, of carrying on a treasonable correspondence with the court of Constantinople, and machinating the ruin of the Gothic empire in Italy. The king, say these writers, probably took umbrage at the uncommon kindness shown them at Constantinople; and perhaps had some intimation of their having encouraged the emperor to take advantage of the king's

---

[166] Vide Auct. Supra citatos.

[167] Heydegger. Hist. Papat. in Joan. The pope dies in prison; - [Year of Christ, 526.] Great disturbances and divisions about the election of a new pope. As the parties could not agree, Theodoric names one, Felix III. The pope, and the other bishops of Italy, henceforth chosen by the people and clergy; but ordained till confirmed by the king.

old age, or the minority of his grandson, to deliver
Italy from the dominion of the Arian Goths, and re-
unite it to the empire. This conjecture may have adopted,
as of all the most plausible, and, considering the present situation of affairs, the best grounded. But from
the anonymous writer, quoted above, we may yet perhaps account, on a better foundation, for the king's
wrath and resentment against his ambassadors. They
were strictly enjoined by Theodoric, as he informs us,
to insist with the emperor on his [327] declaring those,
who through fear or compulsion had quitted the
Arians, free to return to them, and resume unmolested
their ancient religion. This the king thought a just and
reasonable demand; nothing more being thereby required, as he well expressed it, than that men might be
allowed to pull of a mask, which fear, prevailing in
some over conscience, obliged them to wear. With that
demand, however, the bigoted emperor did not comply; and to his not having complied with it we may, I
think, with better reason, ascribe the indignation of the
king, and the treatment the ambassadors met with,
than to any other provocation. For Theodoric well
knew, that the emperor would have granted them that,
as he had done their other demands, had they urged it
as they ought, and as they were by him expressly commanded to do. It was therefore, most probably, their
disobedience to the express command of their sovereign that provoked his wrath, and brought indiffer-
ently on them all, as they were all joined in the same
commission, the woeful effects of his royal displeasure. What became of the others, we know not; but
the pope died in prison on the 18th of May of the following year 526.[168]

His body was translated from Ravenna to Rome,
and deposited in the basilica of St. Peter, where he is
honored to this day as a martyr; but whether he deserved that honor, I leave the reader to judge. Two letters are ascribed to this pope; but they are now both
universally rejected, even by the Roman Catholic writ-

[168] Anonym. Vales. Anast. Marcell.Chron.

ers, as inconsistent with chronology, with history, and with common sense,[169] though quoted by Baronius as genuine."[170]

Catholic historians, those historians who are sympathetic to Rome, or those who wish to remain politically correct often whitewash or altogether dismiss this section of history lest the reader should understand the real issue that ushered in the horrors of the dark ages was the rejection of religious liberty (even though this principle was still in its primitive form). This principle was upheld by the Ostrogoths, the last of the first three main Arian kingdoms according to Procopius.[171] Justinian, the nephew of Emperor Justin, was now the sole ruler and emperor of the east and his resolve to see his dream fulfilled of a universal empire with a one-world religion would know no bounds, even at the expense of his kingdom. In order to establish this new order and secure this objective of a one-world religion, Justinian, along with the Orthodox

---

[169] See Du Pin, Nouvelle Bibl.des Aut. Eecles.tom.

[170] [Baronius quote] "Of this pope Gregory the Great relates, that, being distressed, on his landing at Corinth, in his way to Constantinople, for want of a gentle horse to pursue his journey, a man of distinction lent him that which his wife used to ride; but on condition that he sent him back when he had reached a certain place. The pope sent him back accordingly; but he might as well have kept him; for the horse, knowing his rider, and proud of so great an honor, could never afterwards be brought to debase himself as to carry so mean a burden as a woman; and the husband, moved with the miracle, returned him to the pope.

[171] This miracle, as well as the cure of a blind man, said by the same writer to have been performed by this pope, in the sight of the whole people of Constantinople[172] has escaped all the contemporary historians."

Archibald Bower- Samuel Hanson Cox, D.D., *A History of the Popes*, (Philidel-phia, PA: Griffith & Simon, 1847), 1:324-327. See also, Archibald Bower, *A History of the Popes from the Foundations of the See of Rome to the Present Time* (London, England), 1750, 2:312-318.

[171] Procopius. *History of the Wars*. Translated by H. B. Dewing. Bks. 1-8. In Loeb Classical Library, edited by Jeffrey Henderson. Cambridge, MA: Harvard Univ. Press, 2000-2001, III. ii. 1-8.

Church, would have to remove from the hearts and lives of the Arian Ostrogoths this so-called heretical teaching of religious liberty found in their dualistic[172] code of law:

> *We cannot order a religion, because no one is forced to believe against his will.*"[173]

In order for that to be accomplished, there would have to be a new order of government. And that was just exactly what Justinian and the church set out to complete.

With two out of the three major Arian kingdoms out of the way, the nobles, priests, and populace were exuberant. With such a speedy removal of the Vandals, the Romans fancied the thought of a united kingdom that would usher in a lasting peace and security, while the church sought to regain her lost supremacy from the old world.

For the benefit of continuity on these events that led up to the war with the Ostrogoths and the results from this war itself, we will supply for the reader excerpts from non-biased authoritative historians that will accurately trace the successive steps that led up to the climactic, prophetic year of A.D. 538 and beyond. While a decisive battle was won by Justinian's army in 538, the war was far from over, and here is where some have misapplied the event for the commencement of the 1260-day/year prophetic period. This mistaken identity will be presented in bold relief as we proceed. Justinian sends a letter to the Franks to form an alliance with them to fight against the Ostrogoths:

> "And he also sent a letter to the leaders of the Franks as follows: "The Goths, having seized by violence Italy, which was ours, have not only refused absolutely to give it back, but have committed further

---

[172] Like the Franks who were under Roman and Salica law, the Ostrogoths were under Roman and Gothic law.
[173] Cassiodorus, Magnus Aurelius, Hodgkin, Thomas, *The Letters of Cassiodorus*. London: Henry Frowde, 1886, Book II–27. 185-6.
[174] Procopius. *History of the Wars*. Translated by H. B. Dewing. Bks. 1–8. In Loeb Classical Library, edited by Jeffrey Henderson. Cambridge, MA: Harvard Univ. Press, 2000–2001, V. v. 5-10, 3:45.

acts of injustice against us which are unendurable and pass beyond all bounds. For this reason we have been compelled to take the field against them, and it is proper that you should join with us in waging this war, which is rendered yours as well as ours not only by the orthodox faith, which rejects the opinion of the Arians, but also by the enmity we both feel toward the Goths." Such was the emperor's letter; and making a gift of money to them, he agreed to give more as soon as they should take an active part. And they with all zeal promised to fight in alliance with him."[174] Appendix175

"We know how the death of Atharlic, the grandson and the successor to Theodoric the Great (534) brought the regent Amalasuntha to bring his cousin Theodahad to the throne, the last male representative of the Amales family; and how also, after several months of trouble, Theodoric's daughter was, by the order from his royal spouse, imprisoned on an island in Bolsena lake and a little later, assassinated (April 535).[176] Justinian, who, had already been attentively following Italy's affairs and looking for a way to intervene,[177] did not hesitate to consider as *csus belli* the murder of a princess to whom he had formally offered [182] and accepted his imperial protection.[178] By his orders, his ambassador Peter declared to Theodahad

---

[174] Procopius. *History of the Wars*. Translated by H. B. Dewing. Bks. 1–8. In Loeb Classical Library, edited by Jeffrey Henderson. Cambridge, MA: Harvard Univ. Press, 2000–2001, V. v. 5-10, 3:45.

[175] For an overview of significant events of the rise and domination of the Catholic Franks in Gaul after the reign of Clovis and up to the present year of A.D. 535-6 see **APPENDIX I** pg. 315.

[176] Procopius, *De Bello. Gothico*, ed. De la Byzantine de Bonn., 23-25. [Hereafter - *B. G.*, 23-25.] The murder of Amalasuntha served the interests of the Polusitical empire so well that public rumor in Byzantium attributed the initiative to Theodora and his favorite person, ambassador Peter (*Hist. arc.*, 16). This seems to be questionable, although Theodora conversed with Theodahad and his wife through a fairly mysterious correspondence (Cass., *Var.*, X, 20, 21, 23, 24) and that Peter was completely devoted to him (*Ibid.*, X, 23).

[177] *B. G.*, 18, 24.

[178] *B. G.*, 25.

that, after such a crime, all negotiation became impossible, and only a war without mercy could avenge such an attempt;[179] and resolutely, turning from threats into action, the emperor put two armies en route; one to penetrate Dalmatia, the other, larger—it was comprised of 7500 men, without counting the general's personal guard—was entrusted to Belisarius; it was to go by sea and descend into Sicily by surprise.[180] At the same time, the imperial diplomacy, as it had once done to fight the Vandals, searched for the Ostrogothic alliance, striving to secure another barbaric alliance against the Ostrogoths and soliciting gold for the support of the Merovingian Theudebert.[181]

By rare good fortune, he again found that the king of the Goths, Theodahad, as Gelimer before in Africa, was, in all the world, the man the least capable of resisting an imperial attack. Also, he, as the Vandal king, offered a characteristic example of what contact with the Roman civilization had done to the barbarians. One no longer found in him any of the native energies of his race: he understood nothing of war, he had disgust and contempt for arms. Raised in the Roman way, fostered, since his youth, the love of letters,[182] proud of his Latin culture and Platonic philosophy,[183] he was happily detached and blasé, declaring that power tired and left quickly, and that royalty was not worth what it dirtied, its hands becoming full of innocent blood in order to defend itself. Deep down, his weak and cowardly soul was scared of battles; he felt more at ease in diplomatic negotiations, where his perfidy extended itself with ease; and provided that he preserved and accrued his fortune, his greed got a good price for his dignity. His spirit motivated by this,[184] impressionable, changing, he discouraged himself and regained confidence with equal ease, incapable of firm resolutions, of

---

[179] *Ibid.*, 25.
[180] *Id.*, 26-29.
[181] *Id.*, 27.
[182] *B. G.*, 31.
[183] *Id.*, 16-17.
[184] *Id.*, 34.

a constant will, barely covering a pretentious philosophical varnish that would hardly [183] fool a shrewd ob-
server, he had a lack of energy, of courage, of character.
Faced with such an adversary, Belisarius was in
luck. Without striking a blow, he occupied Sicily; Pa-
lermo, which alone attempted to defend itself, capitu-
lated after a short resistance; after the end of 535, the
large island, that Jordanes called "The Goths' Nanny,"[185]
again became a Byzantine province. Against this sudden aggression, Theodahad did not even try to defend
himself; instead of acting, he humbly negotiated, trou-
bled by fear, "already feeling Gelimer's fate in his
head;"[186] and to appease Justinian, he gave in to the
most ample concessions, so worried, so quivering to
see his propositions rejected by the emperor that, right
behind the Byzantine envoy, he rushed in all haste to
get Pope Agapit himself to Constantinople as a media-
tor.[187] Then all of a sudden, with his ordinary inconsis-
tency, on the rumor of a success won by the Goths in
Dalmatia, perhaps also knowing that Belisarius was
going to quickly be recalled to Africa, he regained
courage, showed himself to be insolent and haughty, and
believing it to be acceptable, he had the ambassadors of
Basilus imprisoned.[188] The decisive battle began.

To stop the imperials, something else was necessary for Theodahad's late and transient energy. One
saw it well. While the emperor's general was recon-
quering Dalmatia, Belisarius entered Italy through
Rhegium, in the month of May 536, and the Italian
populations who hated the Ostrogoths greeted him like
a liberator.[189] He successively attacked and stormed
the large city of Naples, cruelly pillaged by the Byzantines,[190] without Theodahad having, in order to save it,

---

[185] Jordanes, *Getica*, 60.
[186] *B. G.*, 29.
[187] *Id.*, 29-32.
[188] *Id.*, 36.
[189] *Id.*, 38-29. Belisarius presented himself as such in his proclama-
tions (*id.*, 40-41).
[190] *B. G.*, 53-55; *Liber pont.*, *Vita Silv.*, 3; Jordanes, *Romana*, 370;
Marcel. comes, a. 536.

done anything other than vainly consulting oracles. Becoming the leader through the storming of this most important city in all of southern Italy, this leader, at the end of 536, went [184] one step further: to call to the Roman population, encouraged especially by the envoys that Pope Silverius delegated to him,[191] Belisarius marched to Rome, and on December 10, without the Ostrogoth garrison attempting any semblance of resistance, he reestablished Justinian's authority in the eternal city.

These most rapid and resounding successes seemed to guarantee the prompt conquest of all of Italy, and one was so persuaded of this in Constantinople that the emperor already believed the moment had come to organize Sicily as a province.[192] But the Ostrogoths has preserved more energy than the Vandals. Even before the storming of Rome by the Byzantines, a military revolution had deposed the incapable Theodahad, and the barbarian army, returning to old Germanic traditions, had elected as king one of the Vitiges leaders.[193] He was a soldier from an obscure family, but who had proven his bravery; he had illustrated it in one hundred combats,[194] and "the people's free judgment," as Cassiodorus says, was naturally drawn to this man so different from Theodahad, to this warrior "who knew as his comrades the bravest of his soldiers and had fought elbow to elbow with them on the day of the battle."[195] Unfortunately, this energetic soldier, who had done well in the role of a follower, had only a few of the qualities of a general and Polusitician. He did not understand that the supreme goal was to stop, at any cost, Belisarius' march; particularly preoccupied with the progress of the Frankish invasion, he believed him-

---

[191] *B. G.*, 73-74.
[192] *Nov.* 75 (a. 537). See the titles that the emperor takes. *Nov.* 17 (April 535), 42 (July 536), 43 (May 537).
[193] Jordanes, *Romana*, 372.
[194] *B. G.*, 58.
[195] Cassiod., *Var.*, X, 31, 33. Cf. The praise that Cassiodorus gives him in an official discourse pronounced in front of the new king and that has a few fragments that remain (ed. Mommsen, p. 473-480).

self capable of first shaking off the enemy who came
from the north, in order to then throw himself with all
this strength on the Byzantines. In addition, not feeling
well assured of his new royal status, he aspired to le-
gitimize his apparent usurpation through a marriage a
princess of Theodoric's bloodline. In the middle of all
these concerns, he lost precious time. Instead of
marching [185] towards the South, he withdrew to
Ravenna, believing to have done enough, the loyal and
naïve barbarian that he was, in asking the Romans for
a solemn oath of fidelity;[196] and meanwhile, with the
rumor of his retreat, Belisarius pushed ahead, he lost
precious days celebrating his wedding in Ravenna,[197]
negotiating with the Franks whose march he stopped
by relinquishing of Provence,[198] and even sending ambassadors to Justinian. The fall of Perugia awakened
his imprudent inaction: then energetically, "like a furious lion," says the chronicler Jordanes,[199] he threw
himself into battle: but he was no match for Belisarius.
His obstinate and inept bravery was no less fatal to the
Ostrogoths than Theodahad's cowardice.[200]

Vainly, Vitiges, with 150,000 men, went to lay siege
to Rome (March 537),[201] in vain, for more than a year,
[one year and nine days[202]] he camped under the walls
of the eternal city; all his efforts failed in front of

---

[196] *B. G.*, 61.
[197] Jord., *Rom.*, 373; *B. G.*, 61; Marc. comes, a. 536: plus vi copulat
quam amore.
[198] *B. G.*, 73.
[199] Jord., *Get.*, 138.
[200] *B. G.*, 273.
[201] *Id.*, 82.
[202] Procopius dates the beginning of the siege of Rome to February 21,
537. Procopius. *History of the Wars*. Translated by H. B. Dewing. Bks.
1–8. In Loeb Classical Library, edited by Jeffrey Henderson.
Cambridge, MA: Harvard Univ. Press, 2000–2001, V. xvii. 12-14. And
Procopius concludes the siege of Rome on March 1, 538: "Now it was
about spring equinox, one year had been spent in the siege and nine
days in addition, when the Goths, having burned all their camps, set
out at daybreak. And the Romans, seeing their opponents in flight,
were at a loss how to deal with the situation." Ibid, VI. x. 13-14.

Belisarius' admirable energy. The leader had 5,000 men: that was all he needed. Neither the breaking of the aqueducts, which the Goths cut to take water away from the besieged, nor the furious assault, nor the long blockade, nor the illnesses exhausting the soldiers, could bend his resistance: as he said in a letter addressed to Justinian,[203] never, as long as he lived, would Rome fall under the power of barbarians. Such a glorious defense finished by having an impact on the emperor himself; little by little, reinforcements were sent to Italy,[204] which succeeded in forcing the blockade and supplying the besieged city. At the same time, at the beginning of 538, another imperial army, under the orders of John, nephew of Vitalian, debarked on the Adriatic coast, invaded Picenum, and stormed Rimini, ravaging everything in his path with iron and fire; at the archbishop of Milan's call, Byzantine troops made a descent into Liguria and occupied the great city of northern Italy; masters of the sea with their [186] fleets, imperials carrying out decisive victories everywhere. Vitiges, alarmed by this success, and moreover, incapable, with his decimated army, of continuing the siege of Rome any longer, finally decided to retreat (March 538), and Justinian was already speaking of Italy as entirely under his arms,[205] already he was designating a prefect from the court as governor;[206] and in order to finish the conquest, and perhaps also to survey [187] Belisarius, he sent to the peninsula, towards the middle of 538, a new army of 7,000 men, under Narses' orders.[207]

We will now note how the two generals' poor intelligence slowed down the hoped for success by two years. No doubt, one saved Rimini from the attack by Vitiges, but the discord that reigned in the camps paralyzed all other operations and rendered the intelligent plans that Belisarius had employed in northern Italy

---

[203] *Id.*, 114-116.
[204] *Id.*, 116, 125-126, 163-164.
[205] Nov. 69, epil. (Mai 538).
[206] B. G., 101.
[207] *B. G.*, 199.

unsuccessful. Milan was retaken by the Goths and
drowned in an appalling bloodbath; a little later,
Theudebert's Franks, believing the moment had come
to work for themselves, crossed the Alps and atro-
ciously ravaged the Po valley, also appallingly, through
their barbarianism, the Goths and the imperials.
Finally, in 539, Justinian decided to recall Narses and
to leave Belisarius alone in charge of directing the operations.[208] Then events came undone. Successively,
Faesulae in Tuscany and Auximum in Picenum fell, and
after seven months of siege, under Belisarius' threats,
and perhaps because they were exhausted by illness
and family, the Franks retreated.[209] Vitiges, at the end
of his resources and perhaps courage—for this valiant
barbarian seemed to have been singularly overpow-
ered by bad luck[210]—threw himself at Ravenna; he still
hoped that a diversion from Khosrau, with whom he
had entered into negotiations,[211] would oblige the
Basilus to recall his soldiers from Italy to the Orient.
Belisarius' energy and resolution was going to destroy
this last chance; at the end of 539, he went to besiege
Ravenna with all his forces. The supreme battle had
started. After several months of siege (May 540). ..."[212]

There is no need to present to the reader the history
of this ongoing war, for it serves no further purpose here.
The point has been established that the war with the
Ostrogoths was not over in 538. Officially, this war continued until 553:

> [466] "Thus in 552, in the six and twentieth year of the
> reign of Justinian, in whose time the city, as Procopius re-
> marks, was conquered no less than five times,[213] Rome

---

[208] *Id.*, 235.

[209] *Id.*, 250-251.

[210] *B. G.*, 273.

[211] *Id.*, 237; *B. P.*, 156.

[212] Diehl, Charles. *Justinien et la Civilization Byzantine au Vie Siècle.*
Paris: Ernest Leroux, 1901, 181-187.

[213] In 536 by Belisarius; in 546 by Totila; in 547 by Belisarius; in 549
by Totila and in 552 by Narses.

fell again into the power of the Byzantines. Once more
the victor sent the keys to the Emperor at
Constantinople, and the Emperor [467] accepted them
with a like degree of satisfaction as he had shortly before shown on receiving the bloody robe and royal hel-
met of To-tila. . . . [470] The Greeks bore the bloody
head of the last King of the Goths in triumph on a
lance between the ranks of battle, but although the
sight struck dismay into the hearts of his followers they
soon rallied and continued to fight with unabated energy until night Con- [471] cealed the enemy and themselves. After a brief repose they arose in the early
morning to renew the combat, which raged without interruption until night fell for the second time. As, worn
out with fatigue, they now counted their diminished
ranks, they held a council of war, and decided to nego-
tiate with the enemy. The same night some of their
leaders appearing before Narses said that: "The Goths
recognized that it was useless to fight against the will
of God; they scorned flight and desired a free retreat,
to leave Italy to live, not as subjects of the Emperor but
as free men, in some foreign land. They further demanded permission to take with them their possessions scattered in various towns." Narses hesitated, but
John, who had experienced the determination of the
Goths in a hundred fields, advised him to accept the
proposals of heroes resolved to die. While the treaty
was in progress, a thousand Goths, led by the brave
Indulfus, scorning every stipulation as dishonorable
quitted the camp; and, as the Greeks yielded to the resolution of desperate men and allowed them to pass,
boldly effected their retreat to Pavia. The remainder
promised by a solemn oath to fulfill the provisions of
the treaty and leave Italy. With these events, which
took place in March 553, ended the eighteenth year of
this disastrous war."[214]

---

[214] Here Procopius, after having briefly told us that the Greeks took
Cumae and all the other fortresses, closes his invaluable history of the
Gothic war. Aligern, however, defended Cumae and the Cave of the
Sibyl for fully a year with conspicuous bravery.

As we have just witnessed, the Ostrogoths were not defeated until their last king, Tejas, was killed in 553. In March of 553, the Ostrogoths signed a peace treaty with General Nares and after eighteen long years of fighting, the war was officially over, according to Procopius, in 553.[215] After this, it was nothing more than what historians refer to as mopping up operations and the Ostrogoths faded into oblivion.

Yet, central to the prophecy was an issue not discussed by Diehl or other historians, though it was addressed by the ambassadors of the Ostrogoths and recorded by Procopius, the stenographer and bibliographer of Belisarius who was present at those negotiations for peace over the battle of Rome in 538. The main contentious issue at hand was that of religious liberty. This is glossed over by Catholicism, historians, and the politically correct, yet it is central to the scriptures, Ellen White, and to the Ostrogoths. We now submit the entire dialogue from the pen of Procopius:

> [337] "Now the barbarians straightway began to despair of winning the war and were considering how they might withdraw from Rome, inasmuch as they had suffered the ravages both of the pestilence and of the enemy, and were now reduced from many tens of thousands to a few men; and , not least of all, they were in a state of distress by reason of the famine, and while in name they were carrying on a siege, they were in fact being besieged by their opponents and were shut off from all necessities. And when they learned that still another army had come to their enemy from Byzantium both by land and by sea- not being informed as to its actual size, but supposing it to be as

(*Cont.*)

Ferdinand Gregorovius, Translated from the Fourth German Edition, Mrs. Gustavus W. Hamilton, *History Of The City of Rome In The Middle Ages*, (London, George Bell & Sons, 1900, First Published, 1894. Second Edition, Revised, 1900), 1:466, 470-1.

[215] Procopius. *History of the Wars*. Translated by H. B. Dewing. Bks. 1–8. In Loeb Classical Library, edited by Jeffrey Henderson. Cambridge, MA: Harvard Univ. Press, 2000–2001, VIII. xxxv. 38.

large as the free play of rumor was able to make it, they
became terrified at the danger and began to plan for their
departure. They accordingly sent three envoys to Rome,
one of whom was a Roman of note among the Goths, and
he, coming before Belisarius, spoke as follows:

"That the war was not turned out to the advantage
of either side each of us knows well, since we both
have had actual experience of its hardships. For why
should anyone in either army deny facts of which neither now remains in ignorance. And no one, I think,
could deny, at least no one who does not lack understanding, that it is only senseless men who choose to
go on suffering indefinitely merely to satisfy the contentious spirit which moves them for the moment, and
refuse to find a solution of the troubles which harass
them. And whenever this situation arises, it [339] is the
duty of the commanders on both sides not to sacrifice
the lives of their subjects to their own glory, but to
choose the course which is just and expedient, not for
themselves alone, but also for their opponents, and
thus to put an end to present hardships. For moderation in one's demands affords a way out of all difficulties, but it is the very nature of contentiousness that it
cannot accomplish any of the objects which are essential. Now we, on our part, have deliberated concerning
the conclusion of this war and have come before you
with proposals which are of advantage to both sides,
wherein we waive, as we think, some portion even of
our rights. And see to it that you likewise in your delib-
erations do not yield to a spirit of contentiousness re-
specting us and thus destroy yourselves as well as us,
in preference to choosing the course which will be of
advantage to yourselves. And it is fitting that both sides
should state their case, not in continuous speech, but
each interrupting the other on the spur of the moment,
if anything is said that shall seem inappropriate. For in
this way each side will be able to say briefly whatever it
is minded to say, and at the same time the essential
things will be accomplished." Belisarius replied:
"There will be nothing to prevent the debate from proceeding in the manner you suggest, only let the words
spoken by you be words of peace and of justice."

So the ambassadors of the Goths in their turn said: "You have done us an injustice, O Romans, in taking up arms wrongfully against us, your friends and allies. And what we shall say is, we think, well known to each one of you as well as to ourselves. [341] For the Goths did not obtain the land of Italy by wresting it from the Romans by force, but Odoacer in former times dethroned the emperor, changed the government of Italy to a tyranny, and so held it.[216] And Zeno, who then held the power of the East, though he wished to avenge his partner in the imperial office and to free this land from the usurper, was unable to destroy the authority of Odoacer. Accordingly he persuaded Theodoric, our ruler, although he was on the point of besieging him and Byzantium, not only to put an end to his hostility towards himself, in recollection of the honor which Theodoric had already received at his hands in having been made a patrician and consul of the Romans,[217] but also to punish Odoacer for his unjust treatment of Augustulus, and thereafter, in company with the Goths, to hold sway over the land as its legitimate and rightful rulers. It was in this way, therefore, that we took over the dominion of Italy, and we have preserved both the laws and the form of government as strictly as any who have ever been Roman emperors, and there is absolutely no law, either written or unwritten, introduced by Theodoric or by any of his successors on the throne of the Goths. *And we have so scrupulously guarded for the Romans their practices pertaining to the worship of God and faith in Him, that not one of the Italians has changed his belief, either willingly or unwillingly, up to the present day, and when Goths have changed,[218] we have taken no notice of the matter. And indeed the sanctuaries of the Romans have received from us the highest honor; for no one who has taken refuge* [343] *in any of them has ever been treated with violence by any man; nay, more, the Romans themselves have continued to*

---

[216] 476 A.D. Cf. Book V. i. 6-8 and note.

[217] Cf. Book. V.i.10,11.

[218] The Goths were Christians, but followed the Arian heresy.

hold all the offices of the state, and not a single Goth has had a share in them. Let someone come forward and refute us, if he thinks that this statement of ours is not true. And one might add that the Goths have conceded that the dignity of the consulship should be conferred upon Romans each year by the emperor of the East. Such has been the course followed by us; but you, on your side, did not take the part of Italy while it was suffering at the hands of the barbarians and Odoacer, although it was not for a short time, but for ten years, that he treated the land outrageously; but now you do violence to us who have acquired it legitimately, though you have no business here. Do you therefore depart hence out of your way, keeping both that which is your own and whatever you have gained by plunder."

And Belisarius said: "Although your promise gave us to understand that your words would be brief and temperate, yet your discourse has been both long and not far from fraudulent in its pretensions. For Theodoric was sent by the Emperor Zeno in order to make war on Odoacer, not in order to hold dominion of Italy himself. For why should the emperor have been concerned to exchange one tyrant for another? But he sent him in order that Italy might be free and obedient to the emperor. And though Theodoric disposed of the tyrant in a satisfactory manner, in everything else he shewed an extraordinary lack of proper feeling; for he never thought of restoring the land to its rightful owner. But I, for my part, think that he who robs [345] another by violence and he who of his own will does not restore his neighbor's goods are equal. Now, as for me, I shall never surrender the emperor's country to any other. But if there is anything you wish to receive in place of it, I give you leave to speak."

And the barbarians said: "That everything which we have said is true no one of you can be unaware. But in order that we may not seem to be contentious, we give up to you Sicily, great as it is and of such wealth, seeing that without it you cannot possess Libya in security."

And Belisarius replied: "And we on our side permit the Goths to have the whole of Britain, which is much larger that Sicily and was subject to the Romans in early times. For it is only fair to make an equal return to those who first do a good deed or perform a kindness."

The barbarians: "Well, then, if we should make you a proposal concerning Campania also, or about Naples itself, will you listen to it?"

Belisarius: " No, for we are not empowered to administer the emperor's affairs in a way which is not in accord with his wish."

The barbarians: "Not even if we impose upon ourselves the payment of a fixed sum of money every year?"

Belisarius: "No, indeed. For we are not empowered to do anything else than guard the land for its owner.'

The barbarians: "Come now, we must send [347] envoys to the emperor and make with him our treaty concerning the whole matter. And a definite time must also be appointed during which the armies will be bound to observe an armistice."

Belisarius: "Very well; let this be done. For never shall I stand in your way when you are making plans for peace."

After saying these things they each left the conference and the envoys of the Goths withdrew to their own camp. And during the ensuing days they visited each other frequently and made the arrangements for the armistice, and they agreed that each side should put into the hands of the other some of its notable men as hostages to ensure the keeping of armistice."[219]

So it came to pass that when the three months of armistice or truce had expired with no word from the ambassadors, the Goths resolved to abandon their blockade of Rome. Thus, Procopius describes how the battle for Rome came to its end with the defeat of the Ostrogoths:

---

[219] Procopius. *History of the Wars*. Translated by H. B. Dewing. Bks. 1–8. In Loeb Classical Library, edited by Jeffrey Henderson. Cambridge, MA: Harvard Univ. Press, 2000–2001, VI. vi. 1-36., 3:337-347.

"Now it was about the spring equinox, and one year had been spent in the siege and nine days in addition, [February 21, 537-March 1, 538] when the Goths, having burned all their camps set out at daybreak. And the Romans, seeing their opponents in flight, were at a loss how to deal with the situation. For it so happened that the majority of the horsemen were not present at that time, since they had been sent to various places, as has been stated by me above,[220] and they did not think that by themselves they were a match for so great a multitude of the enemy. However, Belisarius armed all the infantry and cavalry. And when he saw that more than half of the enemy had crossed the bridge, he led the army out through the small Pincian Gate, and the hand-to-hand battle which ensued proved to be equal to any that had preceded it. At the beginning the barbarians withstood their enemy vigorously, and many on both sides fell in the first encounter; but afterwards the Goths turned to flight and brought upon themselves a great and overwhelming calamity; for each man for himself was rushing to cross the bridge first. As a result of this they became very much crowded and suffered most cruelly, for they were being killed both by each other and by the enemy. Many, too, fell off the bridge on either side into the Tiber, sank with all their arms, and perished. Finally, after losing in this way the most of their number, the remainder joined those who had crossed before. And Longinus the Isaurian and Mundilas, the guards of Belisarius, made themselves conspicuous for their valor in this battle. But while Mundilas, after engaging with four barbarians in turn and killing them all, was himself saved, Longinus, having proved himself the chief cause of the rout of the enemy, fell where he fought, leaving the Roman army great regret for his loss."[221]

Hodgkin's concluding remarks over the battle of Rome in 538 revealed to many a historian, and perhaps

---

[220] Chap. vii. 25.

[221] Procopius. *History of the Wars*. Translated by H. B. Dewing. Bks. 1–8. In Loeb Classical Library, edited by Jeffrey Henderson. Cambridge, MA: Harvard Univ. Press, 2000–2001, VI. x. 13-20.

to the Goths themselves, the huge black cloud that over-hung the Gothic nation:

> "So ended the long siege of Rome by Witigis, a siege in which the numbers and prowess of the Goths were rendered useless by the utter incapacity of their commander. Ignorant how to assault, ignorant how to blockade, he allowed even the sword of Hunger to be wrested from him and used against his army by Belisarius. He suffered the flower of the Gothic nation to perish, not so much by the weapons of the Romans as by the deadly dews of the Campagna. With heavy hearts the barbarians must have thought, as they turned them northwards, upon the many graves of gallant men which they were leaving on that fatal plain. Some of them must have suspected the melancholy truth that they had dug one grave, deeper and wider than all, the grave of the Gothic monarchy in Italy."[222]

> "The whole nation of the Ostrogoths had been assembled for the attack, and was almost entirely consumed in the siege of Rome."[223]

The battle of Rome finally ended on March 1, 538, with the defeat of the Ostrogoths, and a significant battle it was, indeed, as Vitiges or Witigis and the remainder of his army retreated to Ravenna. However, the Ostrogoths regrouped numerous times thereafter and the war raged on until 553. We also witness that historians recognized that important legislation was issued about Italy in 538 that established Justinian's judicial authority in the west:

> "Justinian was already speaking of Italy as entirely under his arms,[224] already he was designating a prefect from the court as governor;"[225]

[222] Hodgkin, Thomas. *Italy and Her Invaders.* 8 vols. 1st ed. published 1880–1889. New York: Russell and Russell, 1967, 4:285.
[223] Gibbon, Edward. *The History of the Decline and Fall of the Roman Empire*, (Edited by J. B. Bury. London: Methuen, 1909), 4:346.
[224] Nov. 69, epil. (Mai 538).
[225] Procopius, *De Bello. Gothico*, ed. De la Byzantine de Bonn., 101. Diehl, Charles. *Justinien et la Civilization Byzantine au Vie Siècle.* Paris: Ernest Leroux, 1901, 186.

The primary documents from Justinian himself confirm that it was not December 10, 536, when King Vitiges abandoned Rome without a fight and Belisarius simply went in and occupied Rome. No, the deciding factor that would establish Justinian's judicial authority in the west would be the outcome of the first siege of Rome that began on February 21, 537, and ended in a massive defeat of the Ostrogoths on March 1, 538. It was the outcome of that battle alone that secured for Justinian his judicial authority in the west. Novel 69, issued June 1, 538, confirms that this was the first time in 62 years that a Catholic Emperor had held legal jurisdiction in Italy:

TITLE XXIV.

ALL PERSONS SHALL OBEY THE PROVINCIAL JUDGES IN BOTH CRIMINAL AND PECUNIARY CASES, AND PROCEEDINGS SHALL BE CONDUCTED BEFORE THEM WITHOUT ANY EXCEPTION BASED UPON PRIVILEGE, AND PROVINCIALS SHALL NOT BE SUED HERE UNLESS THIS Is AUTHORIZED By AN IMPERIAL PRAGMATIC SANCTION.

SIXTY-NINTH NEW CONSTITUTION.
The Emperor Justinian to the People of
Constantinople.

PREFACE.

[262] "One of the most perfect of all human virtues is that which dispenses equity, and is designated justice, for no other virtue, when accompanied with this, is worthy of the name; therefore We do not praise fortitude, which is not united with justice, and although the Roman language calls virtue courage in battle, if justice is excluded from it, it becomes a vice, and is productive of no good.

As we have ascertained that justice is treated with contempt in Our provinces, We have deemed it necessary to re-establish it in a proper condition, by means of a law which will be acceptable to God. . . .

EPILOGUE.

[266] "Therefore, as soon as Our Most Glorious Imperial Pretorian Prefects appointed throughout the extent of the entire Roman Empire receive notice of this law, they will publish it in all the departments of their government, that is in Italy, Libya, the Islands, the East, and Illyria; in order that all persons may know how greatly We have their interests at heart. We dedicate this law to God who has inspired Us to accomplish such great things, and who will recompense Us for having enacted this constitution for the security of Our subjects. It shall also be communicated to Our citizens of Constantinople. Given at Constantinople, on the *Kalends* of June, during the twelfth year of the reign of Justinian, and the Consulate of John."[226]

Justinian's Novels reiterates the banishment of religious liberty for Italy and the west, as well:

TITLE XXII.

NO ONE SHALL BUILD HOUSES OF WORSHIP WITHOUT THE CONSENT OF THE BISHOP. ANYONE WHO DOES SO MUST FIRST PROVIDE SUFFICIENT REVENUE FOR THE MAINTENANCE AND REPAIR OF THE CHURCH WHICH HE BUILDS. BISHOPS SHALL NOT ABANDON THEIR CHURCHES. CONCERNING THE ALIENATION OF IMMOVABLE ECCLESIASTICAL PROPERTY

SIXTY-SEVENTH NEW CONSTITUTION.

The Same Emperor Justinian to Menna, Most Holy and Blessed Archbishop of Constantinople, and Patriarch of Its Entire Jurisdiction.

---

[226] Scott, S. P., trans., ed. *The Civil Law [of Justinian]*, 17 vols. Union, NJ: Lawbook Exchange, 2001, Justinian, *The Novels*-69. Vol. 16: 262, 266, June 1, 538. The definitive dating used here was taken from the work of a French Doctor of Law: Noailles, Pierre. *Les Collections de Novelles de L'Empereur Justinien: Origine et Formation sous Justinien.* Paris: Recueil Sirey, 1912.

PREFACE.

[258] "Although We have included matters having reference to the most holy churches in numerous laws, We still have need of another to dispose of difficulties which have arisen, and provide for emergencies. For many persons build churches in order to perpetuate their names, and not with a view to utility, and they do not take care to furnish sufficient means for their expenses, their lights, and the maintenance of those charged with Divine service, but after the churches are constructed they leave them to be either destroyed, or entirely deprived of the ministrations of the clergy.

CHAPTER I.

[259] Therefore We order, before all things, that no one shall be allowed to build a monastery, a church, or an oratory, before the bishop of the diocese has previously offered prayer on the site, erected a cross, conducted a public procession, and consecrated the ground with the knowledge of all persons. For there are many individuals who, while pretending to build houses of worship, contribute to the weakness of others, *and become not the founders of orthodox churches, but of dens for the practice of unlawful religious rites.*

EPILOGUE.

. . . . [260] Your Holiness will, by means of suitable letters, cause this Our law to be communicated to the other Most Holy Patriarchs and metropolitans under Your jurisdiction, who must, in their turn, notify the bishops subject to their authority, so that no one may be unaware of what has been decreed by Us.

Given at Constantinople, on the *Kalends* of May, during the twelfth year of Our Lord the Emperor Justinian, and the Consulate of John."[227]

---

[227] Scott, S. P., trans., ed. *The Civil Law [of Justinian]*, 17 vols. Union, NJ: Lawbook Exchange, 2001, *The Novels*, 67. 16:258-9, 260. May 1, 538.

Procopius, in other writings, confirms that it was Justinian who ended religious freedom for the Arian Christians, and we believe he is here quoting Novel 67 that was issued on May 1, 538, which we just reviewed:

"He [Justinian] seized the best and most fertile estates, and *prohibited the Arians from exercising the rites of their religion.*"[228]

In 538, Malalas recorded in the consular list a number of events that took place in that year:

84. "In the consulship of John the Cappadocian the Arians' Churches were confiscated."

85. "In that year the Chalke Gate of the palace at Constantin-ople was finished, being decorated with various kinds of marble and with mosaic work. The horologion near the Augusteion and the Basilical was moved."

"In that year the office of the praefectus vigilium was abolished and praetor was appointed in his place."

"In that year a quaestor was appointed."

86. "In this consulship the dedication of the Great Church took place."[229]

---

[228] Procopius, *The Secret History of the Court of Justinian* (Boston: IndyPublish.com, n.d.), 62.

[229] Jeffreys, Elizabeth, ed. *The Chronicle of John Malalas. A Translation by* Elizabeth Jeffreys, Michael Jeffreys, and Roger Scott. Melbourne: Australian Asso. for Byzantine Studies, 1986, 285.

John Malalas was a Byzantine chronicler that lived during the reign of Justinian. (A.D. 491-578). The three consular lists are these: (1) Theodor Mommsen, *Chronica Minora SAEC. IV.V.VI.VII* (Berlin: Verlag Hahnsche Buchhandlung (www.hahnsche-buchhandlung.de), vols. 1, 2, 3; 1892, 1894, 1898, respectfully; (2) Carl Frick, *Chronica Minora* (Leipzig: B. G. Teubneri, 1892); (3) Roger S. Bagnall, *Consuls of the Later Roman Empire* (Atlanta, GA: Scholars Press, 1987). See also Elizabeth Jeffreys, Brian Croke and Roger Scott, *Studies in John Malalas* (University of Sydney N.S.W.: Australian Association for Byzantine Studies, Department of Modern Greek, 1990), 143.

Theophanes, of ecclesiastical history, adds this to
Malalas' account of the dedication of the Great Church:

"In this year, on 27, December of the 1st indiction,
the first dedication of the Great Church took place. The
procession set out from St. Anastasia, with Menas the
patriarch sitting in the imperial carriage and the emperor joining in the procession with the people. From
the day when the most holy Great Church was burned
until the day of its dedication was 5 years, 11 months
and 10 days."[230]
"The Montanists, in 529, had burnt themselves in
their own churches. Other heretics were given three
months' grace. All magistrates and soldiers had to
swear that they were Catholics. Arians had to be
spared at first for fear of reprisals by the Goths. But in
533 Justinian attacked the Vandals in Africa, and in
535 the Ostrogoths of Italy. After victory their churches
were taken away; they were forbidden them, and baptism. Their importance as conquerors disappeared and
their sects faded away."[231]

In conclusion, it has been rightly stated by Procopius
that the Arian kingdoms did use the same laws and did
practice a common religion, for they were all of the
Arian faith and did not differ in anything else at all.[232]
They were all unified under the legal ideology of religious
liberty until A.D. 538. Hence, the best kept secret of the
dark ages remains a secret no more.

It has been shown that a military overthrow in and of
itself will not suffice for the commencement of the 1260-
day/year prophetic period. The final event that ultimately
sealed the commencement of the prophetic period according to the scriptures is next to be disclosed. It,
hereby, has been demonstrated again from the primary

---

[230] Theophanes, *Chronographia*, ed. C. de Boor (Leipzig: n.p., 1888).
[231] Dom John Chapman, *Studies on the Early Papacy* (London: Sheed
and Ward, 1928), 222-3. Imprimatur.
[232] Procopius. *History of the Wars.* Translated by H. B. Dewing. Bks.
1–8. In Loeb Classical Library, edited by Jeffrey Henderson.
Cambridge, MA: Harvard Univ. Press, 2000–2001, III. ii. 1-8.

and judicial sources that this was a religious war and that the Ostrogoths were the third of the three horns to be "plucked up by the roots." We close with this remarkable testimony by Procopius, an eye witness to it all:

> "And while I watched the entry of the Roman army into Ravenna at that time, an idea came to me, to the effect that it is not at all by the wisdom of men or by any other sort of excellence on their part that events are brought to fulfillment, but that there is some divine power which is ever warping their purposes and shifting them in such a way that there will be nothing to hinder that which is being brought to pass. For although the Goths were greatly superior to their opponents in number and in power, and had neither fought a decisive battle since they had entered Ravenna nor been humbled in spirit by any other disaster, still they were being made captives by the weaker army and were regarding the name of slavery as no insult."[233]

---

[233] Ibid., VI. xxix. 32–34.

8

Justinian, Canon Law, and the Government of Satan

Church and State united in issuing oppressive religious legislation and thereby outlawed religious liberty. Divinely-ordained free will, acknowledged in the concept of religious liberty, is a vital component of the government of God. This precious freedom was exchanged through legislation for a government of force that denied religious liberty in order to control the consciences of all men.

When a study of the religious policy of Justinian is in order, historians are fully acquainted with and still reference a select authorship even to this day.[234] We, likewise, will from time to time quote from some of those authoritative sources, since they are esteemed as credible sources among the academic community as this will further enhance the truth.

We begin with some background on the life of Justinian:

"Flavius Anicius Julianus Justinianus was born on 11 May of the year 483 at Tauresium,[235] a small place

---

[234] A. Knecht, *Die Religionspolitik Kaiser Justinians I.* (1896); G. Krueger, "Justinian I" in Hauck's Realencyclopedie, vol. 9 (1901). C. Diehl, *Justinien et la civilization Byzantine au sixième siècle* (1901); G. Glaizoll, *Un empereur theologien, Justinien* (1905); Hamilkar S. Abailisatos, *Die kirchliche Gesetzgebung des Kaisers Justinian I.* (Aalen,1973. Reprint of 1913 ed.); H. Schubert, *Geschichte der christlichen Kirche im Frühmittelalter* (Tübingen, Verlag J. C. B. Mohr, 1921, (Paul Siebeck), 1917, pp 96-123; L. Duchesne, L'Eglise au sixième siècle (1925;); E. Grupe, Kaiser Justinian (1923), and others.
[235] Evagrius 1. c. lib. IV, 1. . . .

on the border [6] between Illyria and Macedonia. His father was called Istock or Sabbatius; his mother was Biglenitza or Vigilania, a sister of the emperor Justin I. Through the efforts of this uncle, Justinian came to Constantinople in his early youth, where he devoted himself with great zeal to scientific studies. At the local academy, which at that time was in spirited competition with the schools of Rome, Alexandria, and Athens, he enjoyed lessons in philosophy, in the fine arts, in jurisprudence and mathematics, as well as in general science of war. Attention was also given to theology; this study even developed later into one of the emperor's favorite activities.[236]

After completing his academic studies, Justinian entered the military path. After brief service in the army of Justin, he was promoted to be an imperial bodyguard.

When Emperor Anastasius died in the year 518, and the favor of the soldiers opened the way of General Justin to the throne, a never-expected future began for the imperial nephew. In rapid succession he moved from one position of honor to another. In the year 520 he accompanied the grandeur of a Consul. Shortly thereafter followed his appointment to State [7] minister, then the promotion to head of the private chambers, and finally he was awarded the supervision over the entire army. On 1 April 527 the emperor named him a co-regent. The collective government granted only four months. Justin died and left complete sovereignty to Justinian. After the young emperor had himself and his wife Theodora, a person of lowly origins [a prostitute] and of dubious reputation[237], solemnly

---

[236] Fr. Balduinus, *Justinianus sive de iure novo.* Halae et Lipsiae 1728. p. 5.–E. Gibbon, The history of the decline and fall of the Roman Empire, ed. W. Smith, London 1854. Vol. V. p. 35ss.

[237] Procopius, Hist. arcane sive Anecdota. On the authenticity of the secret history, at the beginning of the 17th century, in the middle of the 18th and 19th centuries, and also in the most recent times, a written feud has been waged. The most relevant literature will be mentioned here. For the rest, I recommend K. Krumbacher, *Geschichte d. byzant. Literatur.* München 1891, p. 42. Giphanius l.c., Ludewig l.c., Rivius,

crowned, he turned his attentions to [8] the execution of far-fetched plans for the government."[238]

"Justinian would re-assemble the fallen Christian empire."[239]

(*Cont.*)
Imp. Justiniani defensio adv. Alemannum. Frankofurti 1628, Corvinus Arnoldus a Bel-deren, *Imp. Justinianus M. Catholicus.* Moguntiae 1668. Vindobonae 1766, Struvius, Bibl. hist. instructa. Vol. V. Pars I. Lipsiae 1790. The authors named here argued in favor of the inauthenticity of the private history. The romanistic jurists recently affiliated themselves with this group ("the appreciative admirers of the emperor of the pandects") and J. H. Reinkens in *Anecdota sintne scripta a Procopio.* . . . Breslau 1858. Seeking to validate the authenticity are Schmidt-Leyser, *Observata diplomatico-historica de iis, quae Justiniano imp* . . . *supposita* Helmstadii 1785, Cardinal Alemannus (d. 1626), Anecdota. Lyon 1632, Venetiis 1729 and most recently Felix Dahn, *Procopiusius von Cäsarea,* Berlin 1865 and K. Krubacher l.c. Cf. also *Procopiusios v. Kaesarea, Gesch. d. Kriege mit d. Persern, Vandalen und Gothen,* translated by Spyr. Destunis and commentary by Gabr. Destunis. *Geschichte der Kriege mit den Vandalen.* Book 1. St. Petersburg 1891 (Russ.)–J. Haury, *Procopiana.* Augsburg 1981. Cf. F. Dahn, *Wochenschrift für klass. Philologie.* 1892.–J. Haury, *Procopiana.* Munich 1893.–J. Scheftlein, *De praepositionum usu Procopiano.* Erlangen 1893. Cf. Byz. Ztschr. 1 (1892). P. 164, 2 (1894).–Invernizi l.c. leaves the question undecided: *id unum contend, nullam esse huic libello sive Procipii sit sive alterius cuiusdam obtrectatoris praestandam fidem,* p. 149, likewise J. Paul Reinhard, Procopiuss Geheimgesch. Erlangen-Leipzig 1753.–L. Engelstoft, *De re Byzantin-orum military sub imp. Justiniani I.* Hauniae 1808. p. 10 and M. J. Doppertus, Selectiora ex Justiniani M. historia and Sneebergae 1714 p. 7 are of the opinion that: Procopius . . . *neutro loco aut negligendus aut temere sequendus.* Tancredi, *S. Ormisda e S. Silverio* . . . *ed I loro tempi,* Roma-Torino 1865, writes: *Procopio.* . . . *or esaltando or profondando Giustiniano* . . . *lasciò dubbio fino oggi quando dobbiano acconciargli fede e quando no solita sciagura degli uomini bifronti e bilingui.* Cf. also Vincenzi, *S. Gregorii Nysseni et Origenis scripta* . . . *imp. Justiniani triumphus in oec.* V. syn. Roma 1865. p. 368 ss.

[238] Knecht, August. *Die Religions-Politik: Kaiser Justinians I: Eine kirchengeschicht-liche Studie.* (Dissert. Würzberg, 1896), 5-8. [Andreas Gobel, *The Religious Politics of Emperor Justinian I,* Wurzburg, 1896.]
[239] Hub. Giphanii *de imp. Justiniano commentarius.* Ingostadii 1591. p. 2 ss.

Those "far-fetched plans for the government" did bring about a "new order" through legislation as Procopius, a 6th century historian, describes Justinian's sweeping changes:

> "When Justinian came to the throne, he straightway succeeded in upsetting everything. What had previously been forbidden by the laws, he introduced, while he abolished all existing institutions, as though he had assumed the imperial robe for no other purpose than to alter completely the form of government."[240]

Knecht accurately describes Justinian's legislative changes, as well:

> "*One* state, *one* law, *one* church should rule the world; an absolute authority should reign in them, and he himself should be this authority.[241] To restore the Roman world-empire within its old borders, to elevate it to the worlds previous power, to win back its earlier glory, was the goal of Justinian's external politics. He had attained this goal. His wars brought him the fame of a *restitutor urbis et orbis* and the title of "a ruler of the Alemanni, Goths, Franks, Germanics, Anten, Alani, and Vandals in Africa."[242]

(*Cont.*)
Knecht, August. *Die Religions-Politik: Kaiser Justinians I: Eine kirchengeschicht-liche Studie.* (Dissert. Würzberg, 1896), 5. [Andreas Gobel, *The Religious Politics of Emperor Justinian I*, Wurzburg, 1896.]
[240] Procopius, *The Secret History of the Court of Justinian* (Boston: IndyPublish.com, n.d.), 37.
[241] Ad. Schmidt. l.c. p. 12.
[242] Nov. (17) XXI ed. C.E. Zachariae a Lingenthal. Lipsiae 1881. pars I. p. 137; Byzant. Ztschr. 3 (1894). p. 21—23.–Georgii Cyprii description orbis Romani ed. H. Gelzer. Lipsiae 1890. Cf. Byzant. Ztschr. 1. (1892) p. 601 ff.–L'Illyricum ecclésiastique par L. Duchesne in Byzant. Ztschr. 1 (1892) p. 531 ss.–G. H. Bruckner, An Justinianus imp. recte usurpaverit titulos Germanici e Alemannici. Jenae 1709.– F. G. Grebel-Leyser, *Defensio Justiniani contra obtrectatores.* Vitenbergae 1748. p. 12 ss: The Roman emperors attached such titles to themselves when they had achieved a victory over a people, even if they

Diehl gives us a true perspective of the man Justinian:

"He was the eminent representative of two great ideas: the imperial idea and the Christian idea, and that alone guaranties his fame. . . . By the mere fact that he is sitting on Constantine's throne, he becomes the direct and legitimate heir of the Ceasars; he claims without fear, the whole heritage.[243] The day after his accession, Justinian dreamt about a universal empire. This antique Roman unity, in which German adventurers had carved out sovereignties, he aspired to reconstitute it in its integrity: these historic undeniable rights, he aimed to reinstate them and make them again into a reality."[244]

"To re-conquer Africa from the Vandals, Italy from the Ostrogoths, Spain from the Visigoths, Gaul from the Franks, that was his dream: "he aspired, said Procopius, to conquer the whole world"[245]; and he himself wrote, the day after the occupation of Africa and of Sicily "we have good hopes that God will allow us to retake the other countries the ancient Romans owned, till the limit of the two oceans."[246]

"If he goes to war, it is not only to bring back in the Roman unity the provinces held captive by the Barbarians: as a Catholic prince, he suffers, even more im-

---

(*Cont.*)
had not brought said people into their power. Justinian did not name himself *pater patriae*, and much less *pontifex maximus*, as had Constantine and his direct successors, but he did likely call himself *servus dei*, l.c. p. 15.

Knecht, August. *Die Religions-Politik: Kaiser Justinians I: Eine kirchengeschicht-liche Studie.* (Dissert. Würzberg, 1896), 8. [Andreas Gobel, *The Religious Politics of Emperor Justinian I*, Wurzburg, 1896.]
[243] Const. Deo auctore, 7
[244] *C.J.* 1, 27, 2, *praef.* Cf. *Bell. Vand.*, p.387.
Diehl, Charles. *Justinien et la Civilization Byzantine au Vie Siècle.* Paris: Ernest Leroux, 1901, 22.
[245] *Bell. Pers.* p. 157.
[246] Nov. 30, 11,
Diehl, Charles. *Justinien et la Civilization Byzantine au Vie Siècle.* Paris: Ernest Leroux, 1901, 23.

patiently yet, to see orthodox princes submitted to Arian heretics "persecutors of bodies and souls"[247] next to the restorer of the historic rights of the empire, there is in him a champion of God. Thus, his military enterprises have something of the enthusiasm of crusades: and similarly, in his government, religion is inseparable from politics. If we want to really grasp this combination of diverse sentiments, which constitute the foundation of the imperial soul, we must read in particular, the preface of the great ordinance that Justinian published the day after the conquest of Africa[248]. Everything can be found in it, the piety of the Christian who gave thanks to that God who had just given him a new and more dramatic mark of his favors, and the pride of the sovereign who glorifies himself for having taken back his lost provinces and re-conquered from the Barbarians the ornaments and the insignias of the empire. Here, it is the prince respectful of religion, who modestly thanks the heavens for deigning to choose him to avenge the wounds of the Church; there, the superb emperor who proudly reminds all that the glory he acquired had been denied to his predecessors and who declares that an era of joy is going to start with his reign for Africa."[249]

"Assuredly, this religious passion which enflamed Justinian has its excesses and perils. It quickly leads to religious intolerance, it engenders persecution against anyone who thinks differently from the prince, and this persecution, no matter how rigorous, then becomes legitimate and saintly. "He did not consider murder, said Procopius,—and here too, we think of Philippe II—the death he inflicted on the men who did not share his beliefs."[250] He himself wrote somewhere: "We have a hatred of heretics"[251]; and his whole life, he proved it,

---

[247] *C.J.* 1, 27, 1, 1.
[248] *C.J.* 1, 27, 1.
[249] Diehl, Charles. *Justinien et la Civilization Byzantine au Vie Siècle.* Paris: Ernest Leroux, 1901, 27.
[250] *Hist. Arc.* p.84.
[251] Nov. 45. *praef.*

persecuting without mercy all the dissidents, Jews, Arians, Donatists, Mono-physites and Pagans.[252] And there is another danger of this religious conception: an absolute emperor who takes an interest in the church really risks tyrannizing it. Justinian, in all times, had taken great pleasure in meddling directly in theological controversy: he was a fine orator, he knew it, and willingly he edified the bishops with his homilies full of unction and softness, and his audience was left marveled. "If I had not, writes a prelate, heard with my own ears, the words which, with the grace of God, came out of the blessed mouth of the prince, I would barely believe it, since we found in it reunited the magnitude of David, the patience of Moses, and the clemency of the apostles."[253]

"To have money, all means appeared justified to Justinian: taxes were multiplied, and were taken with an unpitying rigor "the first duty of the subjects, said the prince expressly, and the best way they have to recognize the imperial solicitude, being to pay with an absolute devotion the public taxes in their integrity"[254]. As long as the money entered the treasury exactly, Justinian left all liberty to the greed and exactions of his officials "giving all his favors, said a chronicler, to those who invented ways to find money"[255] and to meet the requirements of his wars, he himself did not hesitate neither in front of injustice nor in front of the most dishonest practices[256]. It is the ordinary ransom of glory: profound misery, the complete impoverishment of the monarchy."[257]

---

[252] Hist. Arc. p.73-76, 156.

[253] Labbe, IV, 1777. Cf. on the taste of Justinian for polemics, Nov. 132, in which he alludes to his theological writings and Liberatus, *Breviarium* (P.L.t. 68.,p.693).Diehl, Charles. *Justinien et la Civilization Byzantine au Vie Siècle*. Paris: Ernest Leroux, 1901, 28.

[254] Nov. 8, 10

[255] Zonaras, p.152. Cf. Bell. Goth., p.525 Zach. Rhet., p.188.

[256] Evagrius, 4, 30 .

[257] Diehl, Charles. *Justinien et la Civilization Byzantine au Vie Siècle*. Paris: Ernest Leroux, 1901, 31.

From the words of August Knecht, we have the confirmed titles and formula used by Justinian and the church to bring about her one-world order:

> "The titles that Justinian uses in his letters and other writings to address the Bishop of Rome are: παπα,[258] παπα 'Ρωμης,[259] *'Papa'* with and without *'urbis Romae,'*[260] *primus achipontifex et papa urbis Romae,*[261] [262],[5a], *beatissimus atque apostolicus pater, papa urbis Romae,*[263] *beatissimus sanctusque pater, pontifex urbis Romae*[264], *sanctissimus archiepiscopus almae urbis Romae et patriarcha,*[265] *sanctitas,*[266] *beatitudo*[267], *apostolatus.*[268] The titles papa primus *archipontifex, apostolicus pater, apostolus,* are used exclusively for the Pope. The remaining names are also used with other bishops and patriarchs. . . .[269]

Justinian thus accords the Bishop of Rome [64] a higher status than the other bishops and metropolitan bishops, the other patriarchs, as well as the archbishop and ecumenical patriarchs from New Rome. He speaks with regard of the "bishops of Old Rome, who follow in every way the apostolic tradition and have

---

[258] Migne l.c. 1029 C. 1033 B.

[259] l.c. 1079 A.

[260] l.c. ep. 44 p. 833, ep. 68, p. 864.

[261] ep. 114 p. 914.

[262] 1.7 § 1 C. de sum. trin. I, 1.

[5a] Migne l.c. 1127 C.

[263] Thiel l.c. ep. 75, p. 875, ep. 127, p. 939.

[264] l.c. ep. 132 p. 954.

[265] l. 8 § 7 C. de sum. trin. I, 1.

[266] l.c. ep. 120 p. 921.

[267] l.c. ep. 89 p. 886, ep. 99 p. 887.

[268] l.c. ep. 135 p. 957.

[269] l. 7 pr. C de sum. trin. I, 1.

[21a]. παπα [in my dictionary only as "expression of surprise" but "pope" like Latin?; Amer. Heritage Dict. says Latin papa/for pope comes from Greek παππας]

[22a]. παπα 'Ρωμης [pope of Rome]

[23a]. papa urbis Romae [pope of the city Rome]

[24a]. primus archipontifex and papa urbis Romae [first archbishop/archpontiff and pope of the city Rome]

never diverged from one another in their teachings, but have preserved the true and proper faith through the present day."[270] A recognition of the primacy on the part of the emperor cannot be denied. His own words serve as proof of this: "We have some time ago decreed a general law against ... Nestorius and Eutyches ... and have taken care that the unity of the holy church and the Holy Father and patriarch of Old Rome, whom we have informed of this law, remain intact in all areas. For we shall not tolerate the withholding of any information pertaining to the church from his Holiness, because he is the head of all the priests of God and especially because, whenever heretics have appeared in these areas, they have been set right by the valid judgment of the holy chair."[271]

(*Cont.*)

25ª. παπα της πρεσβυτερας Ρωμης και πατριαρχης [pope of the elder/greater/ more important Rome and patriarch]

5a. 'ιερευς της πρεσβυτερας 'Ρωμης [priest of the elder/greater/more important Rome]

26ª. beatissimus atque apostolicus pater, papa urbis Romae [very blessed and apostolic father, pope of the city Rome]

27ª. pontifex urbis Romae [bishop/pontiff of the city Rome]

28ª. sanctissimus archiepiscopus almae urbis Romae et patriarcha [very holy archbishop of the kind city Rome and patriarch]

29ª. sanctitas [holiness]

30ª. beatitudo [blessedness]

31ª. apostolatus [apostolate]

The titles παπα [pope], papa primus archipontifex [pope first archbishop], apostolicus pater [apostolic father], apostolus [apostole] and παπα ... και πατριαρχης [pope ... and patriarch]

32ª. αρχιεπισκοπος και οικουμενικος πατριαρχης [archbishop and patriarch of the whole world]

[270] Migne l.c.:

[271] l. 7 § 2 C. de sum. trin. I, 1 (Letter to Epiphanius) l. §§ 7–22 eod. cf. Corvinus a Belderen l.c. tit. IX de Pontifice Romano p. 90–121: [*Greek text*]

14ª Novella XVII (9) l.c.: *legum originem fontem sacerdoti anterior Roma sortita est ... et summi pontificatus apicem apud eam esse. Ex hac*, the same continues, *in totas catholicas ecclesias, quae usque ad oceani fretum positae sunt, saluberrimae legis vigor extendatur, et sit totius occidentis nec non orientis ...*

.... Justinian boastingly emphasizes that Old Rome was "the source and homeland of the laws, the origin of the priesthood, and that the seat of the highest bishop is found there."[14a] In another writing to the same pope (533), Justinian calls his Holiness "the head of all holy churches."[272] He very [65] clearly expresses the relationship between Rome and Constantinople in an edict from 545: "Be it known that, in accordance with the decisions of the holy councils, the holy pope of Old Rome is first among all priests, but that the archbishop of Constantinople takes second rank after the holy apostolic chair of Old Rome and stands before all others."[273] The primacy of the pope before the patriarchs of New Rome is also established by that which Justinian himself writes, "Anthimus, the heretical patriarch, was replaced by Agapet, the bishop of the holy church of Old Rome."[274] Also of importance is what Pope John II writes to Justinian about the relationship between the pope and the emperor: "In the crown of your wisdom and piety, most Christian sovereign, a star gleams with particular light, this star being that you, in the zeal of faith and Christian love, and precisely acquainted with the church's teachings, uphold the reverence of the Roman seat, seek unity with him, and subordinate everything to him to whose predecessor, the prince of the apostles, the Lord said, 'Tend to my flock!' The holy fathers taught that the Roman seat stands in truth over all churches, and the emperors have declared the same in their laws. You testify to the same through your pious words. Through you the word of the Scripture has been fulfilled: 'Through me the kings rule, and through me the lawgivers prescribe what is right' ... We have learned that you, in apostolic zeal and with the endorsement of our brothers and bishops, have decreed a general law to the faithful in order to eradicate false teachings. Now, because this

---

[272] 1. 8 § 11 C. de sum. trin. I, 1: *caput omnium sanctarum ecclesiarum.*

[273] Nov. CLI (119).

[274] Cov. LVI (42). Cf. Nov. LI (40), CXLVIII (120), Nov. XLV (31), XII (6).

stands in accordance with the apostolic teachings, we confirm it by the power of our office."[275]

The theory which Justinian put forth regarding the primacy and the highest teaching office of the bishop of Rome is clear and correct."[276]

"The empire expanded but still lacked one thing in Justinian's view: the inner vital principle of a unified religion. The universal empire should be borne by a universal religion. To create this within a land so divided about religion was a difficult task. Paganism, Judaism, and Christianity, each of which was further divided into various sects, could not possibly be united. If a uniform state religion should reign, which had to exclude all subordinates, then the collective [13] religious creeds had to give way to a single one. From the perspective of the state, this could only be achieved through battle and the application of violence. Justinian did not shy away from these tactics. For more than thirty years he fought against the non-Christian religions, against the Christian heresies and the conflicts of teachings within the Christian church, in order to bring the true faith of Christ to sole sovereignty. The religious politics of the emperor was a continued politics of battle."[277]

"One state and one religion in the state was the goal to which the politics of the Roman emperors always led. Emperor Augustus was given the following advice from the state-savvy Mäcenas: "You must honor the Godhead yourself always and everywhere according to the wisdom of the fathers and command others to honor it likewise. Those, however, who wish to introduce foreign religious services, those you must hate and punish, not only for the sake of the gods, but rather because those who introduce foreign gods will

---

[275] l. 8 pr. — § 7 C. de sum. trin. I, 1.
[276] Knecht, August. *Die Religions-Politik: Kaiser Justinians I: Eine kirchengeschicht-liche Studie.* (Dissert. Würzberg, 1896), 63-65. [Andreas Gobel, *The Religious Politics of Emperor Justinian I*, Wurzburg, 1896.]
[277] Ibid., 12-13.

convince many others to assume this foreign way of life. From this, conspiracies and rebellions arise, which are in no way acceptable to the monarchy."[278] The successors of Augustus, the pagan as well as the Christian, dealt according to this principle. Equality in the contemporary sense was unknown. The emperors of the pre-Christian time of the Roman world-empire held fast, in a rigid way, to the monopoly of the religious cult. The supreme rulers of the Christian era of the Roman Empire demanded [25] the exclusive right of the state for this new religion and declared war on all non-Christian creeds, the foreign as well as the indigenous.

Justinian approached the religious-political legacy of his predecessors in their sense. The Christian religion should possess unlimited supremacy. All non-Christian cults were, sooner or later, violently or gently, threatened with banishment. He strove not only for a Christian state, but also for exclusively Christian subjects. To the end, he entered into battle against all non-Christian sects that still stood within Roman borders, primarily with paganism and Judaism, with sects of the Samaritans and Manichaeans."[279]

"Christian religious politics in and of themselves are not remarkable for a Byzantine emperor after Constantine I. All of Constantine's successors were proponents of Christianity with the exception of Julian, who reigned briefly. However, not all of them followed the same direction. The Arian, Nestorian and Monophysitic faiths, one after another, all had their followers and proponents among the emperors. The fights between the Latinists and Orientalists had, with the help of the emperors, developed into a schism between east and west.

---

[278] Dio Cassius, 52, 36. Cf. Lasaulx, *der Untergang des Hellenismus.* Munich 1854, p. 35.

[279] We will not consider here the smaller sects of the Borborites, Montanists, Tascodrugen, Ophites, and others that Justinian chastises in his laws.

Knecht, August. *Die Religions-Politik: Kaiser Justinians I: Eine kirchengeschicht-liche Studie.* (Dissert. Würzberg, 1896), 24-25. [Andreas Gobel, *The Religious Politics of Emperor Justinian I*, Wurzburg, 1896.]

In order to come to the correct analysis of Justinian's religious policy it is necessary to know how he positioned himself vis-à-vis the church's sources of belief on the one side and heresies and other religious splinters on the other.

In general there is to say that Emperor Justinian, like his Christian predecessors on the Byzantine throne, did not recognize a parity of various confessions. A legal tolerance of Christian sects was as foreign to him as that of non-Christian sects. His religious policy was also exclusive in relation to those. He decreed that only the true church and no other [55] faith had a right to existence and protection within the empire. That this was so is shown by a government manifest which was later made a religious edict: "As the true faith, in the first order, which the Holy Catholic and Apostolic Church of God teaches, in no way allows any change, we hold it. . . . to be appropriate to make generally known to which confessions we are subject. . . . We believe in three persons united in one being and pray to one Godhead. . . . We believe in the Son of God, eternally begotten of the Father. . . . who came down from Heaven and became man. . . . We condemn all heresies, above all Nestorius who does not recognize Christ as God . . . and Mary . . . as mother of God . . . , also Eutyches, who . . . denies the incarnation and refuses to admit that Christ, with respect to the Godhead, is one being with the Father, and, with respect to mankind, is of the same being as we; furthermore we anathematize Apollinarius, who denies the Son of God human spirit...Those who...are found to be of different belief cannot expect any leniency from us. To the contrary, they should be given the appropriate punishments as heretics."[280]

"Since it is known to us," he writes in a later edict, "that nothing gives our dear God so much honor as when all Christians think one and the same regarding the true and unmolested belief and when no splinters exist within the Holy Church of God, so we consider it necessary to take the opportunity to declare all dis-

---

[280] L. 5. C. de sum. Trin. I, 1; cf. l. 6, l. 7 eodem.

turbers of the peace to be scandalous, and also to rid
ourselves of existing scandals, through the proclamation of the true faith as taught by the Holy Church,
with a single law, with which the true believers remain
steadfast and the enemies of the faith recognize the
truth and unite themselves with the Holy Church as
quickly as possible."[281] "Our efforts remain constant,"
Justinian says at another point, "to keep the true and
incontrovertible Christian faith, to ensure the continuation of the holy catholic and apostolic church and to
protect it from any disturbance [56] of its unity. In our
opinion we have earned God's entrusting of us with the
imperial scepter in this world, and his securing our
power and putting down the enemies of the empire;
through such efforts, we also hope to receive the grace
of God for eternity."[282]

"We want all Christians to accept the faith that the
Holy Catholic Church maintains, so that we, as we
know the one God and Lord, also have one such faith.
For there is only one confession of faith, and it consists
of the recognition and praise of the Father, Christ, the
son of God, and the Holy Ghost."[283]

The following words, with which he closes his
edict of condemnation against Anthimus and his comrades, are telling for the motives from which Justinian's religious policy was derived: "We ordain all of
this in the interest of the general peace of the Holy
Church in connection with the teachings of faith of the
fathers, on which the priesthood may operate unhindered towards its welfare. For when this possesses
peace, the state will also prosper, because it receives
peace from above, which our great God and Savior
Jesus Christ, one of the Holy Trinity and only Son of
God, proclaims and bestows on all to whom grace is
given to praise and pray to him truly."[284]

---

[281] J. P. Migne, *Patrologie Graeca*, 86, I 993 D.
[282] Migne l. c. 945 D–947 A.
[283] Migne l. c.
[284] Migne l. c. 1103 A. cf. 1145 C.
Knecht, August. *Die Religions-Politik: Kaiser Justinians I: Eine kirchen-
geschichtliche Studie*. (Dissert. Würzberg, 1896), 54-56. [Andreas
Gobel, *The Religious Politics of Emperor Justinian I*, Wurzberg, 1896.]

The following procedures were instrumental in establishing this "new order" of force:

A.D. 529 Recodification of the ancient laws was to take place and the task to be accomplished was enormous, for there were no fewer than 2,000 books which formed around three million lines.[285] Justinian selected a group of lawyers, including Tribonian, who reconstructed the *Theodosian Code* published in 438. The result was called the *Codex*. A large number of the new laws constructed in *Codex I* were ecclesiastical. This work was officially ratified by a constitution on the seventh of April.[286]

A.D. 533 These same lawyers completed the *Digest*, or *Pandects*, on the thirtieth of December. In the same year, a manual for students of law, taken largely from the works of Gaius in the second century, was published on the twenty-first of November. This was called the *Institutes*.[287]

A.D. 534 The entire work thus far was revised and enhanced by a number of ordinances decreed by the emperor since 529 and the fourth part of Justianian's legal work, the *Novels*, was begun. These were laws drawn up from 534 to the end of Justinian's reign in 565. The most complete edition of the *Novellae Constitutiones* is the Greek collection of 168 constitutions. The revised version was to eliminate all redundant and nonessential material and in its final state, with the Novels, consists of a little over 6,000 pages in 17 volumes. The completed work was called the *Corpus Juris Civilis* and is the basis of all Roman Catholic canon law:

> "This *Corpus* became the definitive form of Roman law for the empire, and soon for the barbarian West, as well."[288]

---

[285] Const. *Tanta*, I.
[286] H.F. Jolowicz, *Historical Introduction to the Study of Roman Law* (London: Cambridge University Press, 1932), 485.
[287] Ibid., 498.
[288] Warren Treadgold, *A History of the Byzantine State and Society* (Stanford: Stanford University Press, 1997), 185.

"The *Corpus Juris Civilis*, "it is," as it is said, the last product of Roman legal science, the supreme effort of concentration of the law struggling against the slow disintegration that made itself felt since the 3rd century."[289] And there is still something else, and perhaps more significant. In this *Corpus Juris Civilis*, are inscribed the essential principles of law that regulate modern societies, it is its study, obscurely followed for the first centuries of the high Middle Ages, taken up again in the 11th century to an extraordinary degree, that truly revealed to Western barbaric nations the idea of a state founded on the law. From there, through this long chain of events across history—and that is what one must, in spite of the necessary critiques, never forget—Justinian's will accomplished one of the most fertile works for the progress of humanity.

One knows what respect, almost superstitious, Justinian professed for the traditions from Roman antiquity, for this "infallible antiquity"[290] (*inculpabilis antiquitas*), of which he flattered himself with being the representative and legitimate heir. If Rome had been great, it was through two things, through the glory of its arms and through the science of law; in Justinian's eyes, a Roman emperor was a person with two sides, "not only victorious in foreign wars, but knowing to follow, through legal paths, injustice and calumny, together triumphant victor over defeated enemies and scrupulous defender of the law."[291]

"In thanking God, whose protection had allowed him to complete his plans, he ordained that the new legislation would have the strength of the law throughout the entire expanse of the empire,[292] that it would

---

[289] G. May, *Elements of Roman Law*, I, 47.

[290] *Nov.* 8, *jusjurandum*. Cf. *Nov.* 23, 3, and the attention with which Justinian's scholarship notes the traditions. *Nov.* 24, *praef.*; 25, *praef.*, 103, *praef.*, etc.

[291] Const. *Imperatoriam majestatem* (at the front of the *Institutes*), *praef.* Cf. *DeJust. cod.confirmando, praef.*
Diehl, Charles. *Justinien et la Civilization Byzantine au Vie Siècle.* Paris: Ernest Leroux, 1901, 248.

[292] Const. *Deo auct.*, 6. *De. Just. cod. conf.*, 3.

erase all old decrees, that it would be taken as unchangeable and holy: everything that was recorded
would be indisputable, even the mistakes. Justinian ordained, in effect, that between the old and authentic
law text and the modified text that figured in the Digest
and Code, the latter would bring justice."[293]

"Indeed, according to a word of an historian of the
time: "he was the first of the sovereigns of Byzantium,
who, not just in name but in fact, was the absolute master of the Romans"[294] . . . . It is this Justinian legislation
which dominated all the middle ages and supplied
modern Europe with the basis of law."[295]

"The activity in the realm of public law earned the
emperor the title "Father of Jurisprudence.""[296]

Under the reign of Justinian, the reading of the
Scriptures was forbidden:

"For consequently the reading of the Holy Scripture would have to be forbidden, since it is constantly
misused by the heretics."[297]

This same policy was also expressed by Pope Leo the
Great, reinforced by Pope Felix and Gelasius I and became standard protocol throughout the entire dark ages
that only the church can interpret aright the scriptures:

". . . . The Christian religion is not a natural religion, Christian belief and its content may not be
recorded by natural means, even because it is not of
natural origin, but was given by God himself, wherefore only the "dispensators'", as the writing called the

---

[293] *De. Just. cod. conf.,* 3; Const. *Deo auct,* 7.
Ibid., 262.
[294] Agathias, p.306.
[295] Ibid., 24.
[296] Knecht, August. *Die Religions-Politik: Kaiser Justinians I: Eine
kirchengeschicht-liche Studie.* (Dissert. Würzberg, 1896), 11. [Andreas
Gobel, *The Religious Politics of Emperor Justinian I,* Wurzburg, 1896.]
[297] J. P. Migne, *Patrologie Graeca,* 86, I. 1136 A – 1137 B. Ibid., 106.

administrators, could give guidelines; they alone are authorized to spread information about the Christian norms and axioms, to clarify and determine what is Christian and what the Christian norm doesn't correspond to by virtue of their education and their special standing. In the opposition pair of *discere-docere* [to learn to teach] it was manifested the knowledge and awareness element which was essential for Christianity in sharply contoured form. Christian norms must- as the beliefs stated therein made clear- be learned by those who were authorized; they could not be "naturally" understood[298]. The dig at the Henoticon is unmistakable. In matters, over which the leader exercised his knowledge, and those are the godly matters, he can issue no commandments, nor can the laymen or the clerics. But according to the imperial judicial order, the Christian religion is the lone legitimate one, the (Christian) empire and the (Christian) church built a unity. The Roman Empire was the Christian empire. Looking out from this point of view, the repute leader should sacrifice his neck in pious humility before the church administrators for all mortal-temporal matters; *colla summittere* [as they alone are to discharge or to send out] is the clear and understandable expression of [Pope] Felix and Gelasius. By this action, this was a phrase, which should have lead the papal leadership program out of the century. It found inclusion in many legal collections and was eventually decreed by Gratian in his (*Dist.* 10.3) in the 12th Century."[299]

Latin remained the official language of the empire:

---

[298] Exactly this consideration makes it understandable, why LEO the Great had forbidden the preaching of laymen: JK 495. The ban also counted for monks. H. KOCH: *Gelasius im Dienst* 48 A. 1 refers to Seneca as the root of the diastasis *discere-docere* (Ep. 6,62 and Ep. 7,8).

[299] Ullman, Walter von. *Päpste und Papsttum* [*Popes and Papacy*]: *Gelasius I. (492–496)*. Bd. 18. Stuttgart: Anton Hiersemann, 1981, 148.

"One thing strikes us first. For this empire, in large part Eastern, Latin remains the legal language.[300] This feature is characteristic: it is that for Justinian, heir of the Roman emperors, Latin remained the official language, and moreover, the national language of the monarchy.[301] In fact, Greek proved to be more widespread, more intelligible; it was always with a sort of condescendence that the successor of the Caesars consented to use it. And if that is true, until the practice of the current administration, they obstinately used Latin. In a province like Syria, where the majority of the population spoke Syrian, where only the upper classes expressed themselves in Greek, they continued, until the 6th century, to compose the protocols of acts in Latin."[302]

"The majority of novellas were written in Greek: "We have not," said Justinian, in an ordinance from 535, "written this law in the national language, but in the common language, which is Greek, so that it will be recognized by everyone through the ease that they will understand it."[303]

A.D. 528 The Decree that laid the Foundation for the Political Power of the Papacy as described by Gregorovius:

"As Arians, remained outside the Roman Church it came to pass that the Pope, as head of Catholic Christendom, felt himself raised above the heretical

---

[300] Assuredly there is nothing surprising about what the editors of the Code and Digest, compiling works written in Latin, preserved under their original form. But the prefaces that accompanied these compendiums and a large number of Justinian's ordinances that are inserted, are in Latin, and even the *Institutes* could have also been composed in Greek.

[301] *Nov.* 7, I. Cf. *Nov.* 15, *praef.*; 66, 1, 2; between the Greek text and the Latin text of a novella, Justinian declares that the latter is [*words in Greek*]. Cf. on the use of Latin in legislation. Finlay, *Hist. of Greece* (ed. Tozer), I, 215.

[302] Cf. Gelzer, in *Byz. Zeitschr.*, III, 22-24.

Diehl, Charles. *Justinien et la Civilization Byzantine au Vie Siècle.* Paris: Ernest Leroux, 1901, 256-7.

[303] *Nov.* 7, I. Ibid., 266-7.

kings, and thus, standing between them and the orthodox Emperor (whom they recognized at the same time
as their Imperial overlord), he gradually became a
man of importance, and finally acquired a greater degree of influence in the internal affairs of the city.[304]
Among the Prescripts enumerated by Cassiodorus is an
edict of Athalaric appointing the Roman bishop arbi-
trator in disputes between the laity and clergy. Anyone
having a dispute with a member of the clergy in Rome
was directed henceforth to appeal first to the judgment
of the Pope, and only in case the Pope rejected his com-
plaint, was he to carry the action before the secular jurisdiction. Anyone refusing to submit to the decision of
the Pope was sentenced to be fined ten pounds of
gold.[305] Felix IV. [343] appears to have been the Pope
who succeeded in obtaining this decree so favorable to
the influence of the Roman Curia. The Episcopal
power of arbitration between laity and clergy had been
exercised from of old, but the privilege may be regarded as simply exempting the clergy from all secular
jurisdiction. *Such was the decree which laid the foundation of the political power of the Papacy.* It was evident
that the royal government felt itself insecure after the

---

[304] Athalaric's letter to Justin, notifying his accession to the throne, indicates the recognition of the Imperial supremacy. *Var.*, viii. I. The silver coins of the Gothic Kings, bearing on the obverse the head of the
Emperor, on the reverse the monogram. of the King, surrounded by a
wreath or the words INVICTA ROMA, supply us with a further indication. J. Friedlander, *Die Munzen der Ostgothen*, Berlin, 1844.

[305] *Var.*, viii. 24. Muratori refers this law to the year 528. G. Sartorius
(*Versuch uber die Regier. der Ostgothen Italien*, p. 145) considers that
this privilegium, the importance of which he depreciates, only applied to the clergy in the city of Rome. S. Marc, however (*Abrege
chronologique de L'histoire d'.Italie*, p. 62), says: c'est sur cette condescendence des princes pour un etat infiniment respectable en lui-
meme, que dans la suite les Ecclesiastiques ont pretendu qu'ils
etaient de Droit divin exempts de la jurisdiction seculaire. [Chrono-
logical summary of the history of. Italy, p. 62), says: It is on this superiority of the princes for an infinitely sizeable state in itself, that in the
continuation the Ecclesiastics claimed that they were of divine Right
exempt of the secular jurisdiction.]

death of Theodoric, and that it hastened to conciliate and to win the Roman Church."[306]

The actual decree itself:

24. KING ATHALARIC TO THE CLERGY OF THE ROMAN CHURCH.

"For the gift of kingly power we owe an infinite debt to God, whose ministers ye are.

Ye state in your tearful memorial to us that it has been an ordinance of long custom that anyone who has a suit of any kind against a servant of the sacrosanct Roman Church should first address himself to the chief Priest of that City, lest haply your clergy, being profaned by the litigation of the Forum, should be occupied in secular rather than religious matters. And you add that one of your Deacons has, to the disgrace of religion, been so sharply handled by legal process that the Sajo[307] has dared actually to take him into his own custody.

This dishonor to the Ministers of holy things is highly displeasing to our inborn reverence, yet we are glad that it gives us the opportunity of paying part of our debt to Heaven.

Therefore, considering the honor of the Apostolic See, and wishing to meet the desires of the petitioners, we by the authority of this letter decree in regular course[308]:

---

[306] During the reign of Theodoric, however, the clergy remained subject to the secular Forum.

[The Decree of A.D. 528 by King Athalaric, the grandson of Theodoric the Great who became king upon his grandfather's death in 526 is believed to have laid the Foundation for the Political Power of the Papacy.]

Ferdinand Gregorovius, Translated from the Fourth German Edition, Mrs. Gustavus W. Hamilton , *History Of The City of Rome In The Middle Ages*, (London, George Bell & Sons, 1900, First Published, 1894. Second Edition, Revised, 1900), 1:342-3.

[307] In the text, 'Sajus.'

[308] "Praesenti auctoritate moderato ordine definimus." Dahn interprets , moderato ordine," "not so absolutely as the Roman clergy desires." Is not this to attribute rather too much force to the conventional language of Cassiodorus?

That if anyone shall think he has a good cause for going to law with a person belonging to the Roman clergy, he shall first present himself for hearing at the judgment-seat of the most blessed Pope, in order that the latter may either decide between the two in his own holy manner, or may delegate the cause to a Iurisconsultus [a jurist] to be ended by him. And if, perchance, which it is impiety to believe, the [372] reasonable desire of the petitioner shall have been evaded, then may he come to the secular courts with his grievance, when he can prove that his petitions have been spurned by the Bishop of the aforesaid See.[309]

Should any litigant be so dishonest and so irreverent, both towards the Holy See and our authority, as to disregard this order [and proceed first in our tribunals against one of the Roman clergy], he shall forfeit 10 lbs. of gold [£400], to be exacted by the officers of the Count and distributed by the Pope to the poor; and he shall lose his suit in addition, notwithstanding any decree which he may have gained in the secular court.

Meanwhile do you, whom our judgments thus venerate, live according to the ordinances of the Church. It is a "great wickedness in you to admit such crimes as do not become the conversation even of secular men. Your profession is the heavenly life. Do not condescend to the groveling wishes and vulgar errors of ordinary mortals. Let the men of this world be coerced by human laws; do you obey the precepts of righteousness."

[See Dahn, 'Konige der Germanen' iii. 191-2, Sartorius 145, and Bauer's 'History of the Popes' ii. 323-4, for remarks on this important *privilegium*.

---

[309] "Definimus, ut si quispiam ad Romanum Clerum aliquem pertinentem, in qualibet causa probabili crediderit actione pulsandum, ad beatissimi Papae judicium prius conveniat audiendus. Ut aut ipse inter utrosque more suae sanctitatis agnoscat, aut causam deleget aequitatis studio terminandam: et si forte, quod credi nefas est, competens desiderium fuerit petitoris elusum, tunc ad saecularia fora jurgaturus occurrat, quando suas petitiones probaverit a supradictae sedis praesule fuisse contemptas."

[310] Cassiodorus, Magnus Aurelius, Hodgkin, Thomas, The Letters of Cassiodorus. London: Henry Frowde, 1886, Book VIII. 24, pgs. 371-3.

It is clear that it relates to civil, not criminal procedure, and that it does leave a right of final appeal from the Papal Courts to the dissatisfied secular litigant. At the same time, that such an appeal would be prosecuted with immense difficulty is clear even from the words of the decree. The appellant [373] will have to satisfy the King's Judges of a thing which it is almost impiety to believe, that the occupant of the Roman See has spurned his petitions.]"[310]

A.D. 529/530 John Malalas, an authoritative historian who lived and chronicled during the entire reign of Justinian, declares:

"In that year there was a great persecution of Hellenes. Many had their property confiscated. Some of them died. . . . This caused great fear. The Emperor decreed that those who held Hellenic beliefs should not hold any state office, whilst those who belonged to the other heresies were to disappear from the Roman state, after they had been given a period of three months to embrace the orthodox faith. This sacred decree was displayed in all provincial cities."[311]

Unfortunately, Dr. Summerbell dated this three-month period as occurring in 538.[312] But that will not stand under investigation of the primary sources.

A.D. 530 Equally significant is the legislative support of the state that the church canons received. Codex I.3.44 of Justinian's law codes, for example, was implemented

---

[311] John Malalas, *Chronographia*, ed. L. Dindorf (Bonn: n.p., 1831), 449; trans. Elizabeth Jeffreys, Michael Jeffreys and Roger Scott, *The Chronicle of John Malalas* (University of Sydney, N.S.W.: Australian Association for Byzantine Studies, Department of Modern Greek, 1986), 262-63. Malalas (A.D. 491-578) was a Byzantine chronicler that lived during the reign of Justinian.
[312] N. Summerbell, *A True History of the Christians and the Christian Church* (Cincinnati: Office of the Christian Pulpit, 1871), 311.

on October 18, A.D. 530, thereby giving total authority to the canons of the synods.

> "Whatever the holy canons prohibit, these also we
> by our own laws forbid."[83]

This codex alone was sufficient to elevate the laws of the church to equality with the laws of the state. Having been accorded this political backing, church canons had to be obeyed by all.

It must be remembered that when Justinian overthrew the Vandals in 534 his jurisdiction was immediately enforced. In fact, we are told specifically that his Codex was to be regarded as the supreme authority in this newly conquered territory:

> "9. Furthermore we remit all the privileges of the
> sacrosanct church of our Carthago Justiniana which
> the metropolitan cities and their priests are recognized
> to have, which also even when separated from sacro-
> sanct churches in his first book are recognized to offer
> their honor by our *Codex*: so that the city which we re-
> garded should be decorated by the name of our divine
> will bloom while decorated also with imperial privi-
> leges."[313]

The same policy was repeated when the Ostrogoths were overthrown by Justinian and his legal jurisdiction was established in Italy in 538. It was said to be:

> "Through the Code, illuminated for all eyes, a shin-
> ing star."[314]

It is through the revised Codex in 534 and the Constitutions or the Novels of Justinian in the following years that we are brought face to face with this oppres-

---

[313] Schoell, Rudolfus, *Corpus Iurus Civilis, Novellae*, (Berlin: Apud Wiedmannos, 1959), Novel 37:9, 3:245.

[314] *De emend. cod. Just.*, 3.

Diehl, Charles. *Justinien et la Civilization Byzantine au Vie Siècle.* Paris: Ernest Leroux, 1901, 261.

sive religious legislation backed by the church and enforced by the state. There are over 6000 pages in Justinian's Corpus Juris Civilis code of law. From that number we have reduced it dramatically in order to allocate some of the most exhilarating religious edicts of Justinian. Due to a lack of space, we can present only a small selection from Justinian's Corpus Juris Civilis code of law taken from his Codex I, but we will provide enough so the reader can form an intelligent and honest assessment. We begin with the Preface of Justinian's Codex I that establishes some very important precedents in rightly understanding this vast amount of jurisdiction. The following brackets [00] signify page numbering in the original that has been translated from the Latin by S.P. Scott.[315]

THE THREE PREFACES OF THE CODE OF JUSTINIA
FIRST PREFACE. CONCERNING THE ESTABLISH-MENT OF A NEW CODE.

[3] ".... the Gregorian, the Hermogenian, and the Theodosian, as well as in those other Codes promulgated after them by Theodosius of Divine Memory, and by other Emperors, who succeeded him, in addition to those which We Ourselves have promulgated, and to combine them in a single Code, under Our auspicious name, in which compilation should be included not only the constitutions of the three above-mentioned Codes, but also such new ones as subsequently have been promulgated.

SECOND PREFACE.
CONCERNING THE CONFIRMATION OF THE CODE OF JUSTINIAN.

The maintenance of the integrity of the government depends upon two things, namely, the force of arms and the observance of the laws:.... We have pre-

---

[315] Scott, S. P., trans., ed. *The Civil Law* [of Justinian] (Union, NJ: Lawbook Exchange, 2001), Codex I. Vol. 12.

served those already enacted, and afterwards by publishing new ones, have established them most firmly
for the obedience of Our subjects. [4] . . . . (3) Therefore
We have had in view the perpetual validity of this Code
in your tribunal, in order that all litigants, as well as
the most accomplished advocates, may know that it is
lawful for them, under no circumstances, to cite constitutions from the three ancient codes, of which mention has just been made, or from those which at the
present time are styled the New Constitutions, in any
judicial inquiry or contest; but that they are required to
use only the constitutions which are included in this
Our Code, and that those who venture to act otherwise
will be liable to the crime of forgery; [5]

THIRD PREFACE.
CONCERNING THE AMENDMENTS OF THE CODE
OP OUR LORD JUSTINIAN, AND THE SECOND
EDITION OF THE SAME.

[7] (1) But after We decreed that the ancient law
should be observed, [8]. . . . (5) Therefore, having repeated Our order that We shall permit none hereafter
to quote anything from Our decisions, or from other
constitutions, which We have previously promulgated,
or from the first edition of the Justinian Code; [A.D.
529] but that only what may be found written in this
Our present purified and amended Code [A.D. 534] shall
be regarded as authority, and cited in all tribunals."[316]

Included in the 534 code of Justinian was his famous
letter he wrote to Pope John II on March 15, 533. In the
same year, on March 25, he wrote to Epiphanius,
Patriarch of Constantinople, confirming that the pope
was now the head of the church and the corrector of
heretics, and giving the pope all ecclesiastical power and
authority. Included is the entire Codex I, Title 1, with the
pope's reply:

---

[316] Scott, S. P., trans., ed. *The Civil Law* [of Justinian] (Union, NJ:
Lawbook Ex-change, 2001), Codex I. First, Second, Third Preface,
12:3-8.

THE CODE OF OUR LORD THE MOST SACRED EMPEROR JUSTINIAN.

SECOND EDITION.

BOOK I.

TITLE I.

CONCERNING THE MOST EXALTED TRINITY AND THE CATHOLIC FAITH, AND PROVIDING THAT No ONE SHALL DARE TO PUBLICLY OPPOSE THEM.

1. *The Emperors Gratian, Valentinian, and Theodosius to the people of the City of Constantinople.*

"We desire that all peoples subject to Our benign Empire shall live under the same religion that the Divine Peter, the Apostle, gave to the Romans, and which the said religion declares was introduced by himself, and which it is well known that the Pontiff Damasus, and Peter, Bishop of Alexandria, a man of apostolic sanctity, embraced; that is to say, in accordance with the rules of apostolic discipline and the evangelical doctrine, we should believe that the Father, Son, and Holy Spirit constitute a single Deity, endowed with equal majesty, and united in the Holy Trinity.

(1) We order all those who follow this law to assume the name of Catholic Christians, and considering others as demented and insane, We order that they shall bear the infamy of heresy; and when the Divine vengeance which they merit has been appeased, they shall afterwards be punished in accordance with Our resentment, which we have acquired from the judgment of Heaven.

Dated at Thessalonica, on the third of the *Kalends* of March, during the Consulate of Gratian, Consul for the fifth time, and Theodosius.

2. The Same Emperors to Eutropius, Prætorian Prefect.

Let no place be afforded to heretics for the conduct of their ceremonies, and let no occasion be offered for them to display the insanity of their obstinate minds. Let all persons know that if any privilege has been fraudulently obtained by means of any rescript whatsoever, by persons of this kind, it will not be valid. Let all bodies of heretics be prevented from holding unlawful assemblies, and let the name of the only and the greatest God be celebrated everywhere, and let the observance of the Nicene Creed, recently transmitted by Our ancestors, and firmly established by the testimony and practice of Divine Religion, always remain secure.

(1) Moreover, he who is an adherent of the Nicene Faith, and a true believer in the Catholic religion, should be understood to be one [10] who believes that Almighty God and Christ, the Son of God, are one person, God of God, Light of Light; and let no one, by rejection, dishonor the Holy Spirit, whom we expect, and have received from the Supreme Parent of all things, in whom the sentiment of a pure and undefiled faith flourishes, as well as the belief in the undivided substance of a Holy Trinity. . . . These things, indeed, do not require further proof, and should be respected.

(2) Let those who do not accept these doctrines cease to apply the name of true religion to their fraudulent belief; and let them be branded with their open crimes, and, having been removed from the threshold of all churches, be utterly excluded from them, as We forbid all heretics to hold unlawful assemblies within cities. If, however, any seditious outbreak should be attempted, We order them to be driven outside the walls of the City, with relentless violence, and We direct that all Catholic churches, throughout the entire world, shall be placed under the control of the orthodox bishops who have embraced the Nicene Creed.

Given at Constantinople, on the fourth of the *Ides* of Janu-ary, under the Consulate of Flavius Eucharius and Flavius Syagrius.

3. *The Emperor Martian to Palladius, Prætorian Prefect.*

No one, whether he belongs to the clergy, the army, or to any other condition of men, shall, with a view to causing a tumult and giving occasion to treachery, attempt to discuss the Christian religion publicly in the presence of an assembled and listening crowd; for he commits an injury against the most reverend Synod who publicly contradicts what has once been decided and properly established; as those matters relative to the Christian Faith have been settled by the priests who met at Chalcedony by Our order, and are known to be in conformity with the apostolic explanations and conclusions of the three hundred and eight Holy Fathers assembled in Nicea, and the hundred and fifty who met in this Imperial City; for the violators of this law shall not go unpunished, because they not only oppose the true faith, but they also profane its venerated mysteries by engaging in contests of this kind with Jews and Pagans. Therefore, if any person who has ventured to publicly discuss religious matters is a member of the clergy, he shall be removed from his order; if he is a member of the army, he shall be degraded; and any others who are guilty of this offence, who are freemen, shall be banished from this most Sacred City, and shall be subjected to the punishment prescribed by law according to the power of the court; and if they are slaves, they shall undergo the severest penalty.

Given at Constantinople, on the eighth of the *Ides* of February, under the consulship of Patricius.

4. *John, Bishop of the City of Rome, to his most Illustrious and Merciful Son Justinian.*

Among the conspicuous reasons for praising your wisdom and gentleness, Most Christian of Emperors, and one which radiates light [11] as a star, is the fact that through love of the Faith, and actuated by zeal for charity, you, learned in ecclesiastical discipline, have preserved reverence for the See of Rome, and have subjected all things to its authority, and have given it unity. The following precept was communicated to its founder, that is to say, the first of the Apostles, by the mouth of the Lord, namely: "Feed my lambs."

This See is indeed the head of all churches, as the rules of the Fathers and the decrees of Emperors assert, and the words of your most reverend piety testify. It is therefore claimed that what the Scriptures state, namely, "By Me Kings reign, and the Powers dispense justice;" will be accomplished in you. For there is nothing which shines with a more brilliant luster than genuine faith when displayed by a prince, since there is nothing which prevents destruction as true religion does, for as both of them have reference to the Author of Life and Light, they disperse darkness and prevent apostasy. Wherefore, Most Glorious of Princes, the Divine Power is implored by the prayers of all to preserve your piety in this ardor for the Faith, in this devotion of your mind, and in this zeal for true religion, without failure, during your entire existence. For we believe that this is for the benefit of the Holy Churches, as it was written, "The king rules with his lips," and again, "The heart of the King is in the hand of God, and it will incline to whatever side God wishes"; that is to say, that He may confirm your empire, and maintain your kingdoms for the peace of the Church and the unity of religion; guard their authority, and preserve him in that sublime tranquility which is so grateful to him; and no small change is granted by the Divine Power through whose agency a divided church is not afflicted by any grief's or subject to any reproaches. For it is written, "A just king, who is upon his throne, has no reason to apprehend any misfortune."

We have received with all due respect the evidences of your serenity, through Hypatius and Demetrius, most holy men, my brothers and fellow-bishops, from whose statements we have learned that you have promulgated an Edict addressed to your faithful people, and dictated by your love of the Faith, for the purpose of overthrowing the designs of heretics, which is in accordance with the evangelical tenets, and which we have confirmed by our authority with the consent of our brethren and fellow bishops, for the reason that it is in conformity with the apostolic doctrine.

The following is the text of the letter of the Emperor Justinian, Victorious, Pious, Happy, Renowned, Triumphant, always Augustus, to John, Patriarch, and most Holy Archbishop of the fair City of Rome:

With honor to the Apostolic See, and to Your Holiness, which is, and always has been remembered in Our prayers, both now and formerly, and honoring your happiness, as is proper in the case of one who is considered as a father, We hasten to bring to the knowledge of Your Holiness everything relating to the condition of the Church, as We have always had the greatest desire to preserve the unity of your Apostolic See, and the condition of the Holy Churches of God, as they [12] exist at the present time, that they may remain without disturbance or opposition. Therefore, We have exerted Ourselves to unite all the priests of the East and subject them to the See of Your Holiness, and hence the questions which have at present arisen, although they are manifest and free from doubt, and, according to the doctrine of your Apostolic See, are constantly firmly observed and preached by all priests, We have still considered it necessary that they should be brought to the attention of Your Holiness. For we do not suffer anything which has reference to the state of the Church, even though what causes the difficulty may be clear and free from doubt, to be discussed without being brought to the notice of Your Holiness, because you are the head of all the Holy Churches, for We shall exert Ourselves in every way (as has already been stated), to increase the honor and authority of your See.

(1) Therefore, We present to Your Holiness the fact that certain infidels and persons who do not belong to the Holy Catholic and Apostolic Church of God have, like Jews and apostates, dared to dispute matters

which are properly accepted, glorified, and preached by all priests in accordance with your doctrines, denying that Our Lord Jesus Christ is the only begotten Son of God, and that Our Lord was born of the Holy Spirit and of the Holy, Glorious, and always Virgin Mary, the Mother of God, and became a man and was crucified, and that he is one of the persons of the Holy Trinity, who are all of one substance, and who should be adored and exalted along with the Father and the Holy Spirit, and that he is consubstantial with the Father according to divinity, and consubstantial with ourselves according to humanity, and susceptible of the sufferings of the flesh, but not susceptible of the same as a deity. For these persons refusing to acknowledge Our Lord Jesus Christ as the only begotten Son of God, and Our Lord as one of the Holy Trinity, and of the same substance with the other persons composing it, appear to follow the evil doctrine of Nestor, who asserts that there is one Son of God according to grace, whom he styles the Word of God, and another Son whom he calls Christ.

(2) All the priests of the Holy Catholic and Apostolic Church and the most Reverend Abbots of the Holy Monasteries, acknowledging Your Holiness, and solicitous for the prosperity and unity of the Holy Churches of God, which they receive from the Apostolic See of Your Holiness, making no changes in the ecclesiastical condition which has existed up to this time, and still exists; with one voice, confess, glorify, and preach that Our Lord Jesus Christ is the only begotten Son and the Word of God, and that Our Lord, born of His Father before all centuries and times, Who descended from Heaven in the last days, was born of the Holy Spirit and the Holy and Glorious Virgin Mary, the Mother of God; became a man and was crucified; is of the same substance as the Holy Trinity to be adored and glorified with the Father and the Holy Spirit; for we do not acknowledge any other God, Word or Christ, but one alone, and the same of like substance with the Father, in accordance with divinity, and of like substance with us in accordance with humanity, Who

could suffer in the flesh, [13] but could not suffer as a
deity; and Whom, Himself perfect in divinity as well as
humanity, we receive and confess as being what the
Greeks call Greek. And, as the only begotten Son and
Word of God was born of His Father before centuries
and times existed, and as He, in later times, descended
from Heaven, was born of the Holy Spirit and the Holy
ever Virgin Mary, the Mother of God, Our Lord Jesus
Christ having become a man, is properly and truly
God. Hence we say that the Holy and Glorious Virgin
Mary is properly and truly the Mother of God, not for
the reason that God obtained speech and origin from
her, but because in the last days He descended from
Heaven, and, incarnated through Her, became a man,
and was born; whom we confess and believe (as has already been stated), to be of the same substance with
the Father according to deity, and of the same substance with ourselves according to humanity, whose
miracles and sufferings voluntarily sustained by Him
while in the flesh we acknowledge.

(3) Moreover, we recognize four Sacred Councils,
that is to say, the one composed of three hundred and
eighteen Holy Fathers who assembled in the City of
Nicea; and that of the hundred and fifty Holy Fathers
who met in this Imperial City; and that of the Holy
Fathers who first congregated at Ephesus; and that of
the Holy Fathers who met at Chalcedony, as your
Apostolic See teaches and proclaims. Hence, all priests
who follow the doctrine of your Apostolic See believe,
confess, and preach these things.

(4) Wherefore We have hastened to bring to the notice of Your Holiness, through the most blessed
Bishops Hypatius and Demetrius (so it may not be concealed from Your Holiness), that these tenets are denied by some few wicked and judaizing monks, who
have adopted the perfidious doctrines of Nestor.

(5) Therefore We request your paternal affection,
that you, by your letters, inform Us and the Most Holy
Bishop of this Fair City, and your brother the Patriarch, who himself has written by the same messengers
to Your Holiness, eager in all things to follow the

Apostolic See of Your Blessedness, in order that you may make it clear to Us that Your Holiness acknowledges all the matters which have been set forth above, and condemns the perfidy of those who, in the manner of Jews, have dared to deny the true Faith. For in this way the love of all persons for you, and the authority of your See will increase, and the unity of the Holy Church will be preserved unimpaired, when all the most blessed bishops learn through you and from those who have been dispatched by you, the true doctrines of Your Holiness. Moreover, We beg Your Blessedness to pray for Us, and to obtain the beneficence of God in Our behalf.

The subscription was as follows: "May God preserve you for many years, Most Holy and Religious Father."

HERE FOLLOWS THE REMAINDER OF THE LETTER OF THE POPE.

It is then clear, Most Glorious Emperor (as the tenor of your message and the statements of your envoys disclose), that you have de- [14] voted Yourself to the study of apostolic learning, as You are familiar with, have written, proposed and published to believers among the people, those matters having reference to the faith of the Catholic religion, which (as we have already stated), both the tenets of the Apostolic See and the venerated authority of the Holy Fathers have established, and which, in all respects, we have confirmed. Therefore, it is opportune to cry out with a prophetic voice, "Heaven will rejoice with You, and pour out its blessings upon You, and the mountains will rejoice, and the hills be glad with exceeding joy." Hence, you should write these things upon the tablets of Your heart, and preserve them as the apples of your eyes, for there is no one animated by the charity of Christ who will appear to impugn this confession of the just and true faith; as it is evident that You condemn the impiety of Nestor and Eutyches, and all other heretics, and that You firmly and inviolably, with devotion to God and reverent mind acknowledge the

single, true, and Catholic Faith of Our Lord God, as revealed by the agency of Our Savior Jesus Christ; diffused everywhere by the preaching of the Prophets and
Apostles; confirmed by the confessions of saints
throughout the entire world, and united with the opinions of the Fathers and Doctors conformably to our
doctrine.

Those alone who are opposed to your professions
are they of whom the Holy Scriptures speak as follows:
"They have based their hope on lying, and have expected to remain concealed through falsehood." And
also those who, according to the prophet, say to the
Lord, "Depart from us, we are unwilling to follow your
ways"; on account of which Solomon said, "They have
wandered through the paths of their own cultivation
and gathered unfruitful things with their hands." This,
then, is your true faith, this your true religion, which
all the Fathers and heads of the Roman Church of
happy memory (as we have already stated) and whom
we follow in all things, have embraced; this is what the
Apostolic See has preached up to this time, and has
preserved inviolate, and if anyone should appear to oppose this confession, and this Faith, he must show himself to be outside of the communion and the Catholic
Church. We have found Cyrus and his followers in the
City of Rome, who came from the Cumitensian monastery, and whom we have attempted by our apostolic
arguments to recall to the true faith, as sheep who are
about to perish and are wandering, should be brought
back to the fold of the owner. In order that, according
to the prophet, stammering tongues may know how to
speak matters which have reference to peace, the first
of our apostles quotes the words of Isaiah, the prophet,
through us to unbelievers, namely: "Continue in the
light of the fire and the flame which you yourselves
have kindled, but their heart is so hardened (as has
been written), that they do not recognize the voice of
the Shepherd, and the sheep which were not mine are
unwilling to hear." With reference to such persons, we,
observing what was established by the Pontiff on this
point, do not receive them in our communion, and we
order them to be excluded from every Catholic Church,

unless, having renounced their errors, they adopt our doctrine, and announce their [15] adherence to it, after having made a regular profession of the same. For it is just that those who do not show obedience to the laws which we have established should be banished from the churches. But as the Church never closes her heart to those who return to her, I beseech Your Clemency, if they, having renounced their errors and abandoned their wicked designs, should wish to return to the bosom of the Church, to receive them in your communion, and abandon your feelings of indignation, and that through our intercession you pardon them, and grant them your indulgence.

Moreover, we pray God and Our Saviour Jesus Christ, that he may preserve you long in peace in this true religion and in the unity and veneration of the Apostolic See, and that your most Christian and pious Empire may, in all respects, long be maintained. Moreover, O most Serene of Princes, we praise Hypatius and Demetrius, your envoys, and our brothers and fellow-bishops, whose selection has shown that they are acceptable to Your Clemency; for the importance of such an embassy indicates that it could not be entrusted to anyone who is not perfect in Christ, and that You would not have deemed them worthy of a mission involving so much piety and reverence, unless they have been very dear to You.

The favor of Our Lord Jesus Christ, the love of God the Father, and the Communion of the Holy Spirit, remain forever with you, Most Pious son. Amen."

The subscription was as follows, "Most Glorious and Clement Son of the Emperor Augustus, may Almighty God guard your kingdom and your health with His eternal protection.

Given at Rome, on the eighth of the *Kalends* of April, during the Consulate of the Emperor Justinian, Consul for the fourth time, and of Paulinus, Consul for the fifth time."[317]

---

[317] Scott, S. P., trans., ed., *The Civil Law* [*of Justinian*] (Union, NJ: Lawbook Exchange, 2001), Codex I. 1. 12:9-15.

The following primary sources will fully document the ecclesiastical "voice" behind the code of Justinian. With the revised code of 534 then in place, it included many of the decrees or constitutions from former Emperors upholding the orthodox religion:

> "We decree that the privileges conceded by former Emperors under the general terms of constitutions, to all the Holy Churches of the orthodox religion, shall be observed, and remain firm and unimpaired for all time."[318]

And Justinian also recognized that the Pontificate in Rome was the only valid source for all ecclesiastical legislation:

> "No one is ignorant of the fact that, in ancient Rome, legislation originally emanated from the head of the Pontificate."[319]

Ironically, Justinian applied the following terms to the Catholic Church:

> "The mother of religion,"[320] "The mother of our piety, the source of the orthodox religion of all Christians,"[321] "The Mother of Our Empire"[322]

From Codex I Book 1 section 4, we wish to reiterate this most significant piece of legislation that we just read from a letter by Justinian written to Pope John II on March 15, 533.

> "For we do not suffer anything which has reference to the state of the Church, even though what causes the difficulty may be clear and free from doubt, to be discussed without being brought to the notice of Your Holiness, because you are the head of all the Holy

---

[318] Ibid., Codex I. 2.12. 12:18.
[319] Ibid., *The Novels*, 9. 16:65-66, April 14, 535.
[320] Ibid., Codex I. 2.14. 12:20.
[321] Ibid., Codex I. 2.15. 12:26.
[322] Ibid., *The Novels*, 3- chapter *I*. Vol. 16:17, March 16, 535.

Churches, for We shall exert Ourselves in every way (as
has already been stated), to increase the honor and authority of your See."[323]

"We shall exert Ourselves in every way" is legally confirmed by the legislative support from the state that the
church canons received. Codex I.3.44 of Justinian's law
codes, for example, was implemented on October 18,
A.D. 530, thereby giving total authority to the canons of
the synods.

> "Whatever the holy canons prohibit, these also we
> by our own laws forbid."[324]

This codex alone was sufficient to elevate the laws of
the church to equality with the laws of the state. Having
been accorded this political backing, church canons had
to be obeyed by all. This serves as the only explanation as
to why the papacy claims that Justinian's Corpus Juris
Civilis is the basis of all Roman Catholic canon law:

> "So the immortal 'Corpus Juris Civilis' was pro-
> duced. . . . It would be difficult to exaggerate the im-
> portance of this 'Corpus.' It is the basis of all canon
> law . . ."[325]

By reinforcing these ecclesiastical mandates the
reader will understand the full significance of the following primary decrees from Justinian's Codex I.

The reader is to now to witness for himself the real
face of the oppressive papal government when church
and state were united. This is in contrast to the
Biblically-ordained principle of religious liberty and the

---

[323] Ibid., Codex I. 1.4, 12:12.
[324] Paul Krueger, *Corpus Iuris Civilis, Codex Iustinianus*, I.3.44 (decreed Oct.18, A.D. 530) (Berolini Apud Weidmannos, 1888), 2:30. See
also Asterios Gerostergios, *Justinian The Great The Emperor And Saint*
(Belmont, MA: Institute for Byzantine and Modern Greek Studies),
163-4.
[325] *Catholic Encyclopedia*, s.v. "Justinian I" (New York: Appleton,
1910), 8:579.

firm warning against harboring a spirit of intolerance that Christ laid down for the New Testament church and that we witnessed previously. This neglected mandate has cost humanity so dear a price:

TITLE II.
CONCERNING THE MOST SACRED CHURCHES, THEIR PROPERTY AND THEIR PRIVILEGES.

[18] 12. "We decree that the privileges conceded by former Emperors under the general terms of constitutions, to all the Holy Churches of the orthodox religion, shall be observed, and remain firm and unimpaired for all time."[326]

"(1) We command that all pragmatic sanctions which are contrary to ecclesiastical canons and have been obtained through favor or political intrigue, shall be deprived of all their force and authority."[327]

(14). . . .[20] Let them know that, under no circumstances, and at no time, shall they be prevented from disposing of their property under the pretext of liberality or gratitude, or from alienating it to persons who are willing to purchase the same, provided all members of the clergy, including the bishop and the steward, consent to the alienation of said property; for it is proper to preserve reverently and intact all rights which now or may hereafter belong to the Most Blessed Church, just as religiously as the Holy Church itself, for as the mother of religion and faith is herself perpetual, so her patrimony should remain entire and uninjured for all time. . . . it shall be acquired for the profit and the advantage of the Church.

(2) Any steward who has done anything of this kind, or, indeed, permitted it to be done, whether by sale, donation, or exchange (except in the way which we have permitted by the present law), or, finally, who has given his consent to any kind of an alienation, shall be deprived of the administration which has been en-

---

[326] Ibid., Codex I. 2.12. 12:18.
[327] Ibid., Codex I. 2.12.1. 12:18.

trusted to him; and any loss which the Church has sustained shall be repaired out of his property, and his heirs, successors, and descendants shall be liable to an action brought by a competent person appointed by ecclesiastics, whether the damage was caused by his own act, or merely by his acquiescence.

(3) Notaries, who have dared to draw up instruments containing forbidden contracts of this kind, shall be punished with the penalty of perpetual exile.

(4) Judges who have jurisdiction of such matters, and who confirm donations or forbidden contracts of this kind, shall be condemned to lose their office and their property.[328]

[26] . . . . 15. We order and decree that the Holy Church of this most religious community, the mother of our piety, the source of the orthodox religion of all Christians, and the most Sacred See of this Imperial Metropolis, shall legally enjoy all privileges and honors relating to the creation of bishops, in preference to all others, and that it shall be acknowledged to possess and to perpetually and firmly hold, by virtue of this Royal City, all other rights which it possessed before Our reign, or during its existence.

TITLE III.

CONCERNING BISHOPS AND OTHER MEMBERS OF THE CLERGY, SUPERINTENDENTS OP ORPHAN ASYLUMS, OF HOSPITALS AND OF CHARITABLE FOUNDATIONS, MONASTERIES OF ASCETICS AND MONKS AND THEIR PRIVILEGES; CASTRENSE PECULIUM; THE REDEMPTION OF CAPTIVES; AND FORBIDDEN OR PERMITTED MARRIAGES OF ECCLESIASTICS.

[31] 5. If anyone should merely attempt to, I do not say ravish, but marry a consecrated virgin, he shall suffer the penalty of death. . . .

---

[328] Ibid., Codex I. 2.14.-4. 12:20.

[33] According to the new law, a crime of this kind is punished with scourging or exile, but if the culprit interferes with the sacred rites, or prevents them from being celebrated, he shall be put to death.

[34] 15. We forbid persons to hold religious assemblies in private houses, even outside the Church, under the penalty of confiscation of the house, if the owner of the same permitted ecclesiastics to hold new and tumultuous meetings therein outside the church.

TITLE IV.

CONCERNING THE EPISCOPAL TRIBUNAL AND THE DIFFERENT CHARTERS WHICH RELATE TO PONTIFICAL SUPERVISION.

[59] 11. *The Same Emperors to Cæcilianus, Prætorian Prefect.*

"We decree that astrologers shall not only be banished from the City of Rome, but also from all other cities; unless, having burned all the books containing their errors under the eyes of the bishops, they are resolved to embrace the Christian religion, and never to return to their former errors. If, however, they should not do this, and should be found in any city, in opposition to Our Decree, or should teach the secrets of their false doctrines or profession, they shall be punished with deportation. . . .

17. We order that only those shall be selected for the office of defender who have been initiated into the mysteries of the orthodox religion, and have established this in the first place by the testimony of their acts, and by proclaiming their belief with the sanction of an oath, in the presence of a Most Reverend Bishop of the Catholic Church. We order that they shall be appointed in this manner, and that they shall be confirmed by a decree of the Most Reverend Bishop, clerks, nobles, proprietors, and members of the *curiae*.

TITLE V.

CONCERNING HERETICS, MANICHEANS, AND SAMARITANS.

[63] (1) Under the name of "heretics" are included those who ought to be convicted of having violated laws passed against them; or who, on frivolous grounds, have been found to have deviated from the judgment and principles of the Catholic religion.

3. Let all heretics know positively that their places of assembly shall be taken from them, whether these are designated under the name of churches, or are called deaconates, or deaneries, or whether meetings [64] of this kind are held in private houses; for all such private places or buildings shall be claimed by the Catholic Church.

(1) All persons are accordingly forbidden to assemble by day or night, in profane assemblies, for the purpose of conducting alleged religious services; and where anything of this kind is permitted to be done either in a public or a private house, the official who allows it, if he is the Prefect of the City, shall be fined a hundred pounds of gold, or if he is the Governor, shall be fined fifty pounds of gold.

Justinian lists here many of the condemned sects that were to be banned from the empire:

[65] 5. "Arians, Macedonians, Pneumatomachians, Appol-linarians, Novatians or Sabatians, Eunomians, Tetradites or Tessarecaidecadites, Valentinians, Paulians, Papianists, Montanints or Priscillians, Phrygians, Pepuzites, Marcionists, Borborites, Messalians, Euchites, or Enthusiasts, Donatists, Audians, Hydroparastetes, Tascodrogites, Batracites, Hermogenians, Photinians, Paulinists, Marcellians, Ophites, Encratitians, Carpocratitans, Saccophores, and Manicheans, who are to be classed as guilty of the worst of all heretical crimes, shall never have the power to assemble or reside in the Roman Empire. . . .

[66] 6. (1) Let no one venture to either have in his posses-sion, read, or copy, the impious books of the wicked and sacrilegious Nestor, written against the venerated sect of the orthodox, and the decrees of the Holy Convocation of bishops at Ephesus, and which We order shall be diligently sought out and publicly burned; so that no one may mention the above-stated name in any religious discussion, and these sectaries have any opportunity of holding any assembly in their city, country, or suburban houses, or anywhere else, either secretly or openly. We have determined to deprive all such persons of the right to hold assemblies, and they all are hereby notified that any violator of this law will be punished with the confiscation of his property.

[69] 9. We also decree that all such lands and possessions which have been transferred or conveyed to heretics, in any way whatsoever, shall be claimed by our Treasury. . . .

10. We have ascertained that there are many orthodox children neither whose fathers nor mothers belong to the true faith; and therefore, We order that in cases where but one of the parents has embraced the orthodox religion, as well as in those where both parents are members of another sect, only such children as are included under the venerated title of orthodox shall be called to their succession, either under a will or *ab intestato*, and that they alone shall be entitled to receive donations and other liberalities. The other children of those persons who have followed, not the love of Almighty God, but the impious belief of their fathers or mothers, shall be excluded from all benefits. Where, however, no orthodox children are living, the property, or the succession, shall go to their agnates or cognates, provided they are orthodox. But if no such agnate or cognate can be found, then the estate shall be claimed by Our Treasury.

(1) . . . All Our Constitutions which have established penalties against Pagans, Manicheans, Borborites, Samaritans, Montanists, Tascodrogites, Ophytes, and other heretics, are confirmed by this Our law, and shall remain forever valid.

[71] 12. We order that Our Divine Decree by which We have ordered that no one who accepts the error of heretics can receive an estate, a legacy, or a trust, shall also apply to the last wills of soldiers, whether they are made under the Common, or military law."

A very straight forward definition given by Justinian for Heretics:

PREFACE

. . . . Hence We very properly call persons heretics who do not receive the holy sacraments from the reverend bishops in the Catholic Church; for although they may give themselves the name of Christians, still they are separated from the belief and communion of Christians, even when they acknowledge that they are subject to the judgment of God.[329]

TITLE VII.
CONCERNING APOSTATES.

[72] 1. If anyone, after renouncing the venerated Christian faith, should become a Jew, and join their sacrilegious assemblies, We order that, after the accusation has been proved, his property shall be confiscated to the Treasury.

[74] 5. We direct that he who has induced a slave or a freeborn person, against his will or by means of threats, to renounce the Christian religion for any infamous sect or rite, shall be punished with the loss of his property and death.

TITLE IX.
CONCERNING JEWS AND THE WORSHIPPERS OF
THE HEAVENS.

[75] 2. We desire all Jews and worshippers of the heavens, and their heads and patriarchs, to be notified that, if anyone, after the promulgation of this law,

---

[329] Ibid., *The Novels-109*, Preface, 17:27, May 7, 541.

should dare to attack a person who has abandoned his odius sect and betake himself to the worship of God, with stones or with any other manifestation of rage (which We have ascertained has been done), he shall at once be given to the flames, and burned with all his accomplices.

5. No Jew shall marry a Christian woman, nor shall any Christian man marry a Jewess; for if anyone should be guilty of an act of this [76] kind, he will be liable for having committed the crime of adultery, and permission is hereby granted to all persons to accuse him.

[77] . . . . 11. For it is certain that whatever differs from the Christian religion is opposed to the Christian law.

12. *The Same Emperors to Jovius, Prætorian Prefect.*

We order that, upon the Sabbath day, and at other times when the Jews observe the ceremonies of their worship, no one shall either do anything to them, or, under any circumstances, compel them to appear in court; and they themselves shall not be given permission to sue orthodox Christians upon those days, so that Christians may not suffer any inconvenience from being summoned by the officials upon the days aforesaid; for it is evident that the remaining days will be sufficient for the purposes of the Treasury, and the suits of private individuals.

15. *The Same Emperors to Asclepiodotus, Prætorian Prefect.*

[78] Jews who are proved to have circumcised any man belonging to our religion, or to have directed this to be done, shall be condemned to the confiscation of their property, and to perpetual exile.

17. *The Same Emperors to Florentius, Prætorian Prefect.*

[79] (2) . . . . He who has begun the construction of a new synagogue, not with the intention of repairing an old one, shall be condemned to pay fifty pounds of

gold, and be deprived of the work which he is already presumed to do; and, moreover, it is hereby decreed that his property shall be confiscated, and that he shall be condemned to the penalty of death, as one who, by his false doctrine, has attacked the faith of others.

Let it be remembered that the church was responsible for the Jewish anti-Semitic legislation which took place largely after the recognition of Christianity by Constantine and which was due in part to the competition between Judaism, paganism, and Christianity. We continue with Justinian's legislation from his Codex I:

TITLE XI.

CONCERNING THE PAGANS, THEIR SACRIFICES, AND THEIR TEMPLES.

7. *The Emperors Valentinian and Martian to Palladius, Prætorian Prefect.*

[81] No one, for the purpose of reverence or worship, shall reopen the temples of the Pagans, which have already been closed, in order that the honor which was formerly shown to their idols and their infamous and execrable rites may be removed from our age; for it is held to be sacrilege instead of religion to adorn the impious portals of shrines with garlands; to kindle profane fires on the altars; to burn incense upon the same; to slaughter victims there, and to pour out libations of wine from bowls. Anyone who attempts to perform sacrifices contrary to this Our decree, and against the prohibition of the most sacred ancient constitutions, can be lawfully accused of the crime before any judge, and, if convicted, shall suffer the confiscation of all his property, and the extreme penalty. . . ."[330]

Given on the day before the *Ides* of November, during the Consulate of the Emperor Martian and Adelphius, 451."

---

[330] Scott, S. P., trans., ed. *The Civil Law* [of Justinian] (Union, NJ: Lawbook Exchange, 2001), Codex I. 12:18-81.

The work of S.P. Scott stops short here at Codex 1.11.8. Paul Krueger, in his *Corpus Iuris Civilis, Codex Iustinianus*, supplies the two remaining codes of title XI. 9-10 that we will share in part:

> 1.11.9.
> "3. All the punishments which were introduced by former emperors against pagan error or in favor of the orthodox faith shall be valid and in force in the future and are retained in force by the present pious legislation.

> 1.11.10.
> Since some have been found who, imbued with the error of the impious and wicked pagans, do things which move the indulgent God to just wrath, and in order not [to] leave matters pertaining to them unprovided for, and knowing that they, having abandoned the adoration of the true and only God, have, in their insane error, offered sacrifices to statues and performed worship replete with iniquity, and that even those who had been already found worthy of sacred baptism, have committed these sins, we subjected them, in a spirit of kindness, to the punishment adequate to the crime of which they shall be convicted. And by the present law we give notice to all that, if in the future it shall appear that those who have become Christians and have at any time been considered worthy of the holy and saving baptism, still adhere to pagan error, they shall be punished by death."[331]

The following documentation offers some excellent insights on the progressive history of the laws on paganism from the emperors of the fourth century to the reign of Justinian and the closing of the schools not sanctioned by the state. History confirms along with Justinian's Code that the pagan temples had already been shut down and those who remained practicing paganism did so un-

---

[331] Paul Krueger, *Corpus Iuris Civilis, Codex Iustinianus*, (Berolini Apud Weidmannos, 1959), Codex I. 11.9.3. Codex I. 10., 2:63-64.

derground and in secret. Knecht will show how a great persecution (around 529) of the pagans took place. Many were discovered, deposed from office, and some of them were executed. Bishop Johannes of Ephesus recounts that Justinian assigned him to conduct an investigation of the followers of paganism who still remained in Constantinople in secret. Knecht will illustrate how the legislation of Justinian differed from all previous emperors:

[28] "Justinian wanted to lead a final, deciding battle against the remains of paganism. He began an attack with this goal from two angles. He applied himself at the same time against the popular, practical paganism on the one and against the intellectual, theoretical form on the other side. His battle concerned idolatry and pagan philosophy.

Of the legal decrees against the former, some were not new. Justinian's predecessors had already decreed similar ones. Emperor Constantine I, under whose reign paganism suffered the loss of its monopoly in the Roman state as well as of the remains of its vitality as a national religion[332], "considered it ... to be correct to purify the city, to which he had meant to grant particular significance through giving it his name, from all paganism. For that reason, in Constantinople, no statues of their gods could be openly worshiped and no altars could be stained with blood offerings, no burnt offerings could be brought, no festival to honor the idols could be celebrated, and no rites of the superstitious pagans could be observed."[333] The sparks which, to

---

[332] L. Seuffert, *Konstantins Gesetze und das Christentum. Rektoratsrede.* Würzburg 1891, p. 22.

[333] Eusebius, Hist. eccl. III, 54, IV, 48, IV, 56.–F.M. Flasch, *Konstantin d. Gr. als erster christl. Kaiser.* Würzburg 1891. p. 37, 38.–Gaston Boissier, *La fin du paganisme.* Paris 1891. I. p. 59 ss., 199.–A. Beugnot, *Histoire de la destruction du paganisme en occident.* Paris 1835. t. I. p. 70 ss.–V. Schultze, *Geschichte des Unterganges des griech.-röm. Heidentums*, Jena. Vol. 1, 1887, Vol. 2, 1892. Vol. 1, p. 56 ff. Cf. *Tübinger Quartalschrift* 1888, p. 496 ff.–V. Schultze, *Quellenuntersuchungen zur Vita Constantini des Eusebius. Ztschr. f. Kirchengesch.* 14 (1894) p. 505–555.

speak with Libanius, Constantine had ignited, be it purely for the capital city[334], be it through general laws [29] for the entire country,[335] were extended to a violent fire by his son and successor Constantius, driven by a broadsheet dealing with the stately duty of intervention against the pagan religion by Firmicus Maternus[336]; in these flames, a good part of paganism was destroyed forever.[337] The brusquely anti-pagan politics of Constantius, as opposed to the more egalitarian politics of his father, found its briefest expression in a law from the year 354, where it is stated that all temples in the city and country should be closed and all offerings forbidden under punishment of death;[338] for the pagan superstition should cease and the insanity of sacrifices should be destroyed. After the brief privileging of paganism by Julian, which had the advantage that it revealed the inner impotence and decadence of the old idolatry,[339] the subsequent emperors could satisfy themselves by calmly watching the dying out of the same. For that reason, according to a law of Valentinian I (from 11 Sept. 364), everyone could freely practice any religion that had found its way into his heart[340], and the pagan historian Ammianus Marcellinus could praise this emperor in that he had not disturbed anyone in matters of religion and never bent the necks of his subjects with the yoke of his

---

[334] L. Seuffert l.c. p. 11.

[335] Flasch l.c.–Schultze l.c.–Boissier I, 99: *Il est donc vraisemblable que es lois de Constance n'ont guère été executes. le seul résultat de ces attaques violentes et prématurées fut d'irriter les païens et de render une réaction plus facile.*

[336] Jul. Firmicus *Maternus de errore profanarum religionum.* Vindobonae 1867.

[337] Schultze l.c. p. 96.

[338] l. 1 C. de pagan. I. 11. cf. l. 2 C. Theod. de pagan. 16, 10: *cesset superstitio, sacrificiorum aboleatur insania,* likewise l. 5 eod. 9.16.

[339] Lasaulx l.c. p. 89.–Boissier l.c. I, 110. – J. R. Asmus, *Theodorets Therapeudik und ihr Verhältnis zu Julian. Byzant. Ztschr.* 3 (1894) p. 116 ff.

[340] l. 9 C. Theod. 9,16 cf ibid. 7. 8. 10. l. 1 C. Theod. 15, 7. l. 1. C. Theod. 16, 1.

own faith through threatening edicts[341]. Gratian once again began the struggle with the ban on the exhibition of entrails[342] [*Eingeweideschau*] and [30] with the cancellation of the privileges as had been possessed by the pagan priests and vestals. Theodosius the Great closed the temple of the gods in Syria and Egypt, ordered that all subjects should recognize the faith that the apostle Peter had announced to the Romans, and forbade the conversion from Christianity to a pagan religion under the threat of loss of active inheritance.[343]

The subsequent emperors Honorius, Arcadius, Theodosius II, Marcian, Leo I, and Zeno limited themselves to repetition of the decrees of their predecessors[344] and added only a few punishments to these, such as the confiscation of possessions, secularization of temple goods, exclusion from civil offices and military positions, or they directed them against individual persons who had adopted the defense of paganism, as, for example, Leo I did against the writings of Porphyrius, Zeno against Hierocles, Severianus and others. Only Leo I deserves further mention for his laws, in which he declared the practice of the pagan religion to be a public crime.[345] Emperors Anastasius and Justin mention the pagans almost only in connection with the Jews and heretics.

In consideration of that which earlier emperors had taken up against paganism, we recognize that the negative decrees of Justinian offer little that is new. He does not differ from them, firstly, so much through his bans as through his commandments, and secondly, through the factual execution of the given laws. Until his time, the acceptance of the Christian religion was not commanded, but rather the practice of the pagan

---

[341] Ammian. Marcell. *rer. gest. libri qui supersunt.* Lipsiae 1773. XXX, 9, 5, cf. Lasaulx l.c. p. 85.

[342] l. 2. C. de pagan. I, 11.–Schultze l.c. p. 211–221.

[343] l. 1 C. Theod. 16, 7. X. 9. 10.–Lasaulx p. 99,—Schultze p. 266 ff.–Beugnot l.c. p. 347 ss.: *il fut moins empereur que serviteur de Dieu.*

[344] l. 3. 4. 5. 6. 7. 8. C. de pagan. I, 11.

[345] Lasaulx l.c. p. 140. 141.–Schultze p. 437 ff.–"crimen publicum' l. 8 C. de pag. I, 11.

religion was forbidden. Political motives may have
held back Constantine, under whose reign a fifth of
Christians stood opposite four fifths of pagans, as well
as his successors, from taking stronger action against
idolatry. Certainly, however, the precepts concerning
forced religion, which were developed by pagan and
Christian writers of their times, had not remained
without [31] lasting influence on them. "As namely the
church . . . well protects itself and its territory, but in
no single case has given indication of violent ruina-
tion,"[346] as it has always taught, "that the truth should
not be announced through violent weapons, but should
find its way into the human heart through the path of
teaching and conviction[347], because nothing is so
much a necessity of free will as religion,"[348] thus pagans and Christians had raised their voices in writing
against the state's force in religions matters. "The natural right," says Tertullian,[349] "demands that everyone
honor the god in whom he believes. It is not religious
to force religion. A religion must be accepted through
conviction and not through violence; for the worshipping of the Godhead demands the agreement of the
heart." The sophist Themistius called out to Emperor
Jovian: "One must give each over to his own soul,
which will provide the path to piety." A ruler could
force his subjects to do much; a few things, however,
could not be commanded and to these belongs, above
all, religion.[350]

An absolute commandment to accept Christianity
and receive the holy baptism was unheard of until the
6th century; such a decree was reserved for Justinian.
Through this law, he overrode the competency of a
prince on the whole and that of a Christian regent
specifically. This precept of forced religion, expressed

[346] Schultze l.c. 1. B. p. 319.
[347] Athanasius I, p. 363 and 384 and Joh. Chrysostomus in Lasaulx
p. 142 ff. cf. Math. 10, 14; 16, 24.
[348] . . . *nihil est enim tam voluntarium quam religio.* Lactant. Div. inst.
V, 19, 20.
[349] ad. Scap. 2 cf. Boissier I, p. 58.
[350] Lasaulx l.c. p. 86.

at the beginning of his reign, provided direction for his coming religious and ecclesiastical politics.

Justinian differed from the preceding Christian emperors, as mentioned above, also in that he brought the decreed laws against paganism into fulfillment. Between theory [32] and practice, among his predecessors, a contradiction had prevailed. A part of the legal decrees, says Schultze,[351] was only applied intermittently. Word and deed did not match one another in all cases—a proceeding as has analogues in the political and religious-political history of all peoples. The tendency toward threat of punishment was, as the repetition of the law reveals, just intimidation, not enforced; brutal violence was far from the general direction of this politics.[352] It was otherwise with Justinian.

As these emperors effected the Christianization of the remaining pagans, the historians of the time give reports. John Malalas[353] writes: "At this time (around 529), a great persecution of the pagans took place. Many were discovered, deposed of office, and some of them were executed." Bishop Johannes of Ephesus recounts that Justinian assigned him to conduct an investigation of the followers of paganism who still remained in Constantinople in secret. There, after careful research, they found and apprehended, among those most distinguished through birth, riches, and education, among the ranks of the patricians, scholars, and doctors, still many followers of the old superstition. One of these, the patrician Phokas, is said to have poisoned himself upon this discovery, whereupon the emperor commanded that the corpse be buried in a pit with no funeral honors. However, he had lead the other pagans earlier to the church, so that they could be taught there and taken into the Christian congregation.[354]—Justinian was effective in the conversion of pagans more in the provinces than in Byzantium. The aforementioned Bishop Johannes traveled, assigned by

---

[351] l.c.
[352] Schultze 2. B. S. 324. 325.
[353] lib. XVIII ed. Bonn. p. 449.
[354] Lasaulx p. 147.

the emperor, to the Asiatic provinces Caria, Lydia, and
Phrygia, in order to declare the Gospel there. 70,000
pagans are supposed to have converted to Christianity
upon hearing his sermons. The newly converted built
41 churches on their own means. Justinian had a further 55 erected and equipped them with holy vessels
and par aments.[355] The Abasgoi[356] on the Black Sea
[33] and the neighboring Lazier allowed themselves to
be influenced by Justinian, taking up the Christian
teachings.—The Tzanen,[357] who were located at the
source of the Phasis and the Akampsis and were notorious for their raids, could also be led by the emperor
toward civilization and the true religion. Many of them
entered the imperial army after receiving the holy baptism.—In two places on the Egyptian border, Justinian
discovered the vestiges of a pagan cult, in Augila, a city
on an oasis in the Lybian desert, and on the island
Philae, at the first cataract of the Nile. In Augila[358]
there still remained a temple dedicated to Jupiter
Ammon and Alexander the Great, in which a number
of cult priests [Götzenpriester] still brought sacrifices
according to the old customs. On imperial command,
Christian missionaries went there immediately, converted the people, and erected a church devoted to the
holy mother of God. In Philae,[359] where the Egyptian
religion sought the graves of Isis and Osiris, immigrant
Blemmyer attempted to maintain the old religion. On
the occasion of a military raid, Narses drove out the invaders and effected the end of the adoration of Isis.
Justinian then sent the Abbot Theodorus as Bishop to

[355] Johannes v. Ephesus, *Kirchengesch.*, ed. J. M. Schönfelder. Munich
1862, p. 122, 133–135.
[356] Evagr. IV. 20–23.–Nicephorus Callistus. *Eccl. hist. Lutetiae
Parisoir.* 1630. t. II. XVII, 14.–Mansi VIII, 382.–Ludewig l.c. p. 525.
[357] Proc. bell. Pers. I, 15.–Agathias IV, 99. V, 100.–Hergenröther,
Kirchengeschichte I, p. 334.
[358] Joh. v. Eph.–Schönfelder p. 81.–Schultze l.c. II, p. 251.–Procop. de
aedif. VI, 2.
[359] (Marinus, Vita Procli c. 19).–Schultze l.c. II, p. 228 ff.–Procop.
bell. Pers. I, 19.– Joh. v. Ephes.–Schönfelder p. 183.–Hergenröther l.c.
I, p. 333, 334.

Philae.—Of Syria[360], Johannes of Ephesus knows to report that he had found there a temple with a brazen idol, to which citizens at the time of plague had made pilgrimage, and that in Heliopolis, still in the year 554, an idol 150 ells high was destroyed by lightning. Despite strenuous activity, he had not succeeded to eradicate the old beliefs.

The examples presented here prove how seriously Justinian took the conversion of the pagans. He pressed up to the most distant and isolated tribes and worked by mobilizing the best forces, with application of significant sums, and not the least also with the application of violence in the eradication of idolatry, so that some writers even believe, [34] that religious motives were at the heart of many of his military raids.[361] That he nonetheless did not succeed in achieving his goal everywhere is evidenced, among other things, by a large religious trial that was still being played out under Emperor Iberius in the year 579[362], and likewise by the fact that even in Constantinople in the year 659, a century after Justinian, idolaters were arrested, led publicly through the city, and their books were burned along with the idols at the Kynegion.[363]

The second blow that Justinian effected against paganism was directed against pagan philosophy. After idolatry had long disappeared from the Roman public eye, pagan sciences, enemies of the cross, still blossomed.

This also should fall and had to, if idolatry was to cease. The only oven in which the fire of the old world wisdom still flamed stood in Athens. Of the four philosophical schools, which for centuries constituted the center of the scientific world, the stoic, epicurean, peripatetic, and platonic, only the last still existed. Already in 402 Synesius of Cyrene could write from Athens:

---

[360] Assemani, Bibl. orient. II, 85. – Schultze l.c. II, p. 445.
[361] Evagr. IV, 16.–Procop. bell. Pers. I, 12, 15; Procop. aedif. III, 4. 7.. V, 2,3.–Niceph. Call. XVII, 12, 24.–Baronius, Annales eccl. tom. IX, X. Lucae 1749 a. 533. Nr. 41.– Le Beau, Hist. du Bas-Emp. VIII, 547.
[362] Schultze l.c. II, p. 272.
[363] Schultze l.c. II, p. 291 ff.

"Athens has nothing praiseworthy anymore except for
the names of its famous amphitheaters. Like the skin of
the slaughtered and wasted animal is a sign of former
life, so also is there nothing left for one to do, since philosophy has emigrated, except to ramble about and ad-
mire the Academy . . . Athens was formerly a place of
wise men; as it now stands, only the bee-keeping is
laudable. It is similar also with the team of wise
Plutarchians, who attract the youth to their auditori-
ums not through the reputation of their lectures, but
with their jugs of wine from the Hymettus."[364] The
later neo-platonic school of Plutarch [35] still attracted
students. "It had," as Zumpt[365] says, "the luck to have,
with its fortune, which it had received from Plato as a
sort of entail and considerably raised in the course of
time, remained independent from state and city, but
then bound itself all the more to paganism." This connection had, for the most part, its basis in the rapid advance of Christianity. The Christian teachings did not
satisfy only the mind but also the heart. Therein lies
the secret of why, as St. Ambrosius (377) writes, the
philosophers were more and more frequently avoided
by the students, and why one no longer had faith in the
dialecticians but rather the fishers. Christianity indicated that philosophy was life wisdom, that its teachings should not just be empty theories presented and
heard in schools, but rather should regulate practical
life. Philosophy must be religious just as religion is

---

[364] Synes. ep., 136.–H. Zumpt, *Über den Bestand der philos. Schulen in
Athen und die Succession der Scholarchen*, in the essays of the
Akademie der Wissenschaften in Berlin 1842, p. 27.–Lasaulx l.c. p. 143.
[365] l.c. p. 52, cf. Gibbon l.c. V, 91: an annual rent which in eight centuries was gradually increased from three to one thousand pieces of
gold.
[366] Here we in no way concede that L. v. Ranke (*Weltgeschichte*, 4. B.
Abt. 2, *D. Kaisertum in Konst. u. d. Ursprung rom.-germ. Königreiche*.
Leipzig 1883. p. 29 ff.) was right when he said: "The Christian religion
emanated from the conflict of religious opinions of the peoples of the
earth, and developed itself into a church in opposition of the same. . . .
With Greek philosophy, the original development of Christian theology also experienced a standstill." Even less do we accept what

philosophical.[366] Pagan philosophy had undergone a
transition in particular under the favor of Emperor
Julian. At the time, they no longer strove for purely logical thinking, but rather for mysticism, intuition, and
ecstasy. "Whereas with Plotinus," says Schultze,[367]
"Neo-Platonism still stood at the peak of philosophy,
with the godly Iamblichus it had already transformed
from a philosophy to a theological doctrine, [36] which
sought its goal in the restoration of polytheism."
From the beginning of the Fifth Century, the curricu-
lum in the philosophical Academy at Athens was such
that mathematics were pursued first, and then the
reading of Platonic and Aristotelian texts. The most
outstanding students were led to theurgist through declarations from oracles. The gods appeared in dreams
and visions to souls which had been purified by recognition and virtue. "Thus the school externally preserved itself as a philosophical institution, in secret as
a colony of priests of Hellenism."[368]

In this consideration of philosophy, the reason
should be sought as to why Emperor Justinian advanced legally upon the teachers of the same. In order
to clog one source of paganism, in 529 he sent a letter
of his own to Athens bearing the message that no one
else could teach philosophy or declare rights. Accordingly, in the same year in which St. Benedict brought
down the last pagan national sanctuary in Italy, the

(*Cont.*)
Harnack, *Dogmengesch.* II, p. 38n, remarks on this: "Hellenistic science in connection with a monkish worldview ruled the spiritual life
of the church as much before Justinian's time as after – they were in
the deepest sense no contradiction, but possessed common roots."
[367] l.c. I, 161. 447. Cf. Zeller, *Gesch. der Philosophie d. Griechen* III. 2,
849.–A. Neander, *Allgem. Gesch. d. Religion u. Kirche.* Hamburg.
1825. I, 1, p. 252 ff.
[368] Zumpt l.c. p. 59, 119.–Gibbon l.c. V, 93: Proklus, for example,
taught in this direction: But in the intervals of study he personally
conversed with Pan, Aesculapius and Minerva, in whose mysteries he
was secretly initiated and whose prostrate statues he adored; in the
devout persuasion that the philosopher, who is a citizen of the universe should be the priest of its various deities.

temple of Apollo in the holy heath of Monte Casino,[369] the high fortress of antique paganism in Greece was destroyed.

"On this Agathius reports[370], Damascius, the Syrian, relies, as well as his students Simplicius of Sicily, Eulamius of Phrygia, Pricianus of Lydia, Hermias and Diogenes from the land of the Phoenicians, and Isidor of Gaza, the blossoms of the philosophy of our time, as well as the Roman empire. They decided to live under Persian rule, which seemed to them, according to the generally accepted opinion, as a connection between Platonic philosophy and kingdom,[371] and where the people would be righteous and moderate. But the found everything [37] to be otherwise than they had expected: in the people they found the same and even greater immorality, arrogance of the nobility, and in King Khosroes they found a penchant for philosophy but lack of higher education and a limited command of the national conventions. They wanted longingly to return, although Khosroes liked them and requested that they remain. However, they had the significant advantage that they could live further at their own discretion. For because precisely at that time a treaty was being negotiated between the Romans and Persians, it was presented to Khosroes as a condition of keeping peace[372] that the men could return to their homes and live for themselves in the future, without being forced to accept what ran against their convictions, or change their paternal faith." In 533 the aforementioned philosophers came back to Athens; their school, however,

---

[369] Beugnot l.c. II, 286.
[370] Agathias l.c. lib. IV, 31.–Gibbon l.c. V, 93.–Zumpt l.c. p. 62.–Procop. Arcana c. 11. 26.–Lasaulx l.c.
[371] They gullibly believed that Plato's Republic could be realized in the despotic Persian state. Gibbon l.c. V. 94.
[372] Schultze l.c. p. 448.

was never reopened. Simplicius is believed to have held further philosophical lectures. Closer details about this, however, remain unknown. Justinian, through the cancelation of the school of Athens, bore pagan philosophy formally to the grave. Materially, the same had already been suffering from long illness for quite some time. None of the earlier emperors had dared to do this, and some could not take this step because the number of pagan philosophy students was still too large. What was decisive and commanding about their actions against paganism was the idolatrous element.[373] Justinian not only set the axe to the few sparsely sprouting branches of paganism but also sought to pull out the last roots of the same. What helped him advance so massively was not devaluation or lack of recognition of the value of philosophy; greed[374] for the fortune of the Academy of Athens did not motivate his abolishment of it; rather, he was led by the same motive that summoned him to battle against idolatry: the hatred of paganism as such and the striving towards a unified Christian state."[375]

Justinian made short work of all institutions and schools[376] in opposition to a unified Christian state and they were systematically closed and subject to the state and/or church treasury. Justinian indeed had gone where none of the earlier emperors had dared to go. We continue with Justinian's legislation from his Codex I:

---

[373] Schlutlze l.c. p. 93. Cf. Neander l.c. II p. 178 ff.
[374] Gibbon V, 89: some reproach may be justly inflicted on the avarice and jealousy of a prince by whose hand such venerable ruins were destroyed.
[375] Knecht, August. *Die Religions-Politik: Kaiser Justinians I: Eine kirchengeschicht-liche Studie.* (Dissert. Würzberg, 1896), 28-37. [Andreas Gobel, *The Religious Politics of Emperor Justinian I*, Wurzburg, 1896.]
[376] Ellen White, *Testimonies for the Church*, (Boise, Idaho, Pacific Press, 1948), 5:156. "All schools among us will soon be closed up."

TITLE XVII.

CONCERNING THE EXPLANATIONS OF THE ANCIENT LAW AND THE AUTHORITY OF THE JURISTS WHO ARE MENTIONED IN THE DIGEST.

[92] . . . . "(10) Where, however, any laws contained in the ancient books have already fallen into desuetude, We, under no circumstances, permit you to insert them; for We only wish those to remain in force which frequent decisions have established, or the long-continued custom of this Fair City has confirmed; in accordance with the statement of Salvius Julianus, which says that all cities should observe the customs and laws of Rome, which is the capital of the world, but that Rome should not observe the customs of other cities. We understand by Rome, not only the ancient City, but also our Imperial Capital, which, by the grace of God, was founded under the most fortunate auspices.

(11) Therefore, We order that everything shall be governed by these two codes, one that of the Constitutions, the other that of the revised law, which is about to be compiled in a Code; or if anything else should afterwards be promulgated by Us in the form of institutes. . . .

This ends the selection of the primary sources of Justinian's Codex I issued in 534 that attest to the fact that oppressive religious legislation had been enacted by the state and received the full backing of the church.

Our next selection of the primary sources from Justinian's Novels will further confirm that oppressive church and state legislation had entirely outlawed religious liberty and more. The Novels of Justinian are also called Constitutions; the collection that we have on hand number up to 168 with a few extant. Unlike the Codex that came out in 534 in a completed form, the Novels were progressive in that they were issued as needed from 535 to the end of Justinian's reign in 565. The Novels, unlike the Codex, are simply numbered from 1-168, are designated as Preface, Chapter, and/or Epilogue and have been dated according to the time of issue. We will share a few of the important ones up to the year 538 in this section. The dating of the Novels in the work of S.P. Scott[377] is some what inaccurate, but it is otherwise a good primary source from which we will quote unless otherwise noted. Supplied for the reader is a valuable chart that correctly dates the Novels of Justinian.[378] Novel 3, also called Constitution 3, will give a glimpse into the vast "host" given over to the priesthood in Constantinople at the time:

THE NOVELS

CONCERNING THE NUMBER OF ECCLESIASTICS
ATTACHED TO THE PRINCIPAL CHURCH AND
THE OTHER CHURCHES OF CONSTANTINOPLE.

THIRD NEW CONSTITUTION.

PREFACE.

[17] ". . . . We have ascertained that on this account the principal church of this Imperial City, the Mother of Our Empire. . . .

CHAPTER I.

[18] (1) Wherefore We order that not more than sixty priests, a hundred deacons, forty deaconesses, ninety sub-deacons, a hundred and ten readers, or twenty-five choristers, shall be attached to the Most Holy Principal Church, so that the entire number of most reverend ecclesiastics belonging thereto shall not exceed four hundred and twenty in all, without including the hundred other members of the clergy who are called porters. Although there is such a large number of ecclesiastics attached to the Most Holy Principal Church of this Most Fortunate City, and the three other churches united with the [19] same, none of those who are now there shall be excluded, although their num-

---

[377] Scott, S. P., trans., ed. *The Civil Law [of Justinian]*, 17 vols. Union, NJ: Lawbook Exchange, 2001, *The Novels*, Vols. 16:1-99, 17:100-168.
[378] The following chart is supplied that correctly dates the release of each and every Novel with month, day, and year when provided in the original and is illustrated in **APPENDIX II**, pg. 321.

ber is much greater than that which has been established by Us, but no others shall be added to any order of the priesthood whatsoever until the number has been reduced, in compliance with the present law.[379]

CONCERNING MONKS.

FIFTH NEW CONSTITUTION.

CHAPTER VIII.

MONKS SHALL NOT MARRY OR KEEP CONCUBINES.

[28] Where anyone leading a monastic life proves worthy of being ordained a priest, he shall continue to observe the rule of his order [29] absolutely. If, however, having become a priest, he should abuse the confidence reposed in him, and presume to marry, although there are certain ranks of the clergy who are allowed to do this and to enter the matrimonial state (We refer to the orders of choristers and readers, but have forbidden the marriage of all others in accordance with the rules of the Church. . . .[380]

HOW BISHOPS AND OTHER ECCLESIASTICS SHALL BE ORDAINED, AND CONCERNING THE EXPENSES OF CHURCHES.

SIXTH NEW CONSTITUTION.

CHAPTER I.

CONCERNING THE MORALS, THE LIFE, THE HONOR, AND THE STATUS OF ONE WHO IS TO BE CONSECRATED A BISHOP.

---

[379] Scott, S. P., trans., ed. *The Civil Law [of Justinian]*, 17 vols. Union, NJ: Lawbook Exchange, 2001, *The Novels*, 3. Preface, Chapter I. Vol. 16:17-19, March 16, 535.

[380] Ibid., *The Novels*, 5. Chapter VIII, 16:28-29, March 17, 535.

[31] . . . . We order that the sacred canons shall be observed hereafter when anyone is presented to be consecrated a bishop. . . .

[32] (8) When the candidate has been selected and prepared for the episcopate, he must, before his consecration, be familiar with the ancient and accepted canons which Our faith acknowledges as just and inviolate, and the Catholic and Apostolic Church has established and transmitted to Us. When, after having frequently read them previous to his ordination, the official in charge of the same must interrogate him, and ascertain if he is capable of complying with the said rules and of doing what they prescribe. If he should state that he cannot observe these sacred precepts he shall, by no means, be consecrated. . . .[381]

THE ROMAN CHURCH SHALL ENJOY THE PRESCRIPTION OF A HUNDRED YEARS.

NINTH NEW CONSTITUTION.

[65] No one is ignorant of the fact that, in ancient Rome, legislation originally emanated from the head of the Pontificate. Hence We now deem it necessary to impose upon Ourselves the duty of showing that [66] We are the source of both secular and ecclesiastical jurisprudence by promulgating a law consecrated to the honor of God, which shall be applicable not only to this city but to all Catholic Churches everywhere, and exert its salutary vigor over them as far as the Ocean, so that the entire West as well as the East, where possessions belonging to Our churches are to be found, or may hereafter be acquired by them, shall enjoy its advantages.

. . . . This Our law, enacted in honor of Omnipotent God and the venerable See of the Apostle Peter, shall be observed in all lands of the entire West, and be applicable to the most distant islands of the Ocean; and Our solicitude for the subjects of Our Empire induces Us to declare it to be perpetual.[382]

---

[381] Ibid., *The Novels*, 6. Chapter I, 16:31-32, April 15, 535.
[382] Ibid., *The Novels*, 9. 16:65-66, April 14, 535.

CONCERNING THE DEPOSITION OF ANTHIMIUS,
SEVERUS, PETER, ZOARAS, AND OTHERS.

FORTY-SECOND NEW CONSTITUTION.

After the church synod of 536 deposed Monophysite,
Patriarch of Constantinople, Anthimos and his followers,
Emperor Justinian declared in the same year:

Without doing anything unusual in the basileia, we
now come to the present law. Whenever a sentence by
priests has removed from their sacred sees unworthy
occupants, like Nestorius, Eutyches, Arius, Macedonius,
Eunomius, and others no less guilty, the basileia always supported the decisions and the authority of the
priests, in order that the human and the divine should
concur in harmonizing the pronouncement of right decisions.[383]

CONCERNING THE WAREHOUSES OR SHOPS OF
THE CITY OF CONSTANTINOPLE, OF WHICH
ELEVEN HUNDRED ARE SET APART FOR THE
PURPOSE OF DEFRAYING THE EXPENSES OF
FUNERALS CONDUCTED IN THE PRINCIPAL
HOLY CHURCH, ALL THE OTHERS, No MATTER
TO WHOM THEY BELONG, SHALL ONLY BE
SUBJECT TO ORDINARY CHARGES.

FORTY-THIRD NEW CONSTITUTION.

CHAPTER I.

Hence We order that the eleven hundred shops
charged with defraying the funeral expenses incurred
by the Holy Principal Church, as well as to provide it
with deans or pallbearers shall, by all means, be main-

---

[383] Rudolf Schoell and Wilhelm Kroll, *Corpus Iuris Civilis, Novellae
XLII* (decreed Aug. 8, A.D. 536) (Berolini Apud Weidmannos, 1928),
3:196, Gr. text. For the Latin version see S. P. Scott, preface to
"Novella XLII," *The Civil Law [of Justinian]*, 16:199. See also Asterios
Gerostergios, *Justinian The Great The Emperor and Saint* (Belmont,
MA: Institute for Byzantine and Modern Greek Studies), 164.

tained intact and free from any other burden; and that no other church but this shall be entitled to demand any deans, whether the said church belongs to heretics or not. What We have already determined shall also be valid, namely, that eight hundred shops shall be set apart to provide pallbearers for the service of the Principal Church, and that three hundred shall pay their share in money, the disposal of which has already been made by Our pragmatic sanction. Any shops which may be destroyed shall be rebuilt in the manner prescribed by the orders of Anastasius of pious memory. The said eleven hundred shops devoted to the service of the Principal Holy Church shall continue to be free and exempt from every species of taxation; nor shall they, or the quarters which furnish them, be compelled to pay tribute. suffer any loss, or recognize any other authority. . . .[384]

THE NAME OF THE EMPEROR SHALL BE PLACED AT THE HEAD OF ALL PUBLIC DOCUMENTS, AND THE DATE SHALL BE WRITTEN PLAINLY IN LATIN CHARACTERS.

FOURTY-SEVENTH NEW CONSTITUTION.

CHAPTER I.

. . . . At present the eleventh year of Our reign is written; but from the beginning of next April, the day upon which God invested Us with the government of the Empire, the twelfth year shall be stated; and so on, as long as God may permit Us to reign, so that this name may survive the laws, and the mention of the latter may remain immortal, while the commemoration of the Empire shall be introduced in all transactions for all time. . . .[385]

---

[384] Scott, S. P., trans., ed. *The Civil Law [of Justinian]*, 17 vols. Union, NJ: Lawbook Exchange, 2001, *The Novels*, 43. Chapter I, 16:204. May 17, 537.

[385] Ibid., *The Novels*, 47. Chapter I, 16:214. August 31, 537.

AD 538

SACRED MYSTERIES SHALL NOT BE CELEBRATED IN PRIVATE HOUSES.

FIFTY-EIGHTH NEW CONSTITUTION.

PREFACE.

It has been provided by former laws that sacred mysteries shall, under no circumstances, be celebrated in private houses, but that the belief in and the worship of God shall be professed in public, in accordance with the custom which has been handed down to Us with regard to the observance of religious ceremonies; and We, by this present law, do provide that what We wish shall be strictly complied with. For We forbid the inhabitants of this great city, as well as all others in Our Empire, to have any kind of chapels in their houses, or to celebrate sacred mysteries there, and to do nothing which may be opposed to Catholic and Apostolic tradition."[386]

The submitted primary legislation has most assuredly sustained the claim of the scriptures that church and state united in issuing oppressive religious legislation and, thereby, did outlaw religious liberty. We will continue to accentuate certain codes and will pick up from Justinian's Novels where we left off (at the year 538) after we continue to address and document the final specifications of the scriptures.

---

[386] Ibid., *The Novels*, 58. Preface, 16:237. November 2, 537.

9

The Man of Sin thinks to change
the Law of God

The Catholic Church has changed the fourth commandment of God, the 7th day Sabbath, from Saturday to
Sunday, the 1st day of the week. This will be revealed to
be the "MARK" of her ecclesiastical authority in religious
things.

In order to establish that the Catholic Church
changed the fourth commandment of God, the 7th day
Sabbath, from Saturday to Sunday, the 1st day of the
week, we must go back to the very early history of the
church. But first a few comments from the pen of Ellen
White:

> "I saw that the Sabbath commandment was not
> nailed to the cross. If it was, the other nine command-
> ments were; and we are at liberty to break them all, as
> well as to break the fourth. I saw that God had not
> changed the Sabbath, for He never changes. But the
> pope had changed it from the seventh to the first day of
> the week; for he was to change times and laws" [Daniel
> 7:25].[387]

> "The pope has changed the day of rest from the
> seventh to the first day."[388]

---

[387] Ellen White, A *word to the Little Flock*, 18. See also *Early Writings*,
(Washington, D.C: Review and Herald, 1945), 32.
[388] Ellen White, *Early Writings*, (Washington, D.C: Review and Herald, 1945), 65.

These quotes, taken by themselves, have caused some readers to misread and misrepresent what she was really conveying by interjecting private interpretations contrary to her intended meaning. We shall allow her to qualify her intended meaning:

> "It was in behalf of the Sunday that popery first asserted its [447] arrogant claims (see Appendix); and its first resort to the power of the state was to compel the observance of Sunday as "the Lord's day.""[389]
> "Royal edicts, general councils, and church ordinances sustained by secular power were the steps by which the pagan festival attained its position of honor in the Christian world."[390]

Ellen White qualified her earlier statements by clearly stating that the *first arrogant claims* asserted by the *pope* were to *compel* the observance of *Sunday* as "the Lord's day." She then further clarified that this would be accomplished in increments or *steps*. In other words, it would be progressive and it would be *sustained by the secular power*. Her statement immediately moves us out of the first three centuries because she fully understood that this event could not take place until a union was formed between church and state. She also understood that Sunday-keeping did not begin in the fourth century. On the contrary, historians and Mrs. White correctly understood that Sunday-keeping had been witnessed in the first centuries along-side those who were keeping the Biblical Sabbath:

> "In the first centuries the true Sabbath had been kept by all Christians. They were jealous for the honor of God, and, believing that His law is immutable, they zealously guarded the sacredness of its precepts. But with great subtlety Satan worked through his agents to bring about his object. That the attention of the people

---

[389] Ellen White, *The Great Controversy*, (Nampa, ID: Pacific Press, 1911), 446-7.
[390] Ibid., 574.

might be called to the Sunday, it was made a festival in honor of the resurrection of Christ. Religious services were held upon it; yet it was regarded as a day of recreation, the Sabbath being still sacredly observed. . . . While Christians generally continued to observe the Sunday as a joyous festival, he led them, in order to show [53] their hatred of Judaism, to make the Sabbath a fast, a day of sadness and gloom."[391]

We have already established in our *A.D. 508 Source Book* that Roman Christianity for the first three centuries experienced complete religious liberty, and it was not until Constantine recognized Christianity in the fourth century with the edict of Milan in A.D. 313 that the steps were taken which brought about a union of church and state for the first time in the pagan Roman empire. Only then, with the legal arm of the state behind the church, would she have any hope of seeing the compelling of Sunday as "the Lord's day." This was rightly understood by Mrs. White:

"In the early part of the fourth century the emperor Constantine issued a decree [March 7, 321] making Sunday a public festival throughout the Roman Empire. (See Appendix.) The day of the sun was reverenced by his pagan subjects and was honored by Christians; it was the emperor's policy to unite the conflicting interests of heathenism and Christianity. He was urged to do this by the bishops of the church, who, inspired by ambition and thirst for power, perceived that if the same day was observed by both Christians and heathen, it would promote the nominal acceptance of Christianity by pagans and thus advance the power and glory of the church."[392]

One must understand that there were four steps in bringing to fruition the compulsion of Sunday worship

---

[391] Ellen White, *The Great Controversy*, (Nampa, ID: Pacific Press, 1911), 52-3.
[392] Ibid., 53.

under the union of church and state that began in the Western Roman Empire:

1. Recognition—Sunday was first recognized and generally accepted by the clergy as it quickly became a sign of anti-Judaism.

2. Official—It became official through church councils, ordinances, canon law, and or ratified by the pope.

3. State Legislation—Church edicts, council resolutions, ordinances, bulls, and canon law, sustained and enforced by the secular power.

4. It would not come to fruition until the ten horns came on the stage of action according to Daniel 7:8, 20, and 24 and that would not be until sometime after A.D. 476.

The second step can be verified from the following treatise from Pope Gelasius I:

"It would be the Popes wish, as he assured, that the leader of the world would reach the salvation longed for by him, and would lead with Christ evermore.[393] Gelasius went so far that he restored the unrest and the confusion in the East on the breach of the fundaments and teachings represented by the Roman church. The thriving of community requires a mistake-free, common faith, and that would be defended by the Roman church.[394]

"The fourth treatise of Gelasius was probably writ-

---

[393] [JK = Phillip Jaffe ed. *Regesta Pontificum Romanorum*, [*Records of the Roman Pontiffs*], (Leipzig, 1885).] JK 632: "Ut regnum quod temporaliter adsecutus es, velim te habere perpetuum, et qui imperas saeculo, possis regnare cum Christo" (PS 21 Z. 4-5 Nr. 8). This wording is, what is seldom recognized, included over the doxology in many crowning ordinances of the middle-age. Consider also the same concept of FELIX III.: JK 591 (PS 68 Z. 26 f. Nr. 20): here the concept appears in connection with the rebirths ideal.
[394] JK 632 (PS 21 f. Nr 8)

ten or at least originated in temporal proximity to him in context with this letter. The main objective lay in the evidence that the condemnation of Acacius and Petrus (Mongus) would legally stand and that *the absolution of the final ones by the Emperor would have no validity.* The tract[395] begins with the *no longer surprising statement that the resolutions of Chalcedon only held validity in so far as they are recognized by the Roman church,* with which he agreed upon every virtue with the 28th "Canon" and would already for this reason, would have liked not to acknowledge the measures of the chair of Constantinople against the other oriental chairs. *What the Roman church didn't acknowledge would have no validity and would be ineffective.*"[396]

As we have shown in our *A.D. 508 Source Book,* Revelation 17:3 is a Biblical illustration of the union of church and state, and the prophecy does not recognize the beast power until such a union exists. Ellen White understood this Biblical premise and stayed within the parameters of the scriptures. This is why she so forcefully clarified her statements by accurately stating that Sunday observance was to be *"sustained by the secular power."* This she understood would be accomplished only through a union of church and state. This brings us to the hard realization that any so-called church edicts, council

---

[395] JK 701 (PS 7 ff. Nr. 6). Other details, below pg. 250 ff.

[396] JK 701: "Quae, sicut dictum est, sedes apostolica non receipt, quia quae privilegiis universalis ecclesiae contraria probantur, nulla ratione subsistent" (PS 8 Z. 8 f. Nr. 6). Further in the same place: "Quod firmavit in synodo sedes apostolica, hoc robur obtinuit; quod refutavit, habere no potuit firmatatem (PS 12 Z. 25 f. Nr. 6).

[JK "701 (382) In fragments, which are inscribed "a tome concerning the bond of anathema", he teaches, that only those things from the Chalcedon statutes are valid, which the apostolic seat approved; that the communion was not returned to Acacius, because he did not repent. Great works of Leo III. 321 (Migne 56 p. 617), Mansi VIII. 88, Migne 59 p. 102, Thiel I. 557.—"Lest by chance because they are in the habit."

Phillip Jaffe ed. *Records of the Roman Pontiffs,* (Leipzig, 1885), 91.]

Ullman, Walter von. *Päpste und Papsttum* [Popes and Papacy]: *Gelasius I. (492–496).* Bd. 18. Stuttgart: Anton Hiersemann, 1981, 204.

resolutions, ordinances, demands for Sunday Easter observance, or Sunday-keeping of the church during the first three centuries is without substance simply because there was no recognition of the church from the state and neither was there any secular legislation enforcing the dogmas of the church until the beginning of the fourth century. In other words, there was no union of church and state during these first three centuries. Our search must commence, then, from the fourth century and onward as we look for the official declaration from the church with the sustained recognition or legislation from the state. The following documentation compiled by Mary Ann Collins, a former Catholic Nun, will help us in that search. She freely acknowledges the source she pulled from in her work was Malachi Martin's book, *The Decline and Fall of the Roman Church*. Their combined work will serve the truth well:

Chapter 7

CONSTANTINE

"On October 28, 312 A.D., the Roman Emperor Constantine met with Bishop Miltiades. (Catholics would later refer to him as Pope Miltiades. But at the time he was known as the Bishop of Rome.) Miltiades was assisted by Sylvester, a Roman who spoke educated Latin, and acted as interpreter. The previous day, Constantine had seen a sign in the heavens: a cross in front of the sun. He heard a voice say, "In this sign you will conquer." He painted crosses on the shields of his soldiers. Constantine won an important battle. He was convinced that it was because of the power of the sign that he had seen. He asked for two of the nails that were used to crucify Jesus. One nail was made into a bit for his horse. Another nail was made a part of his crown, signifying that Constantine ruled the Roman Empire in the name of Jesus. He allowed Miltiades to keep the third nail.[397]

---

[397] Malachi Martin, *The Decline and Fall of the Roman Church*, (New York: G.P. Putnam's Sons, 1981), 31-33. A major theme of this book is the radical change which occurred in the Church as a result of

The fact that Constantine saw the cross and the sun together may explain why he worshiped the sun god while at the same time professing to be a Christian. After his "conversion," Constantine built a triumphal arch featuring the sun god (the "unconquered sun"). His coins featured the sun. Constantine made a statue of the sun god, with his own face on it, for his new city of Constantinople. He made Sunday (the day of the sun god) into a day of rest when work was forbidden.[398]

Constantine declared that a mosaic of the sun god (riding in a chariot) represented Jesus. During Constantine's reign, many Christians incorporated worship of the sun god into [23] their religion. They prayed kneeling towards the east (where the sun rises). They said that Jesus Christ drives his chariot across the sky (like the sun god). They had their worship services on Sunday, which honored the sun god. (Days of the week were named to honor pagan gods. For example, Saturday is "Saturn's day," named for the Roman god Saturn.) They celebrated the birth of Jesus on December 25, the day when sun worshipers celebrated the birthday of the sun following the winter solstice.[399]

Historians disagree as to whether or not Constantine actually became a Christian. His character certainly did not reflect the teachings of Jesus Christ.

(Cont.)
Constantine. Malachi Martin recently died. He was a Catholic priest, a theologian, [Rome's Pontifical Biblical Institute] and a Vatican insider. He was the personal confessor of Pope John XXIII. [Malachi Martin also served three popes as diplomat and spy, speaks seventeen languages and helped translate the Dead Sea Scrolls.]

[398] Paul Johnson, *A History of Christianity*, (New York: Touchstone, Simon & Schuster, 1995), 67-68. Paul Johnson is a Catholic and a prominent historian.

[399] Malachi Martin, *The Decline and Fall of the Roman Church*, 33. Paul Johnson, *A History of Christianity*, 67. Information about the days of the week being named for pagan gods and goddesses can be found in a good dictionary. Look up each day of the week, and "Saturn". I used *Webster's Dictionary*, 1941 edition, which gives the origins of words.

Constantine was vain, violent, and superstitious. His combination of worshiping the Christian God and the sun god may have been an attempt to cover all the bases. (A similar spirit can be seen in wealthy Americans who financially support both opposing candidates during an election. No matter who wins, they expect to have the favor of the person in power.) Constantine had little respect for human life. He was known for wholesale slaughter during his military campaigns. He forced prisoners of war to fight for their lives against wild beasts. He had several family members (including his second wife)[400] executed for doubtful reasons. Constantine waited until he was dying before he asked to be baptized. Historians disagree as to whether or not he actually was baptized.[401]

Constantine wanted to have a state Church, with Christian clergy acting as civil servants. He called himself a Bishop. He said that he was the interpreter of the Word of God, and the voice which declares what is true and godly. According to historian Paul Johnson, Constantine saw himself as being an important agent of salvation, on a par with the apostles. Bishop Eusebius (Constantine's eulogist) relates that Constantine built the Church of the Apostles with the intention of having his body be kept there along with the bodies of the apostles. Constantine's coffin was to be in the center (the place of honor), with six apostles on each side of him. He expected that devotions honoring the apostles would be performed in the church, and he expected to share the title and honor of the apostles.[402]

Constantine told Bishop Miltiades that he wanted to build two Christian basilicas, one dedicated to the Apostle Peter and one dedicated to the Apostle Paul.

---

[400] Paul Johnson, *A History of Christianity*, (Athenum-New York, 1979), 68. [I have personally inserted the actual reading from Johnson here: "He had no respect for human life, and as emperor he executed his eldest son, his own second wife, his favorite sister's husband and 'many others' on doubtful charges." Johnson is a prominent historian and English Roman Catholic writer.]
[401] Ibid., 68-69.
[402] Ibid., 69.

He offered a large, magnificent palace for the use of Miltiades and his successors. Miltiades refused. He could not accept the idea of having Christianity be promoted by the Roman Empire.[403]

Constantine rode off to war. By the time that he returned in 314 A.D., Miltiades had died. Bishop Sylvester was Miltiades' successor. Sylvester was eager to have the Church be spread using Roman roads, Roman wealth, Roman law, Roman power, and Roman military might. Constantine officially approved of Sylvester as the successor of Miltiades. Then he had a coronation ceremony for Sylvester and crowned him like a worldly prince. No bishop had ever been crowned before.[404] Constantine's actions give the impression that he believed that he had authority over the Church.

[24] Before Constantine's "conversion," Christians were persecuted. Now, instead of facing persecution, Bishop Sylvester lived in the lap of luxury. He had a beautiful palace, with the finest furniture and art. He wore silk brocade robes. He had servants to wait on him. Near his palace was a basilica which served as his cathedral. This luxurious building had seven altars made of gold, a canopy of solid silver above the main altar, and 50 chandeliers. The imperial mail system and transportation system were placed at Sylvester's disposal. It was now possible to have worldwide church councils.[405]

Read the Book of Acts and the Epistles and compare the Church shown there to the Church of Bishop Sylvester. Here is how the Apostle Paul described the kinds of things that he had to endure, as a leader in the early Church.

"Of the Jews five times received I forty stripes save one. Thrice was I beaten with rods, once was I stoned, thrice I suffered shipwreck, a night and a day I have been in the deep; In journeyings often, in perils of

---

[403] Malachi Martin, *The Decline and Fall of the Roman Church*, 33-34.
[404] Ibid., 34-35.
[405] James G. McCarthy, *The Gospel According to Rome*, (Eugene, Oregon: Harvest House Publishers, 1995), 231-232. James McCarthy is a former Catholic.

waters, in perils of robbers, in perils by mine own countrymen, in perils by the heathen, in perils in the city, in perils in the wilderness, in perils in the sea, in perils among false brethren; In weariness and painfulness, in watchings often, in hunger and thirst, in fastings often, in cold and nakedness." (2 Corinthians 11:24-27)

After Constantine's "conversion," the Church was radically changed. Suddenly, being Christian resulted in power, prestige, and promotion (whereas previously it had resulted in persecution). Suddenly, by the Emperor's decree, Christianity became "politically correct". So ambitious people joined the Church for worldly reasons. The Bishop of Rome was supported by the military might, political power, and wealth of the Roman Emperor. Worldwide church councils were convened.

This was the birth of the Roman Catholic Church. It was created in the year 314 A.D. by Emperor Constantine and Bishop Sylvester.

A TALE OF TWO BISHOPS

The degree of change which Constantine caused in the Church can be illustrated by looking at the lives of two Bishops of Rome. So let's go back in history for about 100 years before Christianity became "politically correct," to look at the life of Bishop Pontian. Then we will compare Pontian's life with the life of Bishop Sylvester, who lived during the time of Emperor Constantine.

(The following information about Bishops Pontian and Sylvester comes from Malachi Martin, "The Decline and Fall of the Roman Church," pages 19-38.)

[25] Pontian became the Bishop of Rome in the year 230 A.D. He was made bishop suddenly and unexpectedly when his predecessor was arrested and killed by Roman authorities.

On September 27, 235 A.D., Emperor Maximinus decreed that all Christian leaders were to be arrested. Christian buildings were burned, Christian cemeteries were closed, and the personal wealth of Christians was confiscated.

Bishop Pontian was arrested the same day. He was put in the Mamertine Prison, where he was tortured for ten days. Then he was sent to work in the lead mines of Sardinia.

When prisoners arrived at Sardinia, their left eye was gouged out and a number was branded on their forehead. Iron rings were soldered around their ankles, linked together with a six-inch chain which hobbled them. A tight chain around their waist was fastened to their ankle-chain in such a way that they were permanently bent over.

The prisoners worked for 20 hours a day, with four one-hour breaks for sleep. They had one meal of bread and water per day. Most prisoners died within six to fourteen months from exhaustion, malnutrition, disease, beatings, infection, or violence. Some went insane or committed suicide.

Pontian only lasted four months. In January, 236 A.D., Pontian was killed and his body was thrown into the cesspool.

What happened to Pontian was not unusual. Many Christians were sent to the Sardinian lead mines, or persecuted in other ways. If a man accepted the position of being a Christian leader, he knew that his life from that time on was likely to be short and painful. There were 14 Bishops of Rome in the 79 years between Pontian and Sylvester.

Then along came Constantine.

In 314 A.D., Emperor Constantine crowned Sylvester as Bishop of Rome. Sylvester lived in luxury, with servants waiting on him. Constantine confessed his sins to Sylvester and asked for his advice. Sylvester presided over worldwide Church councils. He had a splendid palace and a sumptuous cathedral. He had power, prestige, wealth, pomp, and the favor of the Emperor.

Churchmen wore purple robes, reflecting the purple of Constantine's court. That was an external change. The most important change was an internal one. The Church took on the mentality of Rome. Under Sylvester, the internal structure of the Church took on the form and practice and pomp of Rome.

Sylvester died in December, 335 A.D. He died peace-fully, in a clean, comfortable bed, in the Roman Lateran Palace. He died surrounded by well dressed bishops and priests, and attended by Roman guards. His body was dressed in ceremonial robes, put in an elegant casket, and carried through the streets of Rome in a solemn pro-cession. He was buried [26] with honor and ceremony, attended by the cream of Roman society and by the Roman people.

It is understandable that many Christians would have preferred an officially approved status for the Church. But what was the result?

Before Constantine, the church was a band of heroic men and women who were so committed to serve the Lord Jesus Christ that they would endure any hardship. After 314 A.D., the Church became infil-trated by opportunists who were seeking power and political advancement. Church leaders were no longer in danger of persecution. Rather, they enjoyed all the trappings of power and luxury.

Historian Paul Johnson asks, "Did the empire sur-render to Christianity, or did Christianity prostitute it-self to the empire?[406]

The temptation for an ungodly alliance with Rome was very great. But at what cost?"[407]

Johnson destroys many myths of early church history prior to this marriage or union of church and state in A.D. 314 and replaces them with facts:

"Was there a conscious bargain? Which side ben-efited most from this unseemly marriage between Church and State? Or, to put it another way, did the empire surrender to Christianity, or did Christianity prostitute itself to the empire? It is characteristic of

---

[406] Paul Johnson, *A History of Christianity*, (Athenum-New York, 1979), 69.

[407] Mary Ann Collins a Former Catholic Nun, *The Spirit of Roman Catholicism-What Lies Behind the Modern Public Image?* Copyright 2002, 22-26, PDF.

the complexities of early Christian history that we cannot give a definite answer to this question. It is not at all clear why the empire and Christianity came into conflict in the first place. The empire extended toleration to all sects provided they kept the peace. Jewish Christianity may have been penetrated by Zealotry and Jewish irredentism, but the gentile Christianity of the Pauline missions was non-political and non-racial. Its social implications were, in the long run, revolutionary, but it had no specific doctrines of social change. Jesus had told his hearers to pay taxes. Paul, in a memorable passage, advised the faithful, while waiting for the *parousia,* to obey duly-constituted authority. As early as the mid-second century, some [70] Christian writers saw an identity of interests between the burgeoning Christian movement, with its universalist aims, and the empire itself. Christians might not yield divine honors to the emperor, but in other respects they were loyal Romans. Tertullian claimed:

"We are for ever making intercession for the emperors. We pray for them a long life, a secure rule, a safe home, brave armies, a faithful senate, an honest people, a quiet world, and everything for which a man and a Caesar may pray. . . . We know that the great force which threatens the whole world, the end of the age itself with its menace of hideous sufferings, is delayed by the respite which the Roman Empire means for us when we pray for its postponement we assist the continuance of Rome I have a right to say, Caesar is more ours than yours, appointed as he is by our God."

By Tertullian's time *(c.* 200), as he pointed out, the Christians were numerous enough to overthrow the Empire, had their intentions been hostile:

"We are but of yesterday, and we fill everything you have—cities, tenements, forts, towns, exchanges, yes! and camps, tribes, palace, senate, forum. All we leave you with are the Temples!" Christians were, he urged, a docile as well as a loyal element in society.

And of course for the most part they were left alone. As a rule, the Christians, like the Jews, enjoyed complete freedom from persecution.

. . . . [71] Under weak and vulnerable rulers, like Caligula, Nero and Domitian, they became scapegoats for failure or disaster. As Tertullian put it: "If the Tiber reaches the walls, if the Nile fails to rise to the fields, if the sky doesn't move, or the earth does, if there is famine or plague, the cry is at once: "The Christians to the Lion!"' Prejudice was much stronger in the central and western Mediterranean than in the east, but certain rumors were current everywhere.

. . . . If they were strong and secure [Roman governments] they were less inclined to yield to prejudice. Undisavowed Christianity remained a capital offence, but government did not, as a rule, force Christians into the choice between avowal and apostasy. It left them alone. One reason why the Church strove for uniformity, and so against heresy, was that non-orthodox practices tended to attract more attention and therefore hostility. . . . [72] There was no systematic persecution of the Christians before the second half of the second century. The worst episodes were isolated incidents, as in the Rhone Valley in 177."[408]

Malachi Martin describes how Constantine won the decisive battle at one of Rome's bridges, the Milvian, in the year 312, and the victory assures him the crown. The first thing Constantine requests is to be taken to this obscure little man, the head of Rome's Christians, their bishop, Miltiades. Constantine has had a vision and attributes his great victory to Christ's intervention. He immediately determines to reverse the empire's policy toward Christianity and Christians. Accompanied by his chief priest, Sylvester, Constantine, having made a decision, wastes no words. Constantine reveals to Miltiades and Sylvester that he plans to build a basilica dedicated to Peter and more. Martin continues:

"Miltiades nods, but he is too dazed to answer. The idea of a Christian basilica is too much for him. All his

---

[408] Paul Johnson, *A History of Christianity*, (Athenum-New York, 1979), 69-72.

life, he has only known the little churches and chapels, the "dominica" houses of the Lord-really little back rooms. For Miltiades a basilica has always been a pagan building in whose central portion, the apse, there was the *Augusteum*, a place filled with the statues of the emperors who were worshiped as divinities by the Romans. For Miltiades, a Christian basilica is a square circle, and he [34] will never change, never accept the emperor turning everything upside down and making the world a pleasant and easy place for Christians.

But Sylvester has another view: perhaps this Constantine could serve in Jesus' plan of universal salvation. . . .

There are a few more words between the emperor and the pope. Then Constantine rides off. He has battles to fight and an empire to consolidate. His parting words are for Sylvester: "The Godhead," he says, "wills us two to do great things in the name of Christ. Be here when we return.

By January of 314, only fifteen months later, the frail Miltiades is dead. He dies without ever having changed his mind. Lands and buildings given to the church by Constantine he could accept. But he could not accept a Christianity sanctioned and propagated by civil and military power.

Sylvester, however, by now has seen a new form for the Church: it could spread by means of Roman roads, Roman arms, Roman law, Roman power. The world would belong to Jesus entirely. Thus the triumph and the blessing could be prepared. Besides, Sylvester remembers, no one knows when Jesus will reappear. Therefore, why not make straight the way of the Lord?

A month after Miltiades's death, Constantine returns to Rome and assembles all Christians-priests, deacons, people. He tells them simply: "We have chosen to approve of Sylvester as successor to Miltiades and to Peter the Apostle, as representative of Jesus the Christ." The assembly of Christians confirms the emperor's choice.

After his coronation-Sylvester is the first pope to be crowned like a temporal prince-Sylvester sits down in the Lateran Palace with Constantine. It is the first and last time the two men will talk together at any length. They have decisions to make. Constantine makes a full confession of his whole life, asking for Sylvester's advice and the forgiveness of Christ for his sins. Sylvester takes the first step toward a genuinely universal church. He accepts an alliance between church and empire, so that the church can spread everywhere. The 232 successors to Sylvester will never modify or deviate from that fateful step. From that day to this their spiritual power will be entangled in temporal alliances. Essentially, obstinately, blindly, they will stand in Sylvester's shoes down to the late twentieth century. We have accounts although only secondhand-of the conversation between pope and emperor, but those accounts seem to agree on essentials."[409]

The first possible candidate of the church to have wielded the power of the state to enforce the papal sabbath would have been Pope Sylvester I who reigned from A.D. 314-335.We are now ready to authenticate our second specification of the scriptures, and we begin from a work by Odom to see if Pope Sylvester I was that man:

[196] "Rahanus Maurus, an archbishop of Mainz, Germany, who lived from 776 to 856 A.D., is said to have been "probably the most cultured man of his time, and exceptionally learned in patristics." A perusal of his works will convince anyone that he was a learned man. He says:
"Likewise also *feriae* is derived from *fando*, for

---

[409] Malachi Martin, *The Decline and Fall of the Roman Church* (New York: G.P. Putnam's Sons, 1981), 33-35. [Malachi Martin, *The Decline and Fall of the Roman Church* (New York: G.P. Putnam's Sons, 1981). A major theme of this book is the radical change which occurred in the Church as a result of Constantine. Malachi Martin recently died. He was a Catholic priest, a theologian, and a Vatican insider. He was the personal confessor of Pope John XXIII.]

which reason Pope Sylvester I ordained among the Romans that [concerning] the names of the days, which they previously called after the names of their gods, that is. *Solis* [of the Sun], *Lunae* [of the Moon]. *Martis* [of Mars], Mencurii [of Mercury], *[Iovis* (of Jupiter)]. Veneris [of Venus], [and] *Saturni* [of Saturn], that they should therefore call [them] feriae, that is, first *feria*, second *feria*, third *feria*, fourth *feria*, fifth *feria*, sixth *feria*, because in the beginning of Genesis it is written that God said [197] on each day: on the first, Let there be light; on the second, Let there be a firmament; on the third, Let the earth bring forth green herbs, etc. But he [Sylvester] commanded to call the Sabbath by the ancient term of the law, and [to call] the first *feria* 'Lord's day,' because that on it the Lord rose [from the dead]. Moreover *the same pope decreed that the Sabbath rest should be transferred to the Lord's Day,* in order that on that day we should rest from earthly works to the praising of God."[410]

The same writer repeats this concerning Sylvester in another of his works.

Bede's Testimony About Sylvester

[197] Bede, the noted English monk and ecclesiastical writer (672-735 A.D.), repeatedly declares that Sylvester attempted to change the pagan names of the days of the week. He says: "But the holy Sylvester ordered them to be called *feriae,* calling the first day the 'Lord's [day]'; imitating the Hebrews, who named [them] the first of the week, the second of the week, and so on the others."[411]

---

[410] Rabanus Maurus, *De Clericorum Inslitutione,* book 2, chap. 46, in J. P. Migne, *Patrologia Latina,* Vol. 107, col. 361, author's translation. See also Rabanus Maurus, *Liber de Computo,* chap. 27, "De Feriis," in J. P. Migne, *Patrologia* Latina, Vol. 107 col. 682.

[411] Bede, *De Temporibus,* chap. 4 in J. P. Migne, *Patrologia Latina,* Vol. 90, col. 281. author's translation. See also Bede, *De Divisionibus Temporum,* chap. 10; *De Temporum Ratione,* chap. 8, in J. P. Migne, *Patrologia Latina,* Vol. 90, cols. 657, 658, 326-332.

Bede says also in another work: "*Question:* Who first taught to observe *feriae? Answer:* Pope Sylvester instructed the clergy to observe *feriae,* to whom, resting only to God, it was allowed to engage in no military service or worldly business. . . . And indeed because light in the beginning was made on the first day, and the resurrection of Christ [being] celebrated [on it], he called [it] the 'Lord's [day]:"[412]

Sicard, bishop of Cremona, Italy, about 1221 A.D., also says: "Besides, he [Sylvester] changed the names of the days into *feriae,* and he decreed [that] the fast [be observed] on the fourth [Wednesday], on the sixth [Friday], and on the Sabbath on account of the Lord's burial; but on the Lord's day [he [198] decreed that there he observed] a solemnity on account of the resurrection, and on the fifth *feria* [Thursday] on account of [His] ascension."[413]

In an ecclesiastical manual written in Anglo-Saxon in 1011 A.D., Byrhtferth said: "The reverend Bishop Sylvester altered the names of these days into *feria* (holiday); and said that Sunday was God's day and called it *feria prima;* and Monday (he called) *feria secunda,* that is the second holiday; and all the others he named as we call them in Latin."[414]

In the ecclesiastical terminology of the Roman Catholic Church, the nomenclature recommended by Sylvester is still in use. "The ecclesiastical style of naming the week days was adopted by no nation except the Portuguese, who alone use the terms *segunda Feira,* etc."[415]

Sylvester did not institute Sunday observance among Christians. Rabanus Maurus, already quoted in this chapter, says that "Pope Sylvester instructed the clergy to observe *feriae.* And indeed from an old custom he called the first day 'the Lord's [day],' on which

---

[412] Bede, *De Ratione Computi,* chap. 5, in J. P. Migne, *Patrologia Latina,* Vol. 90. col. 584, author's translation.
[413] Sicard, *Chronicon,* ad anno 310, "De Constantio et Galerio," in J. P. Migne, *Patrologia Latina,* Vol. :213, col. 467, author's translation.
[414] *Byrhtferth's Manual,* p. 131.
[415] *The Catholic Encyclopedia,* Vol. 6, p. 43, art. "Feria,"

light was made in the beginning, and [on which] the resurrection of Christ has been celebrated."[416]

The Roman Breviary *(lect. 6 in festis S. Sylvestri)* remarks: "Retaining the names Sabbath and the Lord's day, and distinguishing the remaining days of the week by the term *feriae*, he [Sylvester] wished them to be called what the [Roman] Church had already previously commenced to name them."[417]

Odom correctly stated that Pope "Sylvester did not institute Sunday observance among Christians. . . . [he simply] instructed the clergy to observe *feriae*." The recognition stage of Sunday observance was already in place long before the fourth century, as Ellen White correctly stated. What we are witnessing here is the second step of instituting Sunday worship under the union of church and state when the pope made it official. Odom's first reference of the *Patrologia Latina*, Vol. 107, col. 361 holds great significance when he quoted the following:

> "Moreover *the same pope decreed that the Sabbath rest should be transferred to the Lord's Day*, in order that on that day we should rest from earthly works to the praising of God."[418]

This is a cornerstone statement and must be seen in its entirety. Therefore, we submit the full document of Rahanus Maurus translated from the Latin:

---

[416] Rabanus Maurus, *liber de Computo*, chap. 27, "De Feriis," in J. P. Migne, *Patrologia Latina*, Vol. 107, col. (182, author's translation.
[417] J. N. Andrews, *History Of the Sabbath*, p. 474. See *The Catholic Encyclopedia*, Vol. 6, p. 43, art. "Feria."
   Robert Leo Odom, *Sunday in Roman Paganism*, (New York: Teach Services, Inc. 1944, 2003), 196-198.
[418] Rabanus Maurus, *De Clericorum Inslitutione*, book 2, chap. 46, in J. P. Migne, *Patrologia Latina*, Vol. 107, col. 361, author's translation. See also Rabanus Maurus, *Liber de Computo*, chap. 27, "De Feriis," in J. P. Migne, *Patrologia* Latina, Vol. 107 col. 682.
   Robert Leo Odom, *Sunday in Roman Paganism*, (New York: Teach Services, Inc. 1944, 2003), 197.

[355] "On the holy Sabbath however of Pentecost, just as on the holy Sabbath of Pascha, baptism should be celebrated, with readings of the Old Testament recited before, and orations and litanies performed before, with the holy celebration of mass following. The holy Sabbath of Pentecost should be revered well also with a celebration similar to the holy Sabbath of pascha, because . . .

Chapter 42. About the day Sunday.

"The apostles have made holy the day of Sunday likewise with religious solemnity because our Redeemer rose from the dead on that day, and thus it is called "Dominicus"/of the Lord, so that on it abstaining from earthly works or the enticements of the world, we serve only divine worships, namely giving honor and reverence to this day, on account of the hope of our resurrection, which we have in it.

[356] However we read that the Sabbath which has been celebrated by an earlier people in leisure for the body, so that the figure may have rest, whence also rest interprets the Sabbath. The day of Sunday however, has been declared not by Jews but by Christians for the resurrection of the Lord, and begins to have its festivity from that. It itself indeed is the first day, which is found as the eighth after the seventh, whence it is called also in Ecclesiastes for the signification of two Testaments: Those say seven, just as those say eight. Indeed at first only the Sabbath was handed over to be celebrated, because before it was the rest of the dead, there was however the resurrection of no one until Christ the Lord, who "rising from the dead, is not dead, his death will not prevail over beyond that one." Now such resurrection has later been made in the body of the Lord, so that it takes the lead at the head of the Church, because the body of the Church hoped in the end, the eighth day of the Lord, which also first, followed in festivity. However it appears that this day was also solemn in the sacred Scriptures. Indeed the day itself is the first of the age, on the very day also the elements of the world were formed, on itself the Angels were created, on itself also Christ arose from the dead, on itself the

holy Spirit descended from the sky over the apostles, on this day manna was given from the sky in the first wilderness. Thus indeed the Lord says: "You will collect manna for six days, on the sixth however you will collect double (Exod. 16). Indeed the sixth day is Good Friday/day of Preparation, which is placed before the Sabbath, however the eighth day is the Sabbath, which Sunday follows on which manna first came from the sky. Whence the Jews understand now that our Sunday was preferred at the time to the Jewish Sabbath, now then it has been indicated that on the Sabbath of themselves the grace of God descended from the sky to them not at all, but on our Sunday in which the Lord first rained it. . . .

[360]

Chapter 46.
Concerning the festivity of the old/former ones, and whence also the festival or holidays are mentioned.
[dies festi: holiday; festum agere: to observe a holiday]

"Those however were the holidays in the ancient law: the day of the Azyme and the Passover, when, when the moon is fullest, with the yeast left/removed, a lamb was sacrificed. The days of Pentecost, when in the top of the month, the Sinai law was given to Moses, in which the breads of the first intention concerning the fruits [the first breads of the proposition from the harvest] were offered. The day of the Sabbath, on which leisure things were celebrated, and on which it was not allowed to collect manna in the desert. The day of the New Moons, a celebration of the new moon. Always however the Jews in the beginning of the months, that is [on] the first moon [the beginning of the moon], observed a holiday. But for that reason they did this in the beginning of the month, because when the moon was waning, the time is ended, and again when waxing, it is begun. The day however of trumpets is the beginning of the seventh month, when the Jews observing the solemnity more fully were singing with a trumpet, and used to offer more sacrifices on that day than in individual months. In this first month [at first],

on the tenth day of this month, it was a day of propitia-
tions or expiations, when the pontiff once/at some time
in the year entered into the holy of holies, and with the
people praying outside, he alone prayed within, both
for his own as well as for ignorance of the people offering incense to God above the altar of thymiam [with
vessels of incense]. In this month also were the very
celebrated days of the Feast of the Tabernacle (Sceno-
pegia), that is, of the Tabernacles, when from the fifteenth day of this month, they used to live for seven
days in the awnings of the tabernacle, taking up for
themselves branches of palms, and branches of wood
of thick leaves, and willows from the stream, and re-
joiced in presence of their Lord God, in commemoration of their exit from Egypt, which the Lord made
them to live in the tabernacles, since he led them out of
the land of Egypt. The days of fasting, of the first,
fourth, seventh, and tenth month, were celebrated on
account of these reasons among us on account of what
we commemorated above, when we discussed concerning the fast. However they are called holidays
from there, because the divine right is spoken in them,
that is, is said, and legal holidays, [361] on which it is
not spoken. Similarly also the holidays are said by
speaking, because the pope Silvester first among the
Romans established that the names of the days which
were called before according to the names of the gods,
that is, of the Sun, Moon, Mars, Mercury, Venus,
Saturn, from now on should be called holy days of the
week, that is, the first day of the week, the second, the
third, the fourth, the fifth, the sixth, because it was
written in the beginning of Genesis that God declared
for individual days: first, "Let there be light"; second,
"Let there be the firmament"; third, "Let the earth produce green vegetation", similarly, and so forth. The
Sabbath however he instructed to call by the ancient
vocabulary of the law, and the first holy day of the
Lord, because the Lord arose on it. *However the same
pope established to transfer the leisure of the Sabbath
more onto the Lord's Day*, so that on this day in order to
praise God we might be free from earthly work, according to that which was written: "Be idle from work

and know, that I am God" (Psal. 45). According to this custom moreover the holy Church orders us to be idle on the feast days of the saints, that is, for celebrating the praises of God. The one who wants to be free from agriculture for this other thing on these days, in order to be devoted to drunkenness and excess, or to give effort to vain child's play should know that he sins more through such leisure than if he kept at some useful work, with King Solomon as witness, when he says: Woe to those who linger in wine, and are interested in draining wine goblets down to the dregs." (Prov. 23), and likewise: "The servant who is intelligent is welcomed to the king, he says, [while] the unuseful one will sustain [his] wrath (Prov. 14). But because we have now spoken above according to the greater sense concerning the more celebrated festivities, for the instruction of those who serve God in the Church, and are in charge of the people, concerning the origin also of song, and of readings, and authority of the Symbol, we shall in addition speak of in the present."[419]

"However the same pope [Sylvester I] *established to transfer the leisure of the Sabbath more onto the Lord's Day. . . ."*
Quoting from Catholic sources, this document fully establishes the fact that the first official position taken by the Catholic Church in transferring the leisure of the Sabbath to Sunday was ratified by Pope Sylvester I. For those who would take issue with this, we simply ask, why would Pope Sylvester I transfer the leisure of the Sabbath to Sunday if it had already officially been proclaimed? It had not, and this concession to paganism was not made until Constantine (the state) and Pope Sylvester I (the church) came to an agreement. Therefore, we see that Ellen White was correct in her previous statements. This same work was critiqued by Dr. Aloisius Knoepfler in 1900 and because of its implications we submit the entirety of his document, as well, translated from the Latin:

---

[419] Rabanus Maurus, *De Clericorum Inslitutione,* book 2, chap. 46, in J. P. Migne, *Patrologia Latina, The Catholic Tradition. 9th Century, Year 856 All the Works of B. Rabanus Maurus* 107: col. 355-6, 360-1.

Veroffentlichungen aus dem Kirchenhistorischen
Seminar Munchen
Number 5:
Rabani Mauri
[Rabbi Maurus]
De Institutione Clericorum Libri Tres.
[Three books concerning the institution of the clerics.]
Dr. Aloisius Knoepfler
Reviewed the text, explained with critical annotations
and exegeses, added an introduction and index.

[152]

Chapter 46.
Concerning Festivities of the Ancients, and whence they were called either festivals or holidays.

"Those festal days however were in ancient law: a day of unleavened and the phase, when with the moon at its fullest a lamb was sacrificed when yeast was refused; the day of Pentecost when[420] the law was given to Moses on the top of the mountain Sinai the law was given to Moses, "on which the "loaves of bread from the grains[421] of the" first "laying forth (b: Isid. Etym. VI, 18.) were offered"; the day of the Sabbath[422] on which in activities were celebrated[423] and on which to collect manna in the desert was not allowed; the day of New moons; the celebration of the "new moon." Always however the Jews in the beginning of the months, this is the first moon, held a festal day; but they did this therefore [153] on the beginning of the month, because when the moon is waning the time is finished and it is begun again when it is born. "The day of the trumpets" however is the beginning "of the seventh month," when the Jews performing a solemnity with a trumpet sang more fully, and offered more sacrifices on it, than in individual months. In this month, it is on the tenth[424]

---

[420] oe has "by which"
[421] J. has "with the new grains"
[422] PP1 have "it is the Sabbath"
[423] M. omits "proposal—were celebrated"; PP1 has present tense
[424] MPP1 have "tenth" in a different gender

day of this month it was a day of propitiations{?} or of atonements, when the pontiff "entered once in the year into the sancta" sanctorum (a: Hebr. IX, 12) and expiated with the holy scattering of blood {the sacred things} and also the sancta sanctorum,[425] and with the people outside praying he himself alone within prayed both "for his own" and also offering for[426] "the ignorance of the people offering incense" to the Lord over the altar of thymiama. In this month also very frequent days were Feasts of the Tabernacle (b: III Esd. V, 51. Levit. XXIII, 40-43.), that is of tabernacles, when from the 15th day of this month "for seven days they lived in shades/bowers, eating twigs of palms for themselves and branches of the wood of dense leaves and willow branches from the brook and were rejoicing in the presence of their lord God" in commemoration[427] of their exit from Egypt, because[428] the Lord made them to live in tabernacles, when he led[429] "them out of the land of Egypt." The days however[430] of fasting, of the first,[431] fourth, seventh and tenth month on account of these reasons were repeated among them, on account of which I remembered above, when I disputed concerning fasting.

They are called festal days however thence, "because the law says in them, that is it is said" (c: Isid., Different. lit. F. Bede, about division. time see under feria, and concerning reasons for times ch. 6. l. c. vol. I. p. 93; vol. II. p. 55.), they are unlawful for business, by which it is not said. Similarly also they are called feriae/holidays from what may be spoken/the act of speaking (c); on account of which Pope Sylvester first established for the Romans, that the names of the days, which [154] before were called according to the names of their gods, that is: Of the Sun, Of the Moon, Of Mars,

---

[425] oe omits "and expiated—sanctorum"
[426] oe omits
[427] hP1 have "with commemoration"
[428] h has a synonym for "because"
[429] h has "led out" in a different tense
[430] oe omits.
[431] MPP1 omits, M has instead: "of the fourth, fifth, seventh."

Of Mercury, Of Jove,[432] Of Venus, Of Saturn, thereafter they called feast days/days of the week, that is[433] the first day of the week, the second day of the week, the third day of the week, the fourth day of the week, the fifth day of the week, the sixth day of the week, because its written in the beginning of Genesis, that God said through individual days, that is the first: let there be light, second: let there be the firmament, third: let the earth produce green grass, and similarly other things. He directed however to name[434] the Sabbath by ay an ancient word of the law, and the first day the day of the lord, because the lord rose again on it. *The same pope established however, that the leisure of the Sabbath be transferred rather onto the Lord's day*, so that on that day we are freed from works of the earth for praising God, according to that which was written (a: Ps. XLV, 11.): "Be idle and know, inasmuch as I am God." According to this custom however the holy church orders us to be free on the birthdays/anniversaries of the saints, that is for the celebrating the praises of God. Still the one who wishes to be free from agriculture on these days for this other thing, so that he may serve devotedly drunkenness and intoxication or may give effort to inane jokes, should recognize, that he errs more through such leisure, than if he persisted in some[435] useful work, with Solomon witnessing[436] who says (b: Prov. XXIII, 30.): "Woe to those, who tarry in wine and are interested in drinking dry the cups"; and likewise (c: Prov. XIV, 35.) "The servant has been[437] accepted to the king," he says," when he understands, he will put off his[438] anger unusefully." But because I have spoken above already concerning the more frequent festivities for the instruction of those, who serve God in the church and are in charge of the people, according to

---

[432] oe omits.
[433] oe exc. h. omits "that is."
[434] "to be called" in h.
[435] MPP1 have "for some"
[436] oe have "as witness"
[437] eo and c. have "is understanding."
[438] oe exc. h. omits

the understanding of the ancestors, I should speak concerning the origin also of song and of readings and the authority of the symbol still in the present book."[439]

"The same pope [Sylvester] *established however, that the leisure of the Sabbath be transferred rather onto the Lord's day,"*

With the transfer of the Sabbath to Sunday officially established by the Catholic Church through Pope Sylvester I, we now need to establish the year of this transfer. Hampson supplies that A.D. 316 is the specific year given for this official declaration by the Catholic Church:

> "Feria.—A day; in the plural, Feriae. In 316, Pope Sylvester prohibited the Christians from naming the days of the week after the Jewish manner- [138] prima, secunda, &c., sabbati; and, as he equally disliked the heathen names from the Gods or planets, Dies Solis, Lunae, &c., Sun-day, Mon, or Moonday, he ordained that, thenceforth, they should call Monday Feria Secunda; Tuesday, Feria Tertia, Wednesday, Feria Quarta; Thursday, Feria Quinta; Friday, Feria Sexta (*Durand. De Off. Div., L.* VII, c. 1.; Pol. Verg., L. VI, c. 5, p. 366-7). Sunday and Saturday had their own names, the first being Dies Dominicus, and the latter, Sabbatum. Feriae, among the ancients, were days on which it was unlawful to work, and were so called from the immolation of sacrifices, "a feriendis hostiis" (*Montan., Disput. Jurid.de Feriis, thes. 1)* or from the banquets which were given at that time "af eriendis epulis" (*Pol. Verg., ut supra*). Hence are derived Fairs, Ferial Days, Foires, &c."[440]

---

[439] Rabani Mauri-Dr. Aloisius Knoepfler, *Veroffentlichungen aus dem Kirchenhis-torischen Seminar Munchen, No. 5., De Institutione Clericorum Libri Tres.*, (Munich, Verlag Der J.J. Lentnerschen Buchhandlung, 1900), 152-154.

[440] R.T. Hampson, *Medii Aevi Kalendarium or Dates, Charters, and Customs of the Middle Ages,* (London, Henry Kent Causton and Co., Birchin Lane 1841), 2:137-8.

The first legislative act of the state enforcing the Venerable Day of the Sun was the law enacted by Constantine:

> "The first public measure enforcing Sunday observance was the law enacted by Constantine. (A.D. 321; see Appendix note for page 53.) This edict required townspeople to rest on "the venerable day of the sun," but permitted countrymen to continue their agricultural pursuits. Though virtually a heathen statute, it was enforced by the emperor after his nominal acceptance of Christianity."[441]

The original decree of Constantine on March 7, 321, as translated by Schaff:

> "On the venerable Day of the Sun let the magistrates and people residing in cities rest, and let all workshops be closed. In the country, however, persons engaged in agriculture may freely and lawfully continue their pursuits; because it often happens that another day is not so suitable for grain-sowing or for vine-planting; lest by neglecting the proper moment for such operations the bounty of heaven should be lost."[442]

Averil Cameron substantiates that the reading from the original reads the "venerable day of the sun." The term coined by Roman sympathizers "the Holy Day of Sunday" or the like does not exist and is being substituted for the "venerable day of the sun." (Cameron's comments will be viewed soon.) The reason for this is because "Catholic Truth" desires to give Sunday some sanctity. In truth, it was a heathen statute fostered by Constantine who was a pagan and remained so until his so-called death bed conversion in 337 (which is also hotly debated among historians).

---

[441] Ellen White, *The Great Controversy*, (Nampa, ID: Pacific Press, 1911), 574.

[442] Philip Schaff, History of the Christian Church, (Peabody, Massachusettes: Hendrickson Publishers, Inc., 1867, 1889, 2002), 3:380, footnote 1.

Eusebius Pamphili, Bishop of Caesarea in Palestine, (born about 260; died before 341) was not only recognized as the "Father of Church History," but also as a church theologian who repeated the claim that the Catholic Church had "transferred" the leisure of the Sabbath to Sunday:

> "The royal mandate not proving a sufficient substitute for divine authority, Eusebius, a bishop who sought the favor of princes, and who was the special friend and flatterer of Constantine, advanced the claim that Christ had transferred the Sabbath to Sunday. Not a single testimony of the Scriptures was produced in proof of the new doctrine. Eusebius himself unwittingly acknowledges its falsity and points to the real authors of the change. "All things," he says, "whatever that it was duty to do on the Sabbath, these we [The Catholic Church] have [past tense] transferred to the Lord's Day."[443]

Eusebius's statement that we have "transferred to the Lord's Day" was undoubtedly repeating Pope Sylvester I when he said:

> "*However the same pope* [Sylvester I] *established to transfer the leisure of the Sabbath more onto the Lord's Day. . . .*"[444]

> "*The same pope established however, that the leisure of the Sabbath be transferred rather onto the Lord's day. . . .*"[445]

---

[443] Robert Cox, Sabbath Laws and Sabbath Duties, page 538. Ellen White, Great Controversy, 574. See also J. P. Migne, *Patrologia Graeca*, (Psalm 92, *A Psalm or Song for the Sabbath-day*) 23:1171-2.
[444] Rabanus Maurus, *De Clericorum Inslitutione*, book 2, chap. 46, in J. P. Migne, *Patrologia Latina, The Catholic Tradition. 9th Century, Year 856 All the Works of B. Rabanus Maurus* 107: col. 361.
[445] Rabani Mauri-Dr. Aloisius Knoepfler, *Veroffentlichungen aus dem Kirchenhistorischen Seminar Munchen, No. 5., De Institutione Clericorum Libri Tres.*, (Munich, Verlag Der J.J. Lentnerschen Buchhandlung, 1900), 154.

We would be remiss not to inquire about a date for the just quoted statement by Eusebius. The Catholic Encyclopedia, although not definitive, supplies us with a date of around A.D. 330:

> "(21) Commentary on the Psalms. There are many gaps in the MSS. of this work, and they end in the 118th Psalm. The missing portions are in part supplied by extracts from the Catenae. An allusion to the discovery of the Holy Sepulchre fixes the date at about 330. Lightfoot speaks very highly of this commentary."[446]

The Council of Laodicea was convened between the years 364-381. Historians are not certain of its dating. Some prefer the year 380 or 381 after Roman Catholicism became the legalized religion of the empire on February 28, 380. The Council produced 60 canons; however, canon 29 is the most pertinent to our study because "Catholic Truth" was determined to give Sunday some sanctity. At the same time, her true character as an intolerant church was being manifest before all:

> "Christians must not judaize by resting on the Sabbath, but must work on that day, rather honouring the Lord's Day; and, if they can, resting then as Christians. But if any shall be found to be judaizers, let them be anathema from Christ."[447]

The following Catholic quotes are supplied to further sustain the said claims:

> "The observance of Sunday by the Protestants is an homage they pay in spite of themselves to the authority of the Catholic Church." *Plain Talk for* Protestants, 213. ~~~"Ques.—How prove you that the church hath power to command feasts and holy days? "Ans.—

446 Eusebius of Caesarea, *Catholic Encyclopedia.* (Albany, New York: Encyclopedia Press, 1909, 1913, 5:621.
447 Council of Laodicea, canon 29.

By the very act of changing the Sabbath into Sunday, which Protestants allow of, and therefore they fondly contradict themselves by keeping Sunday strictly, and breaking most other Feasts commanded by the same church. "Ques.—How prove you that? "Ans.—Because by keeping Sunday they acknowledge the Church's power to ordain feasts, and to command them under sin." *Douay Catechism*, 59. ~~~"If the Bible is the only guide for the Christian then the Seventh-day Adventist is right, in observing the Saturday with the Jew. . . . Is it not strange, that those who make the Bible their only teacher, should inconsistently follow in this matter the tradition of the Catholic Church?" *Question Box*, Ed. 1915, 179. ~~~"The Catholic Church for over one thousand years before the existence of a Protestant, by virtue of her divine mission, changed the day from Saturday to Sunday." *Catholic Mirror*, September 1893. ~~~ ". . . People who think that the scriptures should be the sole authority, should logically become 7th Day Adventists, and keep Saturday holy." *Saint Catherine Catholic Church Sentinel*, May 21, 1995. ~~~ "Of course the Catholic Church claims that the change was her act. . . . And the act is a MARK of her ecclesiastical authority in religious things" H. f. Thomas, Chancellor of Cardinal Gibbons.

With the transfer of the Biblical Sabbath to Sunday confirmed and fully admitted by the Catholic Church that it was "her act. . . . and the act is a MARK of her ecclesiastical authority in religious things," we now turn our attention to the religious circumstances that began in the court of Constantine. Taken from the primary sources of Eusebius, Bishop of Caesarea, on the life of Constantine, we will exhibit a number of brief references by Cameron and Hall that will establish the full recognition from the state on the observance of Sunday backed by the strong influence of Eusebius. Brackets {00} are for the original page numbering in Book IV of Eusebius' historical works of Constantine that we will be referencing. We need to focus only on the conditions laid down for Staff and Military personnel in regards to Sunday:

"**18** (1) He also decreed that the truly sovereign and really first day, the day of the Lord and Saviour, should be considered a regular day of prayer. Servants and ministers consecrated to God, men whose well-ordered life was marked by reverent conduct and every virtue, were put in charge of the whole household, and faithful praetorians, bodyguards armed with the practice of faithful loyalty, adopted the Emperor as their tutor in religious conduct, themselves paying no less honour to the Lord's saving day and on it joining in the prayers the Emperor loved.

(2) The Blessed One urged all men also to do the same, as if by encouraging this he might gently bring all men to piety. He therefore decreed that all those under Roman government should rest on the days named after the Saviour, and similarly that they should honour the days of the Sabbath, in memory, I suppose, of the things recorded as done by the universal Saviour on those days.

(3) The Day of Salvation then, which also bears the names of Light Day and Sun Day, he taught all the military to revere devoutly. {127} To those who shared the divinely given faith he allowed free time to attend unhindered the church of God, on the assumption that with all impediment removed they would join in the prayers. **19** To those who did not yet share in the divine Word he gave order in a second decree that every Lord's Day they should march out to an open space just outside the city, and that there at a signal they should all together offer up to God a form of prayer learnt by heart; they ought not to rest their hopes on spears or armour or physical strength, but acknowledge the God over all, the giver of all good and indeed of victory itself, to whom it was right to offer the lawful prayers, lifting up their hands high towards heaven, extending their mental vision yet higher to the heavenly King, and calling on him in their prayers as the Giver of victory and Saviour, as their Guardian and Helper. He was himself the instructor in prayer to all the soldiery, bidding them all to say these words in Latin:

20. (1) *'You alone we know as God,*

You are the King we acknowledge,
You are the Help we summon.
By you we have won our victories,
Through you we have overcome our enemies.
To you we render thanks for the good things past,
You also we hope for as giver of those to come.
To you we all come to supplicate for our Emperor
Constantine and for his Godbeloved Sons:
That he may be kept safe and victorious for us in long,
long life, we plead.'
(2) Such were the things he decreed should be done by the military regiments every Sunday, and such were the words he taught them to recite in their prayers to God. **21** Furthermore he caused the sign of the saving trophy to be marked on their shields, and had the army led on parade, not by any of the golden images, as had been their past practice, but by the saving trophy alone."[448]

We shall also include three small sections of the commentary of Eusebius by Cameron and Hall that help keep "Catholic Truth" in perspective regarding the previously stated comments of Eusebius:

"**18.2.** He therefore decreed . . . rest on the days named after the Saviour. In March 321 Constantine banned legal and similar business on "the venerable day of the Sun", while encouraging agricultural work to take advantage of the weather (CJ 3. 12. 2). Four months later, acts of emancipation of children and manumission of slaves, which could now be carried out in churches, were also exempted from the ban (CTh 2. 8. I; cf. Stevenson, NE 319). Neither text uses the Christian term 'the Lord's Day', as Eusebius implies. This passage repeats LC 9. 10, and cf. also SC 17. 14, with a very similar presentation of Constantine's role as Christian monarch (see Barnes, CE 249-50).
. . . the days of the Sabbath. Winkelmann, following Valesius, adds a word and reads *(pro) tou sabbatou*,

[448] Cameron, Averil, and Stuart G. Hall, trans. *Eusebius: Life of Constantine.* (Oxford: Clarendon Press, 1999), 159-160.

'the days *before* the Sabbath', on the basis of the fact
that Sozomen later adapts this passage and makes it
refer to resting from legal transactions on Fridays as
well as Sundays, in honour of the crucifixion of Jesus
on that day (Soz., *HE* 1. 8. 11-12; note *ten pro tes heb-
domes)*. There is no other record, however, of rest prescribed on Friday, the Christian fast-day, though
various exemptions down to Justinian in the sixth century relieved Jews of prosecution on the Sabbath. It is
better to keep the unanimous manuscript reading and
assume that Constantine repeated this exemption for
Jews in some form, and that Eusebius gives it a Christian interpretation, just as he interprets the legislation
about the pagan day of the Sun as explicitly Christian.
In contemporary Christian exegesis the rest [318] of
Jesus in the tomb on the Saturday between his crucifixion and his resurrection was taken as a fulfillment of
the Sabbath law and God's own Sabbath rest (Exod.
20:7); see further Hall, 'Some Constantinian Documents', 100-2.

. . . . **19-20.2.** he gave order in a second decree.
Constantine legislates that non-Christian soldiers should
be required to join in a common prayer every Sunday,
for which the wording is here given (20. I); Eusebius
refers to this instruction in more general terms at *LC* 9.
10. The phrase 'just outside the city' suggests that
Eusebius knows this only of the Constantinople garrison, and this fits the description of Constantine's ser-
monizing to the troops. Eusebius does not mind leaving
the impression that it was universal in the army. The
day *(dies solis)*, the hands extended to heaven, and the
address to God chiefly in terms of victories won indicate the cult of Sol Invictus, prominent both on
Constantine's coinage and in features of the vision of I.
28. Eusebius tries to excuse this to his Christian readers
by emphasizing that Constantine pointed the troops beyond heaven (and the sun), 'extending their mental vision yet higher to the heavenly King', who should be
regarded as the true giver of victory. . . ."[449]

---

[449] Ibid., 317-318.

Now with the union of church and state established in the fourth century, for the first time one can witness its maturity by the mass number of legal Imperial Edicts and Constitutions found in the Theodosian law code and the church canons, along with its progressive spirit of intolerance. By credible documentation we have sufficiently sustained the first three of the four steps to be taken, however, the work of Satan was not yet completed:

> "The archdeceiver had not completed his work. He was resolved to gather the Christian world under his banner and to exercise his power through his vicegerent, the proud pontiff who claimed to be the representative of Christ. Through half-converted pagans, ambitious prelates, and world-loving churchmen he accomplished his purpose. Vast councils were held from time to time, in which the dignitaries of the church were convened from all the world. In nearly every council the Sabbath which God had instituted was pressed down a little lower, while the Sunday was correspondingly exalted. Thus the pagan festival came finally to be honored as a divine institution, while the Bible Sabbath was pronounced a relic of Judaism, and its observers were declared to be accursed.

Some of those councils that were held from time to time pressed down the Sabbath a little lower, while the Sunday was correspondingly exalted. This took place after the ten horns came on the scene of action, fulfilling another specification of the prophecy regarding when the compulsion of the Sunday sabbath by the state would come to its climax. From 476 up to 538, the only significant canons by the church on Sunday worship are issued from 506 onward and are found in three church councils prior to 538. None forbid manual labor, and none called issue to the Sabbath as being a Jewish superstition supplanted by the church by the Christian observance of the Lord's Day. The first canon, in 506 at the council of Agde in Southern Gaul, reads thus:

> "Canon 47. On Sundays all laymen must be present at the whole Mass, so that they are not allowed to

depart before the blessing. If, nevertheless, they do so, they shall be publicly censured by the bishop."[450]

Two canons came from the first synod of Orleans I in A.D. 511.

"Canon 26. The people must not leave the church before the end of Mass [on Sunday]; and if a bishop is present, they shall first receive the blessing from him."[451]
"Canon 31. A bishop, unless he is ill, must not fail in attendance at divine service on Sunday in the church which lies nearest to him."[452]

The third canon, from the council of Tarragonin in A.D. 516, referred to nothing more than cases of Christians being heard in the ecclesiastical courts of the church on Sunday.

"Let not any bishop or presbyter or any of the inferior clergy hear causes on the Lord's Day, etc., . . . but let them be occupied in the performance of the solemnities ordained in honor of God."[453]

Nothing else found by this author in an extensive search meets the criteria regarding the Sabbath in the compelling of the conscience or labor being forbidden after A.D. 476 except for the twenty-eighth canon from the church synod at Orleans III in A.D. 538, which we will examine shortly.

However, the contempt for Judaism and the Biblical Sabbath among the Catholic hierarchy is verified from the following:

---

[450] Charles Joseph Hefele, *A History of the Councils of the Church* (Edinburgh: T.and T., 1895), 4:84.
[451] Ibid., 4:91.
[452] Ibid., 4:92.
[453] Ibid., 4:102-6.

"Let the fasting on Friday be extended, lest we should appear to observe any Sabbath with the Jews, which Christ, himself the Lord of the Sabbath, says by his prophets that 'his soul hateth;" which Sabbath he in his body abolished."[454]

Ellen White continues with the narration of Satan's warfare against the government of God:

"The great apostate had succeeded in exalting himself "above all that is called God, or that is worshiped." 2 Thessalonians 2:4. He had dared to change the only precept of the divine law that unmistakably points all mankind to the true and living God. In the fourth commandment, God is [54] revealed as the Creator of the heavens and the earth, and is thereby distinguished from all false gods. It was as a memorial of the work of creation that the seventh day was sanctified as a rest day for man. It was designed to keep the living God ever before the minds of men as the source of being and the object of reverence and worship. Satan strives to turn men from their allegiance to God, and from rendering obedience to His law; therefore he directs his efforts especially against that commandment which points to God as the Creator.

Protestants now urge that the resurrection of Christ on Sunday made it the Christian Sabbath. But Scripture evidence is lacking. No such honor was given to the day by Christ or His apostles. The observance of Sunday as a Christian institution had its origin in that "mystery of lawlessness" (2 Thessalonians 2:7, R.V.) which, even in Paul's day, had begun its work. Where and when did the Lord adopt this child of the papacy? What valid reason can be given for a change which the Scriptures do not sanction?

In the sixth century the papacy had become firmly established. Its seat of power was fixed in the imperial

---

[454] Ante-Nicene Library, 18:390, "On the Creation of the world." J. N. Andrews—L. R. Conradi, *History Of the Sabbath*, (Washington, DC, Review & Herald Publishing Association, 1912), 473.

city, and the bishop of Rome was declared to be the head over the entire church. Paganism had given place to the papacy. The dragon had given to the beast "his power, and his seat, and great authority." Revelation 13:2. And now began the 1260 years of papal oppression foretold in the prophecies of Daniel and the Revelation. Daniel 7:25; Revelation 13:5-7."[455]

From this overview, we are brought to the climax of this warfare against the government of God when, according to Ellen White, the papacy had become firmly established in the sixth century. This then brings us to the fourth step which is described in detail in our final segment. This fourth step signaled the commencement of the 1260-day/year prophetic period.

---

[455] Ellen White, *The Great Controversy*, (Nampa, ID: Pacific Press, 1911), 53-4.

10

A.D. 538

Justinian, the first Catholic Emperor in 62 years to have subdued and reclaimed Rome, established his legal jurisdiction in the west for the first time since the fall of western Rome in A.D. 476. With Rome known to the world at that time as "the capital of the world,"[456] Justinian dethroned the Ostrogoths, the last of those three Arian governments who held to the principle of religious liberty. Justinian's legal jurisdiction included a Sunday law legislated throughout all of Christendom in A.D. 538. With the MARK of the Catholic Church's ecclesiastical authority then enforced, church and state openly defied the God of heaven and earth.

Church and state, once united, issued numerous religious edicts and boycotts with legislation permitting the confiscation of personal property, wills, and inheritance, exile, the burning of books and death. Many of these laws we have already reviewed. The three Arian kingdoms that we have seen experienced all the above and more and were also deprived of their legal code of religious liberty. Humanity was now to experience tyranny at its worst and the crowning act, according to the scriptures, was a vertical assault directed heavenward by the little horn. It was a frontal attack against the government of God by the little horn, urged on by its leader Satan:

---

[456] Scott, S. P., trans., ed. *The Civil Law* [of Justinian] (Union, NJ: Lawbook Exchange, 2001), Codex I. 17. 10. 12:92.

Daniel 8:24 "And his [the little horn] power shall be mighty, <u>but not by his own power</u>: and he shall destroy wonderfully, and shall prosper, and practise, and shall destroy the mighty and the holy people."

Satan's blueprint has always been one and the same, to overthrow the law of God:

"From the very beginning of the great controversy in heaven it has been Satan's purpose to overthrow the law of God. It was to accomplish this that he entered upon his rebellion against the Creator, and though he was cast out of heaven he has continued the same warfare upon the earth. To deceive men, and thus lead them to transgress God's law, is the object which he has steadfastly pursued. Whether this be accomplished by casting aside the law altogether, or by rejecting one of its precepts, the result will be ultimately the same. He that offends "in one point," manifests contempt for the whole law; his influence and example are on the side of transgression; he becomes "guilty of all." James 2:10.

In seeking to cast contempt upon the divine statutes, Satan has perverted the doctrines of the Bible, and errors have thus become incorporated into the faith of thousands who profess to believe the Scriptures. The last great conflict between truth and error is but the final struggle of the long-standing controversy concerning the law of God. Upon this battle we are now entering—a battle between the laws of men and the precepts of Jehovah, between the religion of the Bible and the religion of fable and tradition."[457]

Satan's human agents simply follow their leader, and their aim has always been one and the same, as well: to overthrow the law of God:

Proverbs 28:4 "They that forsake the law praise the wicked: but such as keep the law contend with them."

[457] Ellen White, *The Great Controversy*, (Nampa, ID: Pacific Press, 1911), 582.

The contrast is revealed by those that keep his commandments, for they alone will have the right to the tree of life and will be permitted to enter in through the gates into the holy city:

> Revelation 22:14 "Blessed *are* they that do his commandments, that they may have right to the tree of life, and may enter in through the gates into the city."

As we have previously seen, "time" must be given for Satan to develop the principles which were to be the foundation of his government, the government of force:

> "Time must be given for Satan to develop the principles which were the foundation of his government. The heavenly universe must see the principles which Satan declared were superior to God's principles, worked out. God's order must be contrasted with the new order after Satan's devising. The corrupting principles of Satan's rule must be revealed. The principles of righteousness expressed in God's law must be demonstrated as unchangeable, eternal, perfect."[458]

To find that time allotment given to Satan to demonstrate his oppressive government to the entire universe, we turn to the scriptures, for the account is given there:

> Daniel 7:25 "And he shall speak *great* words against the most High, and shall wear out the saints of the most High, and think to change times and laws: and they shall be <u>given</u> into his hand until a time and times and the dividing of time."

> Revelation 13:5 "And there was given unto him a mouth speaking great things and blasphemies; and power was <u>given</u> unto him to continue forty *and* two months."

---

[458] Ellen White, *Manuscript Releases*, (Silver Spring, Maryland: E.G. White Estate, 1993), 18:361.

John 19:11 "Jesus answered, Thou couldest have no power *at all* against me, except it were <u>given</u> thee from above: therefore he that delivered me unto thee hath the greater sin."

The commencement of the time that heaven granted to Satan to reveal the nature of his government of force for 1260 long years is found in Daniel chapter 8. However, our specifics here will require only a few clauses taken from Daniel chapter 8:

Daniel 8:12 "And it cast down the truth to the ground; and it practised, and prospered."

There are two major clues that determine the chronology of these last two phrases. The first is "the *truth*"[571] (*emeth*). Usage: AV—truth 92, true 18, truly 7, right 3, faithfully 2, assured 1, assuredly 1, establishment 1, faithful 1, sure 1, verity 1; 125 verses, 127 hits. What is the "truth" that the papacy cast down? Certainly it was the truth in the preceding verse concerning the "daily" ministry of Christ and the "place" of his sanctuary where Christ hears prayers and forgives sin that papal Rome cast down or obscured. But the Bible has a much wider and all-encompassing application in mind, for it says:

Ps. 119:142 "Thy righteousness is an everlasting righteousness, and thy law is the <u>truth</u>.[571]

The first clue is that the Bible says the "law is the truth." So why and by whose authority is the law of God introduced in Daniel 8:12? Before we confirm this, we must disclose the second clue that will then define the chronology of verse 12.

After the papacy "cast down the truth to the ground,"— cast down *the law of God*—(Daniel 8:12, thus proceeding in transgression in the fullest sense) the Bible says it "practised, and prospered." That is, for a time and times and the dividing of time or 1260 years. Daniel 7:25 confirms this when the little horn thinks to have changed the law of God:

"And he shall speak great words against the most High, and shall wear out the saints of the most High, and think to change times and laws: and they shall be given into his hand until a time and times and the dividing of time."

Let us remember that 'speaking' in prophecy is an action in progress that represents:

". . . The 'speaking' of the nation is the action of its legislative and judicial authorities."[459]

It was after the man of sin had thought to change times and laws (the law of God) that the Bible says he was to begin his reign and practice and prosper for "a time and times and the dividing of time." As we have seen, this was for 1260 long years. Now the government of Satan was to be displayed before the entire universe. Satan was represented by his earthly ambassador, the Bishop of Rome, who was led on to "destroy the mighty and the holy people" of God (Daniel 8:24).

Turning to an exposition on Daniel 8:12 by Ellen White, we will see how she perfectly mirrors the scriptural account. The italics is in part a direct quote from Daniel 8:12. Her exposition of the text under discussion shows that the law of God was to be cast down and trampled in the dust unimpeded throughout all of Christendom at a specific time in earth's history.

"Among the leading causes that had led to the separation of the true church from Rome was the hatred of the latter toward the *Bible Sabbath. As foretold by prophecy, the papal power cast down the truth to the ground. The law of God was trampled in the dust*, while the traditions and customs of men were exalted. The churches that were under the rule of the papacy were early compelled to honor the Sunday as a holy day. Amid the prevailing error and superstition, many, even of the true people of God, became so bewildered that

---

[459] Ellen White, *The Great Controversy*, (Nampa, ID: Pacific Press, 1911), 442.

while they observed the Sabbath, they refrained from labor also on the Sunday. But this did not satisfy the papal leaders. They demanded not only that Sunday be hallowed, but that the Sabbath be profaned; and they denounced in the strongest language those who dared to show it honor. It was only by fleeing from the power of Rome that any could obey God's law in peace."[460]

Here is the unparalleled statement by Ellen White that fully mirrors our Biblical application and interpretation of Daniel 8:12 as the last prophetic specification to be fulfilled that heaven declared would mark the beginning of the 1260-day/year prophetic period:

> "*The change in the fourth commandment exactly fulfills the prophecy.*"[461]

We now proceed by presenting to the reader the primary definitive historical sources that will sustain the foretold Biblical account of how the papacy orchestrated a universal Sunday law that was legislated throughout all of Christendom in the year A.D. 538. We have already established the fact that the Ostrogoths were uprooted from Rome on March 1, 538, and that Justinian was the first Catholic Emperor since A.D. 476 to have held legal jurisdiction in Rome by designating a prefect from the court to be governor of Rome.[462] With spring beginning the new calendar year, Pope Vigilius (537-555) was exuberant that the Catholic Emperor Justinian had reclaimed Rome by dethroning the Ostrogoths. Pope Vigilius wasted no time writing the following letter to his most beloved brother, Eutherus, in the same month of March in the year A.D. 538:

Letter II. of Vigilius still Pseudopope to Eutherius.

"He responds to the inquiries of Eutherius {with the consultations of Eutherius}.

[460] Ellen White, *The Great Controversy*, (Nampa, ID: Pacific Press, 1911), 65
[461] Ibid., 446
[462] Procopius, *De Bello. Gothico*, ed. De la Byzantine de Bonn., 101.

Vigilius to his most beloved brother * (Eutherus)
(a: Cod. Vatic. Palat. : Profuturus) Eutherius."

VII. The Roman Church is the leader of all the churches.

"For no one believing slightly, or knowing fully is it
doubtful, that the Roman Church is the foundation and
pattern of churches, from which no one of those believing correctly does not know that all churches of
leaders have taken up. In as much as although it is
proper that [33] there be equal election of all apostles,
nevertheless it has been conceded to blessed Peter that
he is preeminent to the others; whence he is also called
Cephas, because he is the head also of all the leading
apostles: and because he has preceded at the head, it is
necessary to follow in the members. Wherefore the holy
Roman Church consecrated deservedly by its voice of
the lord, and strengthed by the authority of the holy
fathers, holds primacy of all churches; and to it the
highest business of the bishops, and judgments, and
complaints, as much as also the greater questions of
the churches should always be referred as if to the head.
For also he who knows that he has been placed before
others, should not take it grievously that someone has
been preferred to him. For the church itself, which is
first, thus has believed that its own {property} must be
bestowed to the rest of the churches, so that they have
been called into the part of solicitude, not into the fullness of power. Whence that the judgment of all bishops
appealing the apostolic seat, and the business of all
greater cases, have been reserved for the same holy
seat is evident: especially when in all of these its advice
should be expected; if any of the priests has tried to
hinder the its way, he should know that he will return
the cases among the same holy seat not without danger
of his own honor. Given on the Kalends of March, when
Volusianus* (Vuilisiarius badly {written}. In the year
of the lord 538) and John very famous men were consuls."[463]

---

[463] Mansi, Joannes Dominicus. *Sacrorum Conciliorum: Nova, et
Amplissima Collec-tio*, bk. 9, facs. ed. Paris: Welter, 1902, 9:32-3.

In March of A.D. 538, Pope Vigilius makes known the position the Catholic Church holds over all of humanity and the authority the pope has over that universal church. On May 1, 538, we witnessed how Justinian clearly prohibited "the practice of unlawful religious rites," meaning, of course, that only the "one and true Catholic faith" was to be recognized among all of humanity as religious liberty was banned and made illegal in the west, as well. Procopius, in other writings, confirms that it was Justinian who ended religious freedom for the Arian Christians, and we believe he is here quoting Novel 67 that was issued on May 1, 538, which we just reviewed:

> "He [Justinian] seized the best and most fertile estates, and *prohibited the Arians from exercising the rites of their religion.*"[464]

In 538, Malalas recorded in the consular list a number of events that took place in that year, however, we will list just one:

> 84. "In the consulship of John the Cappadocian the Arians' Churches were confiscated."[465]

> "The Montanists, in 529, had burnt themselves in their own churches. Other heretics were given three months' grace. All magistrates and soldiers had to swear that they were Catholics. Arians had to be spared at

---

[464] Procopius, *The Secret History of the Court of Justinian* (Boston: IndyPublish.com, n.d.), 62.

[465] Jeffreys, Elizabeth, ed. *The Chronicle of John Malalas. A Translation by* Elizabeth Jeffreys, Michael Jeffreys, and Roger Scott. Melbourne: Australian Asso. for Byzantine Studies, 1986, 285.
John Malalas was a Byzantine chronicler that lived during the reign of Justinian. (A.D. 491-578). The three consular lists are these: (1) Theodor Mommsen, *Chronica Minora SAEC. IV.V.VI.VII* (Berlin: Verlag Hahnsche Buchhandlung (www.hahnsche-buchhandlung.de), vols. 1, 2, 3; 1892, 1894, 1898, respectfully; (2) Carl Frick, *Chronica Minora* (Leipzig: B. G. Teubneri, 1892); (3) Roger S. Bagnall, *Consuls of the Later Roman Empire* (Atlanta, GA: Scholars Press, 1987). See also Elizabeth Jeffreys, Brian Croke and Roger Scott, *Studies in John Malalas* (University of Sydney N.S.W.: Australian Association for Byzantine Studies, Department of Modern Greek, 1990), 143.

first for fear of reprisals by the Goths. But in 533
Justinian attacked the Vandals in Africa, and in 535 the
Ostrogoths of Italy. After victory their churches were
taken away; they were forbidden them, and baptism.
Their importance as conquerors disappeared and their
sects faded away."[466]

Then on May 7, 538, the Catholic Church takes her
boldest step yet in the history of her church councils. A
deliberate frontal attack on the law of God was witnessed
as all of Gaul came under an ecclesiastical Sunday law:

"THIRD SYNOD AT ORLEANS,
A.D. 538.

"The third Synod of Orleans, like the second, was
not merely a provincial Synod, since bishops of several
ecclesiastical provinces took part in it. The president
was the Metropolitan Lupus of Lyons, although the city
and diocese of Orleans did not belong to his province,
but to that of Sens. Besides him were present the
Metropolitans Pantagathus of Vienne, Leo of Sens,
Arcadius of Bourges, and Flavius of Rouen. The
Archbishop of Tours, Injurious, was represented by a
priest. The Acts were subscribed by nineteen bishops,
and seven priests as representatives of absentees. In
the subscription of Archbishop Lupus, the time of the
holding of the Synod is given as *Die Nonarum mensis
tertii, quarto post consulatum paulini junioris V.C. anno
27 regni Domini Childeberti Regis.* This indicates the
year 538, and probably the 7th of May, since in ancient
times it was common to begin the year with the 25th of
March. The assembled bishops declare their aim to be
the reestablishment of the old laws of the church and
the passing of new ones. This they accomplished in
thirty-three canons, many of which contain several ordinances."[467]

---

[466] Dom John Chapman, *Studies on the Early Papacy* (London: Sheed
and Ward, 1928), 222-3. Imprimatur.
[467] Charles Joseph Hefele, *A History of the Councils of the Church*
(Edinburgh: T. and T., 1895), 4:204–9.

It is significant that the third synod of Orleans, France, in AD 538, was not merely a provincial synod, meaning a local one, narrow or limited in scope. The bishops assembled on that date for the specific purpose of reestablishing the old laws and the passing of new ones. They produced thirty-three canons at this synod. Hefele paraphrases the twenty-eighth canon of the new laws of the church with little justice to the original Latin.

> "28. It is a Jewish superstition that it is unlawful to ride or drive on Sunday, or do anything for the decoration of house or person. But field labors are forbidden, so that people may be able to come to church and worship. If anyone acts otherwise, he is to be punished, not by the laity, but by the bishop."[468]

The original wording of the twenty-eighth canon, as it is translated from the original Latin document into fluent English, reads thus:

> "28. Whereas the people are persuaded that they ought not to travel on the Lord's day with the horses, or oxen and carriages, or to prepare anything for food, or to do anything conducive to the cleanliness of houses or men, things which belong to Jewish rather than Christian observances; we have ordained that on the Lord's day what was before lawful to be done may still be done. But from rural work, i.e., plowing, cultivating vines, reaping, mowing, thrashing, clearing away thorns or hedging, we judge it better to abstain, that the people may the more readily come to the churches and have leisure for prayers. If any one be found doing the works forbidden above, let him be punished, not as the civil authorities may direct, but as the ecclesiastical powers may determine."[469]

---

[468] Ibid., 4:208–9.

[469] Joannes Dominicus Mansi, *Sacrorum Conciliorum nova et amplissima collectio.* (A facsimile reproduction of the Florence edition of 1759; reprinted, rearranged, Catholic Church Councils, n.p.: 1901–1927), 9:19 (canon 28) (1902). Translated by A. H. Lewis, *A Critical History of Sunday Legislation* (New York: Appleton, 1888), 64. See also Binius, 2:496.

In these primary source documents of church law, there is irrefutable evidence of the compelling of the conscience by the church. The phrase "we have ordained" is of particular significance. Reasoning from the definition in *Webster's Dictionary*, "ordain" is "to decree, order, establish, enact or to appoint," so Sunday was ordained in direct opposition to the fourth commandment of the Law of God. Rural work was prohibited for the first time in concise detail, thus perfectly fulfilling the prediction of the prophet. Hefele then goes on to paraphrase canon thirty-three thus:

"No bishop may transgress these canons."[470]

The parallel is ironic. God wrote His Ten Commandments in stone, and the church, in this council, wrote her Sunday sabbath in figurative stone when she attested to its implacable intention. The year was A.D. 538 when those blasphemous words ascended unto heaven:

Daniel 7:25 "And he shall speak [by legislation] great words against the most High. . . ."

Ellen White further clarifies and confirms:

"The change in the fourth commandment exactly fulfills the prophecy. For this the only authority claimed is that of the church. Here the papal power sets itself above God."[471]

The power and extended authority of a church council may be better understood from Mary Ann Collins, a former Catholic Nun, under her remarks on Infallibility in reference to the *Catechism of the Catholic Church*, 891:

---

[470] Charles Joseph Hefele, *A History of the Councils of the Church* (Edinburgh: T. and T., 1895), 4:209. See also Joannes Dominicus Mansi, *Sacrorum Conciliorum nova et amplissima collectio.* (A facsimile reproduction of the Florence edition of 1759; reprinted, rearranged, Catholic Church Councils, 1901–1927), 9:20 (1902).
[471] Ellen G. White, *The Great Controversy*, (Nampa, ID: Pacific Press, 1911), 446.

"According to Roman Catholic doctrine, popes and Catholic Church councils are infallible. This means that whenever they make official declarations concerning matters of faith or morals, God supernaturally protects them from making errors. Infallibility applies to all Roman Catholic popes and church councils: past, present, and future."[472]

The source Mary Ann Collins referenced is hereby presented:

891 "The Roman Pontiff, head of the college of bishops, enjoys this infallibility in virtue of his office, when, as supreme pastor and teacher of all the faithful-who confirms his brethren in the faith he proclaims by a definitive act a doctrine pertaining to faith or morals. . . . The infallibility promised to the Church is also present in the body of bishops when, together with Peter's successor, they exercise the supreme Magisterium," above all in an Ecumenical Council.[473] When the Church through its supreme Magisterium [236] proposes a doctrine "for belief as being divinely revealed,"[474] and as the teaching of Christ, the definitions "must be adhered to with the obedience of faith."[475] This infallibility extends as far as the deposit of divine Revelation itself."[476] [477]

Now read the unchangeable fourth commandment, written in stone with the finger of God, reiterating the sanctity of the Seventh-day from creation, the true Lord's Day:

---

[472] Mary Ann Collins a Former Catholic Nun, *The Spirit of Roman Catholicism-What Lies Behind the Modern Public Image?* 2002, 31, note 17, PDF, Infallibility.
[473] 418 LG 25; cf. Vatican Council I: DS 3074.
[474] 419 DV10§2.
[475] 420 LG 25 §2.
[476] 421 Cf. LG 25.
[477] Infallibility, *Catechism of the Catholic Church·* (Liguori, Missouri, Liguori Publi-cations, 1994), No. 891, pgs. 235-6.

Exodus 20:8 "Remember the Sabbath day, to keep it holy."

Exodus 20:9 "Six days shalt thou labour, and do all thy work:"

Exodus 20:10 "But the seventh day *is* the Sabbath of the LORD thy God: *in it* thou shalt not do any work, thou, nor thy son, nor thy daughter, thy manservant, nor thy maidservant, nor thy cattle, nor thy stranger that *is* within thy gates:"

Exodus 20:11 "For *in* six days the LORD made heaven and earth, the sea, and all that in them *is*, and rested the seventh day: wherefore the LORD blessed the Sabbath day, and hallowed it."

The epitome of arrogance and stupidity is projected when any sinful, mortal man, church, or government has the audacity to change or alter any part of the law or government of the universe.

Nevertheless, the Pontifical government (Satan) challenges the entire world:

"Reason and sense demand the acceptance of one or the other of these alternatives; either Protestantism and the keeping holy of Saturday or Catholicity and the keeping holy of Sunday. Compromise is impossible."[478]

However, God himself is soon to confront the entire world over their acceptance or rejection of His universal government. In the soon-coming drama concerning his downtrodden law, this unrelenting battle with dire consequences will be between the laws of men and the precepts of Jehovah, between the religion of the Bible and the religion of fable and tradition. Compromise is impossible.:

Revelation 14:9 "And the third angel followed them, saying with a loud voice, If any man worship the

---

[478] Cardinal Gibbons, *Catholic Mirror*, December 23, 1893.

beast and his image, and receive *his* mark in his forehead, or in his hand,"

Revelation 14:10 "The same shall drink of the wine
of the wrath of God, which is poured out without mix-
ture into the cup of his indignation; and he shall be tor-
mented with fire and brimstone in the presence of the
holy angels, and in the presence of the Lamb:"

Revelation 14:11 "And the smoke of their torment
ascendeth up for ever and ever: and they have no rest
day nor night, who worship the beast and his image,
and whosoever receiveth the mark of his name."

Revelation 14:12 "Here is the patience of the
saints: here *are* they that keep the commandments of
God, and the faith of Jesus."

We have also witnessed that historians recognized
that important legislation was issued about Italy in 538
which established Justinian's judicial authority in the
west:

"Justinian was already speaking of Italy as entirely
under his arms,[479] already he was designating a prefect from the court as governor;"[480]

The primary documents from Justinian himself confirm that it was not December 10, 536, (when King
Vitiges abandoned Rome without a fight and Belisarius
simply went in and occupied Rome) that established
Justinian's judicial authority in the west. No, the deciding factor that would establish Justinian's judicial authority in the west would be the outcome of the first siege
of Rome that began on February 21, 537, and ended one
year and nine days later in a massive defeat of the
Ostrogoths on March 1, 538. It was the outcome of that
battle alone that secured for Justinian his judicial authority in the west. Novel 69, issued June 1, 538, confirms that

[479] Nov. 69, epil. (Mai 538).
[480] Procopius, *De Bello. Gothico*, ed. De la Byzantine de Bonn., 101.
  Diehl, Charles. *Justinien et la Civilization Byzantine au Vie Siècle.*
Paris: Ernest Leroux, 1901, 186.

this was the first time in 62 years that a Catholic Emperor had held legal jurisdiction in Italy:

EPILOGUE.

[266] "Therefore, as soon as Our Most Glorious Imperial Pretorian Prefects appointed throughout the extent of the entire Roman Empire receive notice of this law, they will publish it in all the departments of their government, that is in Italy, Libya, the Islands, the East, and Illyria; in order that all persons may know how greatly We have their interests at heart. We dedicate this law to God who has inspired Us to accomplish such great things, and who will recompense Us for having enacted this constitution for the security of Our subjects. It shall also be communicated to Our citizens of Constantinople.

Given at Constantinople, on the Kalends of June, during the twelfth year of the reign of Justinian, and the Consulate of John."[481]

We will now show the concluding oppressive litigation from Justinian's Codex III that secured for the papacy her universal Sunday law throughout all of Christendom that began in A.D. 538. We begin with Justinian's Sunday laws that were published in Codex III that were issued in A.D. 534:

TITLE XII.
CONCERNING FESTIVALS.

[275]
"*1. The Emperors Constantius and Maximian, and the Caesars, Severus and Maximian, to Verinus.*

As you ask, my dear Verinus, whether the same rule should be observed, so far as the times of appeal are concerned, that apply to the festivals established by Us to celebrate the occurrence of fortunate events, We

---

[481] Scott, S. P., trans., ed. *The Civil Law [of Justinian]*, 17 vols. Union, NJ: Lawbook Exchange, 2001, Justinian, *The Novels*-69, 16:266, June 1, 538.

are pleased to answer you that you should, where cases are appealed, observe the prescribed terms in their regular order, without the addition of days of this kind, for, under such circumstances, additions cannot be made to the observance of the days aforesaid.

2. *The Emperor Theodosius to Vicenus.*

Although it is lawful to manumit and emancipate on Sunday, other business or litigation cannot be attended to on that day. The harvest festival extends from the eighth day of the *Kalends* of July until the *Kalends* of August; and permission is given to institute proceedings in court from the *Kalends* of August until the tenth of the *Kalends* of September. The festival of the vintage lasts from the tenth of the *Kalends* of September until the *Ides* of October. We desire the Holy Festival of Easter, that of the Epiphany, and the birthday of Our Lord, as well as the seven days which precede, and the seven which follow, to be quietly observed; and anything which is done in violation of this provision shall be absolutely void.

3. *The Emperor Constantine to Elpidius.*

Let all judges, the people of cities, and those employed in all trades, remain quiet on the Holy Day of Sunday. Persons residing in the country, however, can freely and lawfully proceed with the cultivation of the fields; as it frequently happens that the sowing of grain or the planting of vines cannot be deferred to a more suitable day, and by making concessions to Heaven the advantage of the time may be lost.

Given on the *Nones* of March, during the Consulate of Crispus and Constantine, Consuls for the second time, 311.

[276]

4. *The Same to Severus.*

No judge shall presume to appoint festival-days by his own authority. Such festivals as a ruler establishes shall be called Imperial holidays, and therefore if they are deprived of the name they should also be deprived of the benefit.

Given during the Ides of April . . .

5. *The Emperors Valentinian, Valens, and Gratian to Olybrius.*

You must proceed with criminal and fiscal cases during the two months of festivals, that is to say, without any interruption.

(1) Hereafter, also, during these same days, examination shall be made of matters in which bakers are interested.

Given on the fourth of the *Nones* of May, during the Consulate of the Noble Prince Valentinian, 368.

6. *The Emperors Gratian, Valentinian, and Theodosius to Lucianus, Vicegerent of Macedonia.*

Every investigation of criminal matters shall be prohibited during the four days which precede the auspicious season of the ceremonies of Easter.

Given at Thessalonica, on the sixth of the *Kalends* of April, during the Consulate of Gratian, Consul for the sixth time, and Theadosius, Consul for the first time.

7. *The Emperors Valentinian, Theodosius, and Arcadius to Albinus,Urban Prefect.*

We order that all days shall be proper for the administration of justice, and that only those shall be considered holidays, which, during two festival months, the year seems to set apart for rest from labor; that is, the days of summer, in order to be better able to endure the heat; and those of autumn, for the purpose of gathering fruit. We also devote to leisure the days of the *Kalends* of January, which it is customary to observe for this purpose, and to these We add the days of the foundation of the great cities of Rome and Constantinople, during which the administration of justice should be suspended, because it owes its origin to them. We include in the same category the sacred day of Easter, and the seven which precede and follow it; the day of the Nativity, and that of the Epiphanies of Christ; and the time when the commemoration of the Apostolic Passion of all Christianity is properly celebrated by the entire world. During the above-mentioned most holy days, We do not permit any public exhibitions to be given. The day sacred to the sun, to which the ancients very properly gave the name of Sunday, which returns after a certain period of revolution, must also be respected, so that there shall be no investigation of legal disputes on that day, either before arbitrators or judges, whether they have been appointed or voluntarily chosen. This rule shall also apply to the days which We first saw the light, or which witnessed the origin of the Empire. During the fifteen days [277] of the celebration of Easter, compulsory distribution of provisions and the collection of all public and private obligations shall be postponed.

Given at Rome, on the second of the *Ides* of August, during the Consulate of Timasius and Promotus, 389.

8. *The* Same *to* Tatian, Praetorian *Prefect.*

All employments, whether public or private, shall be suspended during the fifteen days of the Festival of Easter; still, every person shall have the right of emancipation and manumission during that time, and any proceedings relating to them are not prohibited.

Given on the *Kalends* of January, under the Consulate of Arcadius, Consul for the second time, and Rufinus, 392.

9. *The Emperors Honorius and Theodosius to* Anthemius, *Praetorian Prefect.*

The Governors of provinces are notified that, so far as the torture of robbers, and especially of Isaurians is concerned, they must not think that any of the forty days of Lent, or the venerated Festival of Easter should be excepted, lest the betrayal of the designs of the criminals, which might be obtained by torture, may be deferred. This should the more readily be accomplished, as, during this time, there is greater hope of pardon by the Almighty, and the health and safety of many persons are secured.

Given at Constantinople, on the fifth of the *Kalends* of March, during the Consulate of Bassus and Philip, 408.

10. *The Emperors Leo* and *Anthemius to Armasius, Praetorian Prefect.*

We do not wish holidays dedicated to the majesty

of God to be employed in public exhibitions, or be profaned by any annoyances resulting from collections.

(1) Hence We decree that Sunday shall always be honored and respected, and exempt from all executions. No notice shall be served upon anyone; no security shall be exacted; bailiffs shall remain quiet; advocates shall cease to conduct cases, and this day shall be free from the administration of justice; the harsh voice of the public crier shall be silenced; litigants shall have a respite from their disputes, and enjoy the interval of a truce; adversaries may approach one another without fear; repentance will have an opportunity to occupy their minds, they can enter into agreements and discuss compromises. We do not permit persons who are at leisure during this sacred day to devote themselves to obscene pleasures; and no one shall then demand theatrical exhibitions, the contests of the circus, or the melancholy spectacle of wild beasts; and when Our birthday happens to fall on Sunday, its celebration shall be postponed. If anyone should think that upon this holiday he can venture to interest himself in exhibitions; or the subordinate of any judge, should, under the protest of any public or private business, violate the provisions of this law, he [278] shall suffer the loss of his employment and the confiscation of his property.

Given at Constantinople, on the *Ides* of September, during the Consulate of Zeno and Martian, 469."[482]

These were the codes of Sunday legislation that were enforced in the eastern Roman Empire. Please take special notice of Codex III. 12. 10. After Justinian revised his codex in the year A.D. 534, this code reveals the punishment for the violation of the Sunday sabbath as the loss of one's employment and the confiscation of one's property. However, let us not forget how Justinian's ecclesiastical legislation comes to fruition. From Codex I. 1. 4., we have read the letter by Justinian that he wrote to Pope John II on March 15, 533 as follows:

---

[482] Scott, S. P., trans., ed. *The Civil Law* [of Justinian] (Union, NJ: Lawbook Exchange, 2001), Codex III. 12. 1–10. 12:275–278.

"For we do not suffer anything which has reference to the state of the Church, even though what causes the difficulty may be clear and free from doubt, to be discussed without being brought to the notice of Your Holiness, because you are the head of all the Holy Churches, for We shall exert Ourselves in every way (as has already been stated), to increase the honor and authority of your See."[483]

Church and state legislation was very direct and needed no commentary:

"For it is certain that whatever differs from the Christian religion is opposed to the Christian law.[484]

"No one is ignorant of the fact that, in ancient Rome, legislation originally emanated from the head of the Pontificate. Hence We now deem it necessary to impose upon Ourselves the duty of showing that [66] We are the source of both secular and ecclesiastical jurisprudence by promulgating a law consecrated to the honor of God, which shall be applicable not only to this city but to all Catholic Churches everywhere, and exert its salutary vigor over them as far as the Ocean, so that the entire West as well as the East, where possessions belonging to Our churches are to be found, or may hereafter be acquired by them, shall enjoy its advantages. . . . This Our law, enacted in honor of Omnipotent God and the venerable See of the Apostle Peter, shall be observed in all lands of the entire West, and be applicable to the most distant islands of the Ocean; and Our solicitude for the subjects of Our Empire induces Us to declare it to be perpetual."[485]

There was nothing which has reference to the state of the Church in ecclesiastical matters that did not come first before the pope for approval. This procedure was already established when Justinian declared, "We shall exert Ourselves in every way," and was legally confirmed

---

[483] Ibid., Codex I. 1.4, 12:12.
[484] Ibid., Codex I. 9. 11. 12:77.
[485] Ibid., *The Novels*, 9. 16:65-66, April 14, 535.

by the legislative support from the state that the church canons received. Codex I.3.44 of Justinian's law codes, for example, was implemented on October 18, A.D. 530, thereby giving total authority to the canons of the synods.

"Whatever the holy canons prohibit, these also we by our own laws forbid."[486]

This codex alone was sufficient to elevate the laws of the church to equality with the laws of the state. Having been accorded this political backing, church canons had to be obeyed by all. This serves as the only explanation as to why the papacy claims that Justinian's Corpus Juris Civilis is the basis of all Roman Catholic canon law:

"So the immortal 'Corpus Juris Civilis' was produced. . . . It would be difficult to exaggerate the importance of this 'Corpus.' It is the basis of all canon law . . ."[487]

As Justinian continues to regulate church-sanctioned legislature, his standard protocol for implementing his jurisdiction in a newly conquered territory is seen from his Novel 37. 9., issued on August 1, 535:

"9. Furthermore we remit all the privileges of the sacrosanct church of our Carthago Justiniana which the metropolitan cities and their priests are recognized to have, which also even when separated from sacrosanct churches in his first book are recognized to offer their honor by our Codex: so that the city which we regarded should be decorated by the name of our divine will bloom while decorated also with imperial privileges."[488]

---

[486] Paul Krueger, *Corpus Iuris Civilis, Codex Iustinianus,* I.3.44 (decreed Oct.18, A.D. 530) (Berolini Apud Weidmannos, 1888), 2:30. See also Asterios Gerostergios, *Justinian The Great The Emperor And Saint* (Belmont, MA: Institute for Byzantine and Modern Greek Studies), 163-4.

[487] *Catholic Encyclopedia,* s.v. "Justinian I" (New York: Appleton, 1910), 8:579.

[488] Schoell, Rudolfus, *Corpus Iurus Civilis, Novellae,* (Berlin: Apud Wiedmannos, 1959), 3:244-5.

From Novel 37. 9., we see Justinian's authority implemented in the former Vandal province to, first and foremost, bring honor to his *"Codex"* so "the name of our divine will bloom while decorated also with imperial privileges." This was standard protocol for Justinian when he claimed legal jurisdiction of a newly conquered territory including the land occupied by the Ostrogoths of Italy.

From the following Codex law code that was published and in force in 534, we have Justinian himself affirming that all former laws of previous emperors that were "in favor of the orthodox faith shall be valid and in force in the future and are retained in force by the present pious legislation.":

Codex I. 2.12.
"We decree that the privileges conceded by former Emperors under the general terms of constitutions, to all the Holy Churches of the orthodox religion, shall be observed, and remain firm and unimpaired for all time."[489]

Codex I.11.9.3
"3. All the punishments which were introduced by former emperors against pagan error or in favor of the orthodox faith shall be valid and in force in the future and are retained in force by the present pious legislation."[490]

This especially applied to Justinian's Sunday Laws since all of them were from previous emperors. He wrote nothing of himself on this issue because for him it was already an established precedent of the orthodox faith that was not to be contested. It just simply needed to be enforced. Codex I. 2.12. and Codex I.11.9.3 is the legal proclamation that gave Justinian the legal basis for the enforcement of his Sunday laws which had been estab-

[489] Scott, S. P., trans., ed. *The Civil Law* [of Justinian] (Union, NJ: Lawbook Exchange, 2001), Codex I. 2.12. 12:18.
[490] Paul Krueger, Corpus Iuris Civilis, Codex Iustinianus, (Berolini Apud Weidman-nos, 1888), 2:63-4. Greek text.

lished by previous emperors and were to be found in his subsequent Codex III.12.1-10. Justinian stated that they "are retained in force by the present pious legislation." This legislation was never altered or retracted in any way from 534 to the end of Justinian's reign in 565. Justinian's subjects, from 538 and onward, whether from the east or from the west, all had to observe and reverence the papal sabbath, the first day of the week, or suffer loss of employment, confiscation of property and perhaps even death itself. This proves that Justinian's Sunday laws were part of the enforced jurisdiction implemented in Italy on June 1, 538. With small beginnings in the west, Sunday enforcement was in full swing in the east. However, by the end of the year 538 and just ten days into the New Year, Justinian's jurisdiction was declared by Justinian himself to encompass Italy, the entire West and those of both Romes, meaning Rome and Constantinople:

BEFORE WHOM THE CASES OF MONKS AND AS-
CETICS SHALL BE TRIED.

SEVENTY-NINTH NEW CONSTITUTION.

CHAPTER II.

CONCERNING THE ENFORCEMENT AND
OBSERVANCE OFTHIS CONSTITUTION AND THE
DETERMINATION OF THE LEGAL CONTROVER-
SIES IN WHICH MONKS ARE CONCERNED.

"Litigation in which monks are involved shall be speedily disposed of. This law is of general application, and its enforcement shall be committed to the Most Glorious Prefects having jurisdiction in all dioceses, namely: those of Illyria, Italy, the entire West and those of both Romes, as well as by the Most Glorious Praetors of the People, and the magistrates of the provinces, with their subordinates; and it shall not be evaded in any way but must be observed unchanged for the honor of the most reverend monks."[491]

[491] Scott, S. P., trans., ed. *The Civil Law [of Justinian]*, 17 vols. Union, NJ: Lawbook Exchange, 2001, Justinian, *The Novels*-79, 16:294-5,

The year was AD 538. The entire then-known world of Christendom was under a universal Sunday law just as the scriptures predicted and as Pope Vigilius is to confirm. With the biggest threat of opposition removed and believing that the ongoing threat of war was also removed, the Roman populace was delighted in the uniting of the old empire as one again under one religion. Pope Vigilius (537-555), writes to Justinian on Sept. 17, 540, the following letter of praise for establishing the one and only true faith *"in every corner of the world"*:

> "We have noted in the letter of Your Clemency . . . that you do not permit any differences, any discordance in the Christian faith which honors and worships the Divine Trinity. . . . Not the least of our satisfaction in the Lord is to see that He deigned in his mercy to give you not only an imperial, but a priestly soul. In offering the sacrifice according to ancient tradition, all pontiffs pray that the Lord may deign to unify the Catholic faith and preserve it throughout the world. This Your Piety effected with all possible strength, when you imposed in all your provinces and in every corner of the world the inviolate maintenance of that faith which we know was defined and imposed as Christian confession by the most venerable Synods of Nicaea, Constantinople, the First of Ephesus, and Chalcedon, and when you refused to call Christian whoever severs himself from the unity of those Synods. . . ."[492]

H.F. Thomas, Chancellor of Cardinal Gibbons, correctly states:

---

[492] Guenther, Otto, *Epistulae Imperatorum Pontificum Aliorum, Avellana Quae Dicitur Collectio*, 2 pts. In *Corpus Scriptorum Ecclesiasticorum Latinorum*, vol. 35. Prague: F. Tempsky, 1895, (ep. 92), 348, Sept. 17, 540.

Mansi, Joannes Dominicus. *Sacrorum Conciliorum: Nova, et Amplissima Collectio*, facs. ed. Paris: Welter, 1902, 9:35.

Translatation: Dvornik, Francis. *Early Christian and Byzantine Political Philosophy*, (Washington, DC: Dumbarton Oaks Ctr. for Byz. Studies, 1966), 2:822.

"Of course the Catholic Church claims that the change was her act." He goes on to say, "And the act is a MARK of her ecclesiastical authority in religious things." The Universal Sunday law throughout Christendom in 538 was simply the catalyst or the Mark of her ecclesiastical authority which signaled that the Pontifical government of force or, more accurately stated, the government of Satan, was then fully underway and thereby commenced the 1260 prophetic period in A.D. 538. Previously divorced from Christ, no longer widowed, but married to the state, the Catholic Church was "given" a specified time of 1260 long years-to "practice and prosper." What a witness to the universe of the "new order" of Satan's rule! You cannot have a Sunday law without first denying religious liberty and this is the real issue behind the Sunday law.

> "The man of sin thinks to change times and laws. He is exalting himself above God, in trying to *compel the conscience*."[493]

In AD 538 we now have a perfect application of 2 Thessalonians 2:4:

> "The archdeceiver had not completed his work. He was resolved to gather the Christian world under his banner and to exercise his power through his vicegerent, the proud pontiff who claimed to be the representative of Christ. Through half-converted pagans, ambitious prelates, and world-loving churchmen he accomplished his purpose. Vast councils were held from time to time, in which the dignitaries of the church were convened from all the world. In nearly every council the Sabbath which God had instituted was pressed down a little lower, while the Sunday was correspondingly exalted. Thus the pagan *festival* came finally to be honored as a divine institution, while the Bible Sabbath was pronounced a relic of Judaism, and its observers were declared to be accursed. The great

---

[493] Ellen White, *Review and Herald*, December 24, 1889.

apostate had succeeded in *exalting himself* 'above all
that is called God, or that is worshiped.' 2 Thessalonians 2:4. He had dared to change the only precept of
the divine law that unmistakably points all mankind to
the true and living God. In the fourth commandment,
God is revealed as the Creator of the heavens and the
earth, and is thereby distinguished from all false gods.
It was as a memorial of the work of creation that the
seventh day was sanctified as a rest day for man. It was
designed to keep the living God ever before the minds
of men as the source of being and the object of reverence and worship. Satan strives to turn men from their
allegiance to God, and from rendering obedience to
His law; therefore he directs his efforts especially
against that commandment which points to God as the
Creator."[494]

Please notice that the prophet uses the term "festival," the very term used by Justinian in the original
source for the heading of his Sunday laws. The original
source reads thus:

THE CODE OF JUSTINIAN, BOOK III. 12, 10.
TITLE XII.
CONCERNING FESTIVALS.

"And thou shalt be called, The repairer of the
breach. . . . Now we have to understand what the
breach is. Look at the fourth commandment. . . . Here
comes a power under the control of Satan that puts up
the first day to be observed. God calls him the man of
sin because he has *perpetuated transgression* [*Daniel
8:12*]."[495]

For those who would like to look further into the concepts of "exalt," "magnify," and "truth" in their very close
relationship to the law of God, we suggest a study of those

---

[494] Ellen White, *The Great Controversy*, (Nampa, ID: Pacific Press,
1911), 53–4
[495] Ellen White, *Manuscript Releases* (Silver Spring, Maryland: E.G.
White Estate, 1993), 5:45.

words in the context of Daniel 7:25; 8:11–12; 11:36–37;
and of 2 Thessalonians 2:4, 10, 12.

Having fully sustained and illustrated by the definitive primary sources every specification of the scriptures
pertaining to the identity, nature and commencement of
the 1260-day/year prophetic period, we rest our case.

Nevertheless, there is still a need to see the beast
power in all her infamous glory. This may be witnessed
further by Justinian's legislation that encompassed every
social, religious and private aspect of his subjects. The
following edict against homosexuality in 538 demon-
strates this point well, for homosexuality was sweeping
over the empire. However, Justinian understood correctly from the scriptures "that both cities as well as men
have perished because of wicked acts of this kind.":

MEN SHALL NOT COMMIT THE CRIME AGAINST
NATURE, NOR SWEAR BY GOD'S HEAD, OR ANY-
THING OF THIS KIND, NOR SHALL THEY BLAS-
PHEME GOD.

SEVENTH-SEVENTH NEW CONSTITUTION.

PREFACE.

[288] "We think that it is clear to all men of good
judgment that Our principal solicitude and prayer is,
that those who have been entrusted to Us by God may
live properly, and obtain Divine favor. And as God does
not desire the perdition of men, but their conversion
and salvation, and as He receives those who, having
committed sin, have repented, We invite all Our subjects to fear God and invoke His clemency, for We
know that all those who love the Lord and are deserving of His pity do this.

CHAPTER I.

Therefore, as certain persons, instigated by the
devil, devote themselves to the most reprehensible
vices, and commit crimes contrary to nature, We
hereby enjoin them to fear God and the judgment to
come, to avoid diabolical and illicit sensuality of this

kind;[496] in order that, through such acts, they may not
incur the just anger of God, and bring about the destruction of cities along with their inhabitants; for We
learn from the Holy Scriptures that both cities as well
as men have perished because of wicked acts of this
kind.

(1) And as, in addition to those who commit these
offences which We have mentioned, there are others
who utter blasphemous words, and swear by the sacraments of God, and provoke Him to anger, We enjoin
them to abstain from these and other impious
speeches, and not swear by the head of God, or use
other language of this kind. For if blasphemy when uttered against men is not left unpunished, there is much
more reason that those who blaspheme God himself
should be deserving of chastisement. Therefore We
order all men to avoid such offences, to have the fear
of God in their hearts, and to imitate the example of
those who live in piety; for as crimes of this description
cause famine, earthquake, and pestilence, it is on this
account, and in order that men may not lose their
souls, that We admonish them to abstain from the per-
petration of the illegal acts above mentioned. But if,
after Our warning has been given, anyone should continue to commit these offences, he will in the first place
render himself unworthy of the mercy of God, and will
afterwards be subjected to the penalties imposed by
the laws.

[289] (2) We order the Most Glorious Prefect of this
Royal City to arrest any persons who persist in committing the aforesaid crimes, after the publication of
Our warning; in order that this city and the State may
not be injured by the contempt of such persons and
their impious acts, and inflict upon them the punishment of death. If, after the publication of this law, any
magistrates should become aware of such offences,
and not take measures to punish them, they shall be

[496] This was considered by the Romans as well as by modern legisla-
tors as one of the most odious and reprehensible of crimes. *"Peccata
contra naturam sunt gravissima."*-ED.

condemned by God. And even if the Most Glorious
Prefect himself should find any persons doing anything
of this kind, and not punish them in accordance with
Our laws, he will, in the first place, be subjected to the
judgment of God, and afterwards sustain the weight of
Our indignation."[497]

Now only into the second month of the New Year of
539, Justinian decrees that no private person shall make,

---

[497] The Canon Law treated the crime of blasphemy, which it defined
as the uttering of curses and insults against God, Christ, the Virgin
Mary, or the Saints:

*"Quicunque Deo palam, 8eu publice maledixerit, contumeliosisque
ac obscaenis verbis Dominum nostrum Iesum Christum, vel gloriosam
Virginem Mariam eius Genitricem expresse blasphemauerit,"* with
great severity. Ecclesiastics were temporarily or permanently deprived of their livings, and rendered incapable of-reinstatement.
Members of the laity were heavily fined, and might be imprisoned for
life, or sentenced to the galleys. Sometimes they were compelled to
stand for an entire day before the principal door of the church wear-
ing a paper mitre, m*itra infamis,* as a token of disgrace. Secular
judges who were remiss in prosecuting offenders rendered themselves liable to the same penalties. *(Corpus Juris Canonici* VII, *Decret*
V, VIII.)

Every hierarchy has naturally legislated against blasphemy as
being an attack upon the foundation of its authority. It was a capital
offence among the Hebrews: "And he that blasphemeth the name of
the Lord, he shall surely be put to death, and all the congregation
shall certainly stone him; as well the stranger, as he that is born in the
land, when he blasphemeth the name of the Lord;, shall be put to
death." (Leviticus XXIV, 16.)

The old Castilian Codes in this, as in many other instances, regu-
lated the punishment in accordance with the rank and wealth of the
culprit. A nobleman forfeited the use of his land for a year for the first
offence, for two years for the second, and for all time for the third.
Similar penalties were imposed upon vassals. Citizens were heavily
fined and banished. Those belonging to the lowest order of the people
were scourged, branded on the lips, or condemned to have their
tongues amputated. *"E si fue're otro 0me de los menores que non ayan
nada, por la primera vez denle cinquenta acotes, por la segunda
seinalenle con fierro caliente en los becos, que sea fecho a semejanca de
B. E. por la tercera vegada quo lo faga, cortenle La lengua." (Las Siete
Partidas* VII, XXVIII, II.)

(*Cont.*)

Blasphemy was an indictable offence at Common Law, punishable by fine and imprisonment; "as Christianity is part of the laws of England." The first prosecution for it was instituted in 1617, during the reign of James I, before justices of the peace; but the case was dismissed, after reference to the Attorney General, for want of jurisdiction. (*Vide* Archbold, Criminal Procedure II, Page 209.) In England, the publication of heretical doctrines was long considered as inferentially blasphemous, and the writings of their advocates as libels. Political considerations were always more or less involved in those accusations, as the king was the head of the Church, and the promulgation of false religious dogmas was considered a blow at his supremacy. The penalty, while often severe, was not always as drastic as might seem justifiable under such circumstances. As late as 1812, a man convicted of blasphemy was sentenced by Lord Ellenborough to stand in the pillory for two hours every month, during eighteen months.

The offence is described by a leading English authority as follows: "A wilful intention to pervert, insult, and mislead others by means of contumelious abuse applied to sacred subjects, or by wilful misrepresentations and artful sophistry calculated to mislead the ignorant and unwary, is the criterion and test of guilt." (Starkie on Libel, Page 593.) This is the basis of the American doctrine that the feelings of the hearers must be respected. The penalty is excommunication and imprisonment for not more than six months.

Scotch law punished the blasphemer capitally, if he remained recalcitrant. "Blasphemy, Railers against God, or any of the Persons of the blessed Trinity, shall be likewise punishable by death, if they obstinately continue therein." (Mackenzie, The Laws and Customes of Scotland in Matters Criminal III, V.) The penalties now are mere imprisonment or fine, or both, at the discretion of the court. The offence includes atheism. (*Vide* Erskine, Principles of the Laws of Scotland IV, IV, 7.)

Blasphemy, concisely defined by Kent as "maliciously reviling God or religion," has a more limited application in the United States than elsewhere, in general. "The weight of authority is that blasphemy is only indictable when uttered in such a way as to insult the religious convictions of those at whom it is aimed. The gist of the offense is the insult to the religious sense of individuals, irrespective of the truth of those religious views or the extent of their prevalence." (Wharton, A Treatise on Criminal Law, Page 2121.)

The German Code prescribes a term of imprisonment, not exceeding three years, upon anyone convicted of blasphemy. (*Strafgesetzbuch fur das Deutsche Reich*, Art. 166.) The penalty in Austria is imprisonment for from one to ten years (*Allgemeines Strafgesetz*, Art. 123); in Spain, it is for one year, a month and twenty-one days, to a buy, sell, or own arms. Undoubtedly, Justinian remembers the Nika Revolt of 532 and the difficulties in 536 as he tried to put a check on the abounding iniquity in the streets of his empire. Yet, the following decree certainly goes well beyond that as the "new order" obviously had an agenda all of its own. The regime has put down all opposition and it is determined to keep it down:

CONCERNING ARMS.

EIGHTY-FIFTH NEW CONSTITUTION.

PREFACE.

[314] "Always invoking the aid of Omnipotent God and Our Saviour Jesus Christ, We exert every effort to preserve from all injury and calumny the subjects whose government God has entrusted to Us, and to prohibit the wars which men privately conduct against one another; for, by means of these wars, they cause much reciprocal suffering and are exposed to the double penalty of mutual injury, as well as of undergoing the punishment prescribed by the laws.

CHAPTER I.

Therefore, desiring to prevent men from killing each other, We have thought it proper to decree that no private person shall engage in the manufacture of weapons, and that only those shall be authorized to do so who are employed in the public arsenals, or are called armorers; and also that manufacturers of arms should not sell them to any private individual.

(Cont.)

year and two months, and a fine of from 250 to 2500 *pesetas (Godigo Penal de Espana,* Art. 240); in Italy, the penalty is detention for not more than one year, and a fine of 100 to 3000 *lire (Codice Penale del Regno d'Italia,* Art. 141); in Denmark, it is imprisonment for one month, and, where aggravating circumstances exist, a fine in addition *(Almendelig Straffelov,* Sec. 156).-ED.

Scott, S. P., trans., ed. *The Civil Law [of Justinian],* 17 vols. Union, NJ: Lawbook Exchange, 2001, Justinian, *The Novels-*77, 16:288-290, N.A., 538.

Nor do We permit any persons who, styled *deputati*, are enrolled in the army for the purpose of caring for the arms and are paid out of the Treasury, to manufacture or sell them to anyone whomsoever; but We desire that they shall only have charge of the arms of soldiers, in accordance with the duties assigned to them. If, however, they should manufacture any new weapons, these shall be taken from them, and either deposited in Our Imperial arsenal or in the armory.

CHAPTER II.

We also desire that those who are called *ballistarii*, and whom We have stationed in different cities, and authorized to manufacture weapons, shall only repair and place in good condition those belonging to the government, which are deposited in the public arsenals of each town. Where any workmen have manufactured arms they must surrender them to the *ballistarii*, to be placed with those belonging to the public, but they must by no means sell them to anyone else. The *ballistarii* shall, at the risk of the municipal magistrates of the cities to whom they are subject, observe what We have decreed, and the responsibility for this, as well as for the preservation of the public arsenals, shall attach to these magistrates; and where any of the workmen called *deputati*, or armorers, have been detected in selling weapons, the local magistrates shall subject them to punishment; shall deprive the purchasers of these weapons without refunding the price paid for them; and shall claim them for the benefit of the public.

CHAPTER III.

Therefore, God directing Our thoughts, We decree by the present law that no private individual, or anyone else whosoever shall, in any province or city of Our Empire, have the right to make or sell arms, or deal in them in any way, but only such as are authorized to manufacture them can do so, and deposit them in Our armory.

[315] We order that this rule shall be obeyed by Your Highness, as well as by those who may succeed you in

office, and We appoint five of the chief chartularies
subject to your authority in the Bureau of Armorers,
who are skillful and of good repute, who shall be
charged on their own responsibility to seek men who
are manufacturing arms in this Most Fortunate City,
and in the other towns of Our Empire, in order to prevent private persons, or anyone else whomsoever, from
doing so, with the exception of workmen employed by
the armory; and in order that, if they should find, anywhere in any place, private individuals who are rash
enough to make any weapons, they may seize them
and deposit them in the Arsenal of the Treasury. But if
among private workmen the said chartularies should
discover any persons who are thoroughly skilled in
their trade, they shall employ them in the manufacture
of arms, if the workmen are willing, and shall inscribe
their names upon the list of armorers, and notify Us of
this fact, in order that the said workmen may be assigned by an Imperial Rescript to the Public Arsenal,
for the purpose of manufacturing arms, and receive remuneration from the Treasury. If the aforesaid persons
scrupulously comply with what We have ordered, private individuals residing in towns, or peasants who are
living in the country, will not be permitted to make use
of arms against one another, thereby endangering their
lives; men will cease to commit homicide; work on
public buildings will not be suspended; and the fear of
death will no longer compel the cultivators of the soil
to resort to flight.

(1) Therefore those selected from the above-mentioned Bureau of Armorers, who are directed by Your
Highness to prevent private persons from making
weapons, shall be sworn by the local magistrates, their
subordinates, the defenders of towns, and decurions,
that they will allow nothing which We have forbidden
to take place in the future, and that they will comply
with the provisions of the present law, for the said
magistrates will be liable to a pecuniary penalty, as
well as a corporeal one, if they should violate it.

We order that, if the judge of the great City of
Alexandria should fail to observe these provisions, he
shall be liable to a fine of twenty pounds of gold, and

shall be deprived of his office. His court shall also incur a similar penalty, as well as be subjected to capital punishment. So far as the magistrates of other provinces are concerned, they, together with their courts, shall incur a fine of ten pounds of gold and the loss of their offices. The defenders of municipal magistrates of cities shall pay a fine of three pounds of gold, and run the risk of being put to death if, after having learned of violations of this law, they permit them to remain concealed instead of punishing them, or notifying magistrates who can do so.

CHAPTER IV.

But in order that what has been forbidden by Us to private persons and all others may become clear, We have taken pains to enumerate in this law the different kinds of weapons whose manufacture is forbidden. Therefore We prohibit private individuals from either [316] making or buying bows, arrows, double-edged swords, ordinary swords, weapons usually called hunting knives, those styled *zabes*, breast-plates, javelins, lances and spears of every shape whatever, arms called by the Isaurians *monocopia*, others called *sitinnes*, or missiles, shields, and helmets; for We do not permit anything of this kind to be manufactured, except by those who are appointed for that purpose in Our arsenals, and only small knives which no one uses in fighting shall be allowed to be made and sold by private persons.

Your Highness will publish this general law in this Royal City, as well as in the other cities of Our Empire, in order that all persons, being aware of the provisions which We have been pleased to enact, may observe them.

CHAPTER V.

We notify the chartularies who have been appointed from the aforesaid Bureau of Armorers personally to see that this law is obeyed, for their negligence will not only expose them to pecuniary penalties, but they will also be subjected to corporeal punishment, as well as be deprived of their offices; for

We shall not permit them to longer remain in the Bureau of Armorers, but will appoint others in their stead.

EPILOGUE.

Your Highness, and those who may hereafter succeed you, will hasten to cause what it has pleased Us to enact by the present law to be carried into execution; for unless you take measures for the observance of what is so advantageous to the public welfare, you will have reason to fear the effects of Our indignation."[498]

As mentioned earlier, believing that the biggest threat of opposition had been removed and the ongoing threat of war ended, the Roman populace was delighted in the uniting of the old empire as one again under one religion. You will remember the letter we viewed earlier that Pope Vigilius wrote to Justinian on September 17, 540, praising him for establishing the one and only true faith "in every corner of the world." Hardly had the words gone forth from the pen of Pope Vigilius, when it happened. In the summer of 541 the world-wide epidemic called the Bubonic plague touched down on the Mediterranean at the extreme eastern edge of the Nile Delta. Procopius describes the severity of the plague:

> "During these times there was a pestilence, by which the whole human race came near to being annihilated."[499]

Constantinople remained untouched until March or April of 542, but when it hit like elsewhere, it took out nearly half the empire. Justinian's empire never fully recovered. In the meantime, the Ostrogoths regrouped and the ongoing war cost the ravaged empire dearly, but

---

[498] Scott, S. P., trans., ed. *The Civil Law [of Justinian]*, 17 vols. Union, NJ: Lawbook Exchange, 2001, Justinian, *The Novels-85*, 16:313-316, April 7, 539.

[499] Procopius, *History of the Wars* (London, Cambridge, MA: Harvard University Press, Loeb Classical Library, 1919; reprint, 2000), II. xxii. 1. Or, Vol. 1:451.

Justinian finally prevailed against the Ostrogoths in March of 553. In turn, Pope Vigilius sends another letter to Justinian on *May 14, 553*, in gratitude and with hope that his accomplishments may go down as *a pattern for all future ecclesiastical peace*:

> "Among the many cares that burden your imperial charge, we hear of Your Clemency's praise worthy determination to remove all the seeds of discord which the enemy of the human race has sown in the Lord's field. For this purpose you have hastened to bring to unity and concord all the priests of God by having them make their professions as witness to their conscientious belief, to show that they remain faithful to the definitions and decisions of our holy Fathers, of the four venerable Synods, and of the heads of the Apostolic See. That the form of these professions may go down to posterity as a pattern of ecclesiastical peace. . . ."[500]

Thus officially ended the reign of the Ostrogoths. Ferdinand Gregorovius well illustrates how that smear campaign of hate has still continued against the Arians all because these God-fearing and law abiding citizens were governed by the Biblical principle of religious liberty:

> "Where the last remnant of the Goths wandered at [472] length from the battlefield of Vesuvius, we do not know; their sorrowful exit from the beautiful country for which their fathers had fought, and where innumerable scenes reminded them of glorious deeds in the past, remains shrouded in mystery.

---

[500] Guenther, Otto, *Epistulae Imperatorum Pontificum Aliorum, Avellana Quae Dicitur Collectio*, 2 pts. In *Corpus Scriptorum Ecclesiasticorum Latinorum*, vol. 35. Prague: F. Tempsky, 1895, (ep. 83), 230, May 14, 553.

Mansi, Joannes Dominicus. *Sacrorum Conciliorum: Nova, et Amplissima Collectio*, facs. ed. Paris: Welter, 1902, 9:6.

Translatation: Dvornik, Francis. *Early Christian and Byzantine Political Philosophy*, (Washington, DC: Dumbarton Oaks Ctr. for Byz. Studies, 1966), 2:822.

The kingdom established by Theodoric had lasted only sixty years. During this period the transition from Antiquity to Mediaevalism had been accomplished in Italy, and to the Goths, who stood on the confines of the two ages, belongs the imperishable glory of having been the protectors of the ancient culture of Europe in the dying hours of the Roman world.[501] The Goths themselves remained strangers in Italy on account of the innate opposition which they offered to the nationality and religion of the Latins; further, because they were powerless to infuse a fresh vitality into the land which they had conquered. It is idle to speculate in the face of the facts of history as to what form Italy and the West might have assumed had the Goths been allowed to settle permanently in the conquered land, had opportunities been granted them of self development, of peaceful intercourse, and of fusion with the Italian race. Under their sceptre the country was united for the last time, and in the premature overthrow of the Goths the national unity of Italy perished.

The Goths represented in outward form, customs, and language that primitive race of Zamolxis or [473] Ulfilas, of whom, according to the testimony of Jordanes, Dio said, in his lost history of the Goths, that they were "wiser than all barbarians, and in genius closely resembled the Greeks."[502] To the great facility for culture, which the shortness of their tenure in Italy had not given time to develop, they united the gentleness and also the manliness of the Teutonic character, and, if we but compare the period of Gothic rule with any later foreign government in Italy, further comment is unnecessary.

---

[501] *Gothorum laus est civilitas custodita.* This admission of Cassiodorus (*Var.*, ix. 14) forms the epitaph on the Goths, and ought to be borne in mind by the Italians.

[502] Jordan., *De reb. Get.*, c. 5: *unde et pene omnibus barbaris Gothi sapientiores semper* extiterunt, *Graecisque pene consimiles.* Compare with this statement the memorable letter of the Visigothic King Sisebut to Adelwald, King of the Lombards, where the German character is depicted: *genus inclitum, inclita forma, ingenita virtus, naturalis prudentia, elegantia morum.* Troya, *Cod. Dipl. Long.*, i. p. 571, according to Florez, *Espana Sagrada*, vii. 321-328.

We may, however, add the sentence of the greatest
of Italian historians on the Ostrogoths: "If we mention
the name of Goth in Italy," says Muratori, "some of the
people shudder, chiefly the half-educated, as if we
spoke of inhuman barbarians, destitute of laws and
taste. Old buildings of bad style are called Gothic ar-
chitecture, and Gothic is the rude character of print at
the end of the fifteenth or the beginning of the following century.[503] These are the judgments of ignorance.
Theodoric and Totila, both Kings of the Gothic nation,
were certainly not free from many faults, but [474] each
possessed the love of justice, moderation, wisdom in
the choice of his officials, abstemiousness, sincerity in
his treaties, and other notable virtues to such a degree
as to render him a model in the art of good government. It is sufficient to read the letters of Cassiodorus
and the history of Procopius, himself an enemy of the
Goths. Moreover, these rulers did not in anywise
change the magistrates, the laws or the customs of the
Romans, and the legends of their bad taste are but
childish folly. The Emperor Justinian was more fortunate than the Gothic Kings, but if only half related by
Procopius be true, he was excelled in virtue by these
very Goths."[504] "The Romans," Muratori further says,
"longed for a change of masters; they changed them indeed, but they paid for the fulfilment of their desires by
the incalculable losses inseparable from a long and tedious war; and, what is worse, the change involved the
utter ruin of Italy in a few years, and plunged the country into an abyss of misery."[505] The best apology for

---

[503] In the age of Humanism the so-called Gothic character was exchanged for the Antiqua. Valla expressly designates the pre-humanis-
tic characters as Gothic: *codices Gothice scripti*, and bewails the
depravatio of the Roman handwriting *(Elegant.*, lib. iii. praef.).

[504] Procopius, in the *Historia Arcana*, c. 6, &c., brands Justinian as a
foolish and malicious impostor, greedy alike for gold and blood, and
portrays him as a second Domitian. The notorious description of
Theodora, which almost taxes the belief of the most wanton libertine,
follows in c. 9. Compare the learned comments of Alemannus on
these passages.

[505] *Annal. d' Italia ad Ann.* 555; and the enlightened opinion of La
Farina, *Storia d' Italia*, i. p. 61, &c.

Gothic rule is to be found in the state of tedious and utter misery into which Italy sank, when, after the overthrow of the Goths, the wild Lombard race settled on the ruins of the kingdom of Theodoric.

Throughout the entire course of the Middle Ages, [475] down to later times and even in the age of Humanism, the Romans retained the absurd belief that the Goths had destroyed their city.[506] Of the wonderful fables that were in circulation we are informed by the memoirs of Flaminius Vacca, a Roman sculptor, bearing the date of 1594, and the history of the city exhibits proofs of the ignorance of the Romans concerning their monuments.[507] While the inhabitants surveyed the remains of their ancient city, and knew not that, more even than time, the rude barons of the Middle Ages and even popes had destroyed the monuments of antiquity, they recollected from tradition that the Goths had long ruled Rome, frequently stormed, conquered, and plundered her. They saw the greater part of the ancient buildings, the triumphal arches, and the huge walls of the [476]

Colosseum as we see them now, pierced with innumerable holes; and not being able to explain these

---

[506] This belief was greatly strengthened by the national sentiment fostered in Italy by the Humanists. Nevertheless, Flav. Blondus was sufficiently impartial to acquit the Goths of the reproach of Vandalism. In his *Roma Instaur.*, n. 99, f., he says: *ut per annos septuaginta quibus Ostrogothi regno Romae et Italiae sunt potiti, Octaviani Augusti Trajani Hadriani Antonini Pii aut Alexandri Severi amorem in Romanam rem desiderari non oportuit.* In the face of the popular ignorance he shows that the destruction of the aqueducts was not the work of the Goths, but of the Romans, who were in search of building materials. In the *Italia Illustrata* (Etruria) Blondus has also exonerated Totila from the charge of having reduced Florence to ruins. Leon Battista Alberti also diverts the reproach from the heads of the barbarians to that of the Romans themselves *(De re aedif.,* x. I).

[507] Flaminio Vacca, collecting material for the antiquary, Anastasius Simonetti of Perugia, makes notes of various objects which he had seen discovered or dug up. See Fea in the Miscellan., t. i., and Nibby in the Appendix to Nardini's *Roma Antica:* "Memorie di varie antichita trovate in diversi luoghi della citta di Roma, scritte da Flaminio Vacca nell' anno 1594."

holes, came to the conclusion that they had been made by the Goths, either in order to break out the stones with levers, or (which was more sensible) to tear away the bronze clamps.[508] In Vacca's time were shown the so-called hatchets of the Goths, hatchets with which they had broken the statues; the naive sculptor relating that one day two hatchets had been found in the "vigna" where the so-called temple of Caius and Lucius (called by the people "Galluzi") stood, and that they bore on one side a club and on the other a halberd. "I believe," he adds, "that these were the weapons of the Goths, that the edge served in battle to cleave the shield, the club to destroy the antiquities."[509]

The imagination of the Romans even discovered [477] the funeral urns of the Goths who had fallen at the siege of Vitiges. When, at the gate of San Lorenzo, several sarcophagi of granite and marble were one day found, they were held to be Gothic on account of their workmanship, and "I believe," the same sculptor says, "they belong to the time when poor Italy was ruled by the Goths, and I remember to have read that the Goths received a repulse at this very gate. Perhaps they were funeral urns of the officers who perished in the assault, and who wished to be buried on the spot where they fell."

---

[508] The learned Snares, Bishop of Vaisson, writing his *Diatriba de foraminibus lapidum in priscis aedificiis*, in 1651, puts forward seven suggestions to account for these holes, without being able to decide on any. 1. Envy of the barbarians, who, since they were not able to destroy the monuments, disfigured them. 2. That the holes had originated in the preparations for constructing dwellings. 3. Through barricades in the times of revolution. 4. Through the removal of concealed metal clamps. 5. In the search for hidden treasures. 6. That they had been formed in the original building for the purpose of construction. 7. That they had arisen in the Colosseum when the arches were converted into booths. See also Marangoni, *Delle Memorie sacre e profane dell' Amfiteatro Romano*, Rome, 1746, p. 46, &c. Fea, *Sulle rov.*, pp. 276, 277, speaks with reason of the improbability of the damage having been the work of the barbarian. Vacca naively says: *tutti bucati all' usanza de' Goti, per rubarne le spranghe.* I myself am of opinion that the holes arose in great part from the removal of the clamps in times when there was a great scarcity of metal.

[509] Fl. Vacca, n. 17.

It is amusing to discover fables such as these current in Rome at so late a date; to find that people still believed that the Goths had not only buried their treasures in the city, but had marked the spots where these treasures lay concealed, and that their descendants knew of these hiding places. So great was the popular ignorance that, down to the end of the sixteenth century, it was commonly believed that Goths, living in some unknown quarter, came by stealth to the city in search of the spoils of their forefathers, and prosecuted their excavations with an even greater ardour than many cardinals, without a like knowledge, had already prosecuted theirs. Flaminio Vacca, with naive simplicity, gives us the following anecdote:-

"Many years ago I went to see the antiquities. I found myself beyond the gate of San Bastian at the Capo di Bove (the mausoleum of Cecilia Metella), and, as it was raining, I stepped into a little Osteria below. While waiting there, I talked with the host, who told me that a few months before a man had [478] come for some fuel, and had returned in the evening with three companions for supper. After supper they all went away, the three companions never exchanging a word. The same thing happened three evenings in succession. My host suspected that something was wrong and resolved to accuse them. One evening when they had supped as usual, he watched them by moonlight, and saw them enter some caverns in the Circus of Caracalla (Maxentius). On the following morning, having informed the authorities of what had taken place, search was made in the caverns, when a quantity of loose earth and a deep hole were discovered, and amid the earth numerous recently broken fragments of earthenware vases and iron instruments which had been used in digging. Wishing to convince myself of these facts, and being near the spot, I entered and saw the excavations and the fragments of vases, which resembled tubes. It is supposed that these men were Goths, who, following the same old clues, had here unearthed a treasure."[510]

---

[510] FI. Vacca: n. 81.

Another tale is as follows: - "I recollect that in the time of Pius IV. a Goth came to Rome having in his possession a very ancient book, dealing with a hidden treasure, with a serpent and a figure in bas-relief; on one side of it was a Cornucopiae, and on the other it pointed to the earth. The Goth sought until he found the described bas-relief on the side of an arch; then, going to the Pope, begged for permission to dig for the treasure, which, as he said, belonged to the Romans. After going to the people [479] he received the required permission, set to work with a chisel at the side of the arch, and laboured until he had made a opening. The Romans, suspicious of the enmity of the Goths, believing that they still harboured the desire to destroy the monuments of antiquity, and fearing that the man might undermine the arch, attacked him, in the prosecution of his work, with such violence that, thankful to make his escape, he left his design unfulfilled."[511]

Fables such as these were the only associations retained by the Romans of the glorious period of Gothic rule, and the care displayed by the barbarians for the monuments of antiquity. We shall, however, see hereafter that, during the Middle Ages, the ignorance of the people reached such a depth that even Caesar, Augustus, and Virgil disappeared from the sight of their descendants in the mists of fable."[512]

---

[511] Fl. Vacca, n. 103. The arch itself is not specified, but may have been that of Septimius Severns. The ancient myth concerning buried treasures ever and anon reappears in Rome. I came across it in December 1864, when, with the sanction of the Pope, excavations were made in search of a treasure in the Colosseum. A man feigned to have discovered an old parchment which gave an accurate description of the spot where this treasure lay hid. For fourteen days they dug under the arch of entrance on the side of the Lateran and an engine was incessantly engaged in pumping out the water, which rushed like a stream about the amphitheatre. The search, however, brought to light nothing but the bones of some animals.

[512] Ferdinand Gregorovius, Translated from the Fourth German Edition, Mrs. Gustavus W. Hamilton , *History Of The City of Rome In The Middle Ages*, (London, George Bell & Sons, 1900, First Published, 1894. Second Edition, Revised, 1900), 1:471-479.

Ferdinand Gregorovius has accurately stated that if one would read Cassiodorus or even Procopius, an enemy of the Goths, as we will illustrate with just one example, one can still witness to the true character of these poor maligned and misrepresented people even from the primary sources:

> "Now there is a certain church of the Apostle Paul,[513] fourteen stades distant from the fortifications of Rome, and the Tiber River flows beside it. In that place there is no fortification, but a colonnade extends all the way from the city to the church, and many other buildings which are round about it render the place not easy of access. But the Goths shew a certain degree of actual respect for sanctuaries such as this. And indeed during the whole time of the war no harm came to either church of the two Apostles[514] at their hands, but all the rites were performed in them by the priests in the usual manner."[515]

"Catholic Truth" has wanted us to believe that the Arians were against law, order, and Christianity, a demoralized people. The truth of the matter has shown just the opposite. They were, however, opposed to the tyrannical Pontifical Government of Catholicism that denied religious liberty because the Ostrogoths decreed legislation supporting religious liberty for all men of all faiths. And for that they became the foremost enemy of the Roman Catholic Church. History has certainly shown us that if you can tell a lie long enough it miraculously somehow will turn into truth, "Catholic Truth." The fact of the matter is that if the Biblical principle of religious liberty had been endorsed as the governing principle throughout the 1260-year period as it had been by the Arian governments, there would have never been the

---

[513] The Basilica of St. Paul stood south of the city, outside the Porta Ostiensis which is still called Porta S. Paolo.
[514] St. Peter and St. Paul.
[515] Procopius. *History of the Wars.* Translated by H. B. Dewing. Bks. 1–8. In Loeb Classical Library, edited by Jeffrey Henderson. Cambridge, MA: Harvard Univ. Press, 2000–2001, VI. iv. 7-13. 3:321.

dark ages as we know it today. That means there would
have been no state-sponsored religious terrorism of any
kind because all religious bigots would have been outlawed from society, rendering their societies safe from
extremists. This, in turn, would have secured for all of
Eastern and Western Europe a much different history.
No burning of human beings at the stake or all the other
countless forms of torture that is too gruesome to reiterate here. No exile, no loss of property or wills, no discrimi-
nation, no loss of employment, no loss or denial of or to
the marriage vow, no Inquisition, no Crusades, and no
loss of human life that historians number between 50-
120 million slaughtered, men, women, and children. Oh,
what an account the man of sin will have to render at the
judgment bar of God almighty, for this awful record has
been faithfully chronicled by heaven:

> Revelation 18:24 "And in her was found the blood
> of prophets, and of saints, and of all that were slain
> upon the earth."

The term "Arians" which was given to them and its
implied negative connotation is also suspect and needs
measured by unbiased primary sources, if they are to be
found. As we have also seen in our *A.D. 508 Source Book*,
deception was and is the tool that was used by Satan's
human agents to misrepresent and falsely malign those
who adhered to the Bible and its principles. This has always been the sad lot of the followers of Christ who have
been the minority throughout history:

> Matthew 5:11 "Blessed are ye, when *men* shall re-
> vile you, and persecute *you*, and shall say all manner of
> evil against you falsely, for my sake."
> Luke 12:32 "Fear not, little flock; for it is your
> Father's good pleasure to give you the kingdom."

Unfortunately, this history and the methods of religious bigots and extremist, backed by the state are to
have an enormous recurrence against the faithful just before the second coming of Christ. It has been said that
you can judge a regime from its subjects. With that per-

spective in mind, we shall let those who were the very first subjects under that tyrannical Pontifical Government of Catholicism share their experience. We begin with the testimony of our first eye witness, Procopius:

"While he was stirring up all this strife and war to plague the Romans, he also endeavoured, by various devices, to drench the earth in human blood, to carry off more riches for himself, and to murder many of his subjects. He proceeded as follows. There prevail in the Roman Empire many Christian doctrines which are known as heresies, such as those of the Montanists and Sabbatians and all the others by which men's minds are led astray. Justinian ordered all these beliefs to be abandoned in favour of the old religion, and threatened the recusants with legal disability to transmit their property to their wives and children by will. The churches of these so-called heretics-especially those belonging to the Arian heresy-were rich beyond belief: Neither the whole of the Senate, or any other of the greatest corporations in the Roman Empire, could be compared with these churches in wealth. They had gold and silver plate and jewels more than any man could count or describe; they owned many mansions and villages, and large estates everywhere, and everything else which is reckoned and called wealth among men.

As none of the previous Emperors had interfered with them, many people, even of the orthodox faith, procured, through this wealth, work and the means of livelihood. But the Emperor Justinian first of all sequestrated all the property of these churches, and suddenly took away all that they possessed, by which many people lost the means of subsistence. Many agents were straightway sent out to all parts of the Empire to force whomsoever they met to change the faith of his fore- [39] fathers. These homely people, considering this an act of impiety, decided to oppose the Emperor's agents. Hereupon many were put to death by the persecuting faction, and many made an end of themselves, thinking, in their superstitious folly, that this course best satisfied the claims of religion; but the greater part of them voluntarily quitted the land of their forefathers, and went into exile. The Montanists, who were settled in Phrygia, shut themselves up in their churches, set them on fire, and perished in the flames; and, from this time forth, nothing was to be seen in the Roman Empire except massacres and flight.

Justinian straightway passed a similar law with regard to the Samaritans, which produced a riot in Palestine. In my own city of Caesarea and other cities, the people, thinking that it was a foolish thing to suffer for a mere senseless dogma, adopted, in place of the name which they had hitherto borne, the appellation of "Christians," and so avoided the danger with which they were threatened by this law. Such of them as had any claims to reason and who belonged to the better class, thought it their duty to remain stedfast to their new faith; but the greater part, as though out of pique at having been forced against their will by the law to abandon the faith of their fathers, adopted the belief of the Manicheans, or what is known as Polytheism.

But all the country people met together in a body and determined to take up arms against the Emperor. They chose a leader of their own, named Julian, the son of Sabarus, and for some time held their own in the struggle with the Imperial troops, but were at last defeated and cut to pieces, together with their leader. It is said that one hundred thousand men fell in this engagement, and the most fertile country on the earth has ever since been without cultivators. This did great harm to the Christian landowners in that country, for, although they received nothing from their property, yet they were forced to pay heavy taxes yearly to the Emperor for the rest of their lives, and no abatement or relief from this burden was granted to them.

After this he began to persecute those who were called Gentiles, torturing their persons and plundering their property. All of these people, who decided to adopt the Christian faith nominally saved themselves for the time . . . [45] Although Justinian's character was such as I have already explained, he was easy of access, and affable to those whom he met. No one was ever denied an audience, and he never was angry even with those who did not behave or speak properly in his presence. But, on the other hand, he never felt ashamed of any of the murders which he committed. However, he never displayed any anger or pettishness against those who offended him, but preserved a mild countenance and an unruffled brow, and with a gentle voice would order tens of thousands of innocent men to be put to death, cities to be taken by storm, and property to be confiscated. One would think, from his manner, that he had the character of a sheep; but if anyone, pitying his victims, were to endeavor, by prayers and supplications, to make him relent, he would straightway become savage, show his teeth, and vent his rage upon his subjects. As for the priests, he let them override their neighbors with impunity, and delighted to see them plunder those round about them, thinking that in this manner he was showing piety. Whenever he had to decide any lawsuit of this sort, he thought that righteous judgment consisted in letting the priest win his cause and leave the court in triumph with some plunder to which he had no right whatever; for, to him, justice meant the success of the priest's cause. He himself, when by malpractices he had obtained possession of the property of people, alive or dead, would straightway present his plunder to one of the churches, by which means he would hide his rapacity under the cloak of piety, and render it impossible for his victims ever to recover their possessions. Indeed, he committed numberless murders through his notion of piety; for, in his zeal to bring all men to agree in one form of Christian doctrine, he recklessly murdered all who dissented there from, under the pretext of piety, for he did not think that ,it was murder, if those whom he slew were not of the same belief as himself. . . . [86] Nothing was [87] spoken of in conversation at home, in the streets, or in the churches, except misfortune and suffering. Such was the state of the cities. . . . At first, as has been said, he got all the shops into his own hands, and having established monopolies of all the most necessary articles of life, exacted from his subjects more than three times their value. But if I were to enter into the details of all these monopolies, I should never finish my narrative, for they are innumerable."[516]

Procopius gives a very graphic account of Justinian's wife, Theodora, her birth, how she was brought up, how she married him, and how in conjunction with him she utterly ruined the Roman Empire. However, our purpose here is solely to witness to the true character of the man, Justinian and the graphics supplied by Procopius serve no purpose here:

> [31] As soon, however, as she [Theodora] reached the age of puberty, as she was handsome, her mother sent her into the theatrical troupe, and she straightway became a simple harlot, as old-fashioned people called it; for she was neither a musician nor a dancer, but merely prostituted herself to everyone whom she met, giving up every part of her body to debauchery. . . . [75] for she herself also, from her earliest years, had associated with sorcerers and magician, since her character and pursuits inclined her towards them. She had great faith in their arts, and placed the greatest confidence in them. . . . [35] Thus did Theodora, as I have told you, in spite of her birth and bringing-up, reach the throne without finding any obstacle in her way. Justinian felt no shame at having wedded her, although he might have chosen the best born, the best educated, the most modest and virtuously nurtured virgin. in all the Roman Empire, with outstanding breasts, as the saying is; whereas he preferred to take to himself the Common refuse of all mankind, and without a thought of all that has been told, married a woman stained with the shame of many abortions and many other crimes. Nothing more, I conceive, need be said about this creature's character, for all the vices of his heart are thoroughly displayed in the fact of so unworthy a marriage. When a man feels no shame at an act of this kind, and braves the loathing of the world, there is thereafter no path of wickedness which may not be

---

[516] *The Secret History of the Court of Justinian.* Boston: IndyPublish. com, n.d., 38-9, 45, 86-7.

trodden by him, but, with a face incapable of blushing, he plunges, utterly devoid of scruple, into the deepest baseness.

However, no one in the Senate had the courage to show dissatisfaction at seeing the State fasten this disgrace upon itself, but all were ready to worship Theodora as if she had been a goddess. Neither did any of the clergy show any indignation, but bestowed upon her the title of "Lady." The people who had formerly seen her upon the stage now declared themselves, with uplifted hands, to be her slaves, and made no secret of the name. None of the army showed irritation at having to face the dangers of war in the service of Theodora, nor did anyone of all mankind offer her the least opposition. All, I suppose, yielded to circumstances, and suffered this disgraceful act to take place, as though Fortune had wished to display her power by disposing human affairs so that events came about in utter defiance of reason, and human counsel seemed to have no share in directing them. Fortune does thus raise men suddenly to great heights of power, by means in which reason has no share, in spite of all obstacles that may bar the way, for nothing can check her course, but she proceeds straight on towards her goal, and everything makes way for her. But let all this be, and be represented as it pleases God. "[517]

"That the emperor was not a man but, as I have already pointed out, a demon in human shape, could be demonstrated by considering the magnitude of the calamities which he brought on the human race. For it is by the immensity of what he accomplishes that the power of the doer is manifested. To make any accurate estimate of the number of lives destroyed by this man would never, it seems to me, be within the power of any living being other than God. For sooner could one number all the sands than the hosts of men destroyed by this potentate."[518]

---

[517] Ibid., 31, 75, 35.
[518] Procopius. *The Secret History*. Translated by G. A. Williamson. London: Folio Society, 1990, 83.

The following testimony is from another eye witness:

> "We know this famous anecdote: "When I die,
> asked Napoleon I to one of his courtesans, what would
> be said?—Sire, answered the interlocutor, this will be
> said, that will be said! No, interrupted suddenly the
> emperor, what would be said is: "phew!" The peoples
> said; phew! the day after the death of Justinian. The
> poet Corippus told[519] that, when for the first time the
> successor of the dead sovereign appeared in the Hippo-
> drome, he was greeted by a suppliant and lamenting
> crowd. "Take pity on us, cried these men, because we
> are dying. Come to the rescue of your slaves". "You are
> pious, whined others, you are all-powerful, see our
> tears, ease our misery" It was all those to whom
> Justinian had extorted money, the family of unsolvable
> debtors, the wives and mothers of prisoners, all the
> victims of the preceding regime, imploring the mercy
> of the new emperor. And so profoundly felt was, every-
> where, the impression of deliverance, that the grave
> Evagrius himself wrote as an ending to the story of that
> reign: "Thus died Justinian, after filling the whole
> world with noise and troubles; and, having, as soon as
> he died, received the salary of his misdeeds, we went to
> find, in front of the tribunal of hell, the justice he was
> due.""[520]

Ironically, the testimony of what those subjects had
said at the commencement of the Pontifical Government's reign will be witnessed to have been said by its
subjects at the end of its prophetic rule of 1260 years, as
well. The following is taken directly from the personal
diary of Cardinal Giuseppe Antonio Sala who was a
priest in Rome on February 10, 1798, when General

[519] Corippus, In laud Just., II, 361 sq.
[520] Evagrius V, 1. It must be observed though that inversely, Corippus
sends him directly to the heavens (in laud. Just. I 245-246) Cf. also
Paul Silent., *loc.cit*, 309-310.
   Diehl, Charles. *Justinien et la Civilization Byzantine au Vie Siècle*.
Paris: Ernest Leroux, 1901, 31-32.

Berthier entered that city during the French Revolution. We will begin with his personal testimony on February 15, 1798:

> "There were made a thousand attacks on the coat of arms of the Pope, some of which had been thrown to the ground. The Patriots were shouting: "Let down arms; the tyranny has ended; let us be free," etc. . . .
>
> The Jews have thrown off the former servitude and rejoice for the actual newness [they are now considered equal citizens]. . . . [32] In the afternoon *General Cervoni went to the Pope and said to him that the Roman People had implored the generosity of the French Nation to be freed from the oppression of the Pontific Government; that the French had granted to them their assistance; and that having become free, there remained to the Pope only concern for the spiritual.* His Holiness responded to him with few words, reminding him of Religion, individuals, and propriety."[521]

Quite a contrast to the testimony of Christ:

> Matthew 11:28 "Come unto me, all *ye* that labour and are heavy laden, and I will give you rest.
>
> Matthew 11:29 "Take my yoke upon you, and learn of me; for I am meek and lowly in heart: and ye shall find rest unto your souls."
>
> Matthew 11:30 "For my yoke   easy, and my burden is light."

Such has been the testimony of those who have lived under the oppressive yoke of the Pontifical government when the union of church and state controlled the consciences of all men.

---

[521] Sala, G. A. Diario Romano: degli anni 1798–99. 3 vols. In Miscellanea della Società Romana di Storia Patria. Rome: presso la Società, 1882 (1, 2); 1886 (3). 1:31-32.

CONCLUSION

As witnessed from our Appendix I, the Burgundians were defeated in 532 and annexed in 534 by the Franks for political gain. The Burgundian law code was replaced with the Lex Romana Visigothorum law code to fully cement a uniform jurisdiction of Catholic and Frankish law. Justinian and the Franks then formed an alliance against the Ostrogoths. Justinian sent a letter to the leaders of the Franks as follows:

"The Goths, having seized by violence Italy, which was ours, have not only refused absolutely to give it back, but have committed further acts of injustice against us which are unendurable and pass beyond all bounds. For this reason we have been compelled to take the field against them, and it is proper that you should join with us in waging this war, which is rendered yours as well as ours not only by the orthodox faith, which rejects the opinion of the Arians, but also by the enmity we both feel toward the Goths." Such was the emperor's letter; and making a gift of money to them, he agreed to give more as soon as they should take an active part. And they with all zeal promised to fight in alliance with him."[522]

In 536 came the final establishment of the French monarchy in Gaul[523] and the possession of Provence, and this left the Franks in complete control to freely enforce the Lex Romana Visigothorum law code throughout all of Gaul.

With the last of the three major Arian powers subdued judicially in A.D. 538 when they were forced to relinquish Rome, the capitol of the world as we have just witnessed, the oppressive union of church and state had successfully put down all major opposition and had out-

[522] Procopius. *History of the Wars.* Translated by H. B. Dewing. Bks. 1–8. In Loeb Classical Library, edited by Jeffrey Henderson. Cambridge, MA: Harvard Univ. Press, 2000–2001, V. v. 5-10, 3:45.
[523] Gibbon, Edward. *The History of the Decline and Fall of the Roman Empire,* (Edited by J. B. Bury. London: Methuen, 1909), 4:128, margin, AMS edition.

lawed religious liberty throughout all of Christendom. By this act, the church officially ushered in the horrors of the dark ages. This has been the best kept secret of the dark ages. Another well-kept secret has been that this event then opened the way for the enforcement of a universal Sunday law throughout all of Christendom in A.D. 538. That proved to be the catalyst or the MARK of her ecclesiastical authority which signaled that the Pontifical government of force, or more accurately stated, the government of Satan, was then fully underway and, thereby, commenced the 1260 prophetic period in A.D. 538. You cannot have a Sunday law without first denying religious liberty and this is the real issue behind the Sunday law. Previously divorced from Christ, no longer widowed, but married to the state, the Catholic Church was "given" a specified time to "practice and prosper" for 1260 long years. What a witness to the universe of the "new order" of Satan's rule. This union of church and state continued as such with the state enforcing the dogmas of the church until the deadly wound was administered to the papacy (Revelation 13:10) in 1798. Although there were low and high moments in the career of the papacy, never once for 1260 years did she relinquish the position she held by granting or acknowledging the principle of religious liberty until she was forced to do so for the first time in 1798. That was the year the Catholic Church became a widow because the state divorced itself from the woman (the church) and no longer enforced the dogmas of the church, thus rendering the counterfeit church incapable of persecution. The fulfillment of that prophetic event will be illustrated fully in my *A.D. 1798 1843 Source Book*.

> "But today in the religious world there are multitudes who, as they believe, are working for the establishment of the kingdom of Christ as an earthly and temporal dominion. They desire to make our Lord the ruler of the kingdoms of this world, the ruler in its courts and camps, its legislative halls, its palaces and market places. They expect Him to rule through legal enactments, enforced by human authority. Since Christ is not now here in person, they themselves will

undertake to act in His stead, to execute the laws of His kingdom. The establishment of such a kingdom is what the Jews desired in the days of Christ. They would have received Jesus, had He been willing to establish a temporal dominion, to enforce what they regarded as the laws of God, and to make them the expositors of His will and the agents of His authority. But He said, "My kingdom is not of this world." He would not accept the earthly throne. . . .

Not by the decisions of courts or councils or legislative assemblies, not by the patronage of worldly great men, is the kingdom of Christ established, but by the implanting of Christ's nature in humanity through the work of the Holy Spirit. . . ."[524]

---

[524] Ellen White, *Amazing Grace*, (Hagerstown, MD: Review and Herald, 2001), 13.

Appendix I

In this overview our focus will be on the rise and domination of the Catholic Franks in Gaul up to the conquest of the Ostrogoths. There is much significant legislation by Clovis in the Council of Orleans I in 511 and, in fact, in many of the Merovingian's Church councils, but due to space constraints we will be unable to include them. The reader is directed to my website www.the-sourcehh.org for all the pertinent legislation found in those church councils which will greatly enhance this overview. Here is the list of Merovingian church councils that will be found on my website that may be downloaded with commentary for free:

Council of Agde (Sept. 10, 506)
Council of Orleans (July 10, 511)
Council of Epaone (September 6, 517)
Council of Lyon (518-519)
Council of Arles (June 6 524)
Council of Carpentras (November 6 527)
Council of Vaison (November 5, 529)
Council of Orange (July 3 529)
Council of Marseille (May 26 533)
Council of Orleans II (June 23 533)
Council of Orleans III (May 7, 538)

At the end of the 5th century and into the 6th century there were three established barbarian peoples:

"At the end of the 5th century three barbarian peoples succeeded in founding in Gaul durable establishments: the Visigoths, the Burgunds, and the Franks."[525]

Pontal continues:

"In 511 Merovingian Gaul was therefore composed of:
-the Frankish kingdom that extends from the Rhine to the south of Languedoc and to Provence;
-Gothic countries: Septimanie which remained in Visigoth hands until 711 and shared the destiny of Spain and Provence that belonged to the Ostrogoths;
-the Burgund kingdom : Bourgogne and Franche-Comté."[526]

With the Visigoths uprooted in Gaul in 508 by Catholic Clovis, King of the Franks, as we witnessed in my *A.D. 508 Source Book*, we need to understand the direction and fate of the Burgundians:

"Upon the death of [Arian King] Gondebaud, his son and successor Sigismond, grateful and devoted student of Avit, converted to Catholicism and assured the triumph of the orthodoxy. Following Clovis's example, he wanted to hold a national council of his kingdom. It is in this context that the council of Epaone in 517 was called."[527]

---

[525] Cf. MUSSET, *Les invasions*, 80-92 and 111-132.
    Pontal, Odette. *Histoire des Conciles Mérovingiens*.N.p.: Éditions du Cerf, 1989, 12.
    For the readers information there is a German translation as well and we have supplied that information but we have quoted and translated from the French version:
Pontal, Odette. *Die Synoden im Merowingerrich*. Paderborn, Ger.: Ferdinand Schöningh, 1986.
[526] Cf. EWIG, *Die fränkische Reichsbildung*, 259.
    Pontal, Odette. *Histoire des Conciles Mérovingiens*.N.p.: Éditions du Cerf, 1989, 39.
[527] Pontal, Odette. *Histoire des Conciles Mérovingiens*.N.p.: Éditions du Cerf, 1989, 61.

"Sigismond returned living and victorious. Providence kept him to play the great role that Avitus [the Burgundian bishop Avitus of Vienna] had foretold for him: that of being, after Clovis, the second Western Catholic prince. Gondebaud's death in 516 marked the triumph of Catholicism. The following year, Sigismond authorized the council meeting for the Burgundy kingdom at Epaone. However, one must pay homage to Avitus, who did not abuse his victory, more perhaps from prudence that by a true spirit of tolerance. We have the proof in a long letter that he addressed around 517 to the bishop of Grenoble, Victorius, who had consulted on the opportunity to give the Catholic cult the Arians' basilicas."[528]

[2] "In 516 Gundobad died and was succeeded by his son, Sigismund, who may have shared the rule with his brother Godomar. In 523 the Franks, now under the leadership of Clovis' sons Chlodomir, Childebert, and Clothaire (Chlotar)-renewed their attacks against the Burgundian kingdom. Sigismund was killed, and a part of the Burgundian kingdom was lost while Sigismund's brother, Godomar, became king of the Burgundians. Godomar made repeated efforts to renew the strength of his kingdom, but the Franks were determined to have Burgundy. In 532 the Burgundians were defeated and Godomar driven into flight, and in 534 the Burgundian kingdom was divided among the Frankish rulers. This was the end of the second and the last independent Burgundian kingdom, although her local counts remained strong and from time to time became powerful enough to be able to rule [3] almost independent of their Frankish and later Hapsburg rulers. . . . [5] The Burgundians were evidently willing to live up to the trust which the Gallo-Romans had put in them when they practically invited them to become their rulers, and we find that the

---

[528] *Ep.* VI, p. 35.

Reydellet, Marc. *Royalty in Latin Literature from Sidonius Appolinarus to Isadore of Seville.* Paris: Diffusion de Boccard, 1981, 128.

Burgundians did not forcibly subject the Roman population of their kingdom to the Burgundian customary
law, but rather they attempted to establish codes of law
which would be fair to both Burgundians and Romans.
Leges barbarorum were drawn up to govern relations
between Burgundians, or between a Burgundian and a
Roman; *leges romanae* were to govern relations between the Romans.

In the case of the Burgundians, the compilation of
these laws for both the Burgundians and the Romans
was undertaken by Gundobad, king of the Burgundians
from 474-516. The lawbook for the Burgundians is
known variously as *Lex Burgundionum, Liber Legum
Gundobadi, Lex Gundobada, la Loi Gombette,* and
Gombata; that for the Romans simply as the *Lex Romana
Burgundionum* or, because of an early mistake in man-
uscripts, as the Papian." . . . . [6] after the Frankish conquest of the Burgundians in 532 the *Breviary of Alaric,*
which had been compiled by Alaric for the Roman subjects of his Visigothic kingdom, was used to enlarge or
supplement the *Lex Romana Burgundionum,* and finally even replaced it."[529]

[41] "In Burgundy, the people converted to Catholicism adopted the life of the Franks but kept their own
law[530]. . . . Provence, which belonged to the Ostrogoth
state from 508 to 536 was like Burgundy the model of
a dualist state[531]: Goths and Romans were subject to

---

[529] Harold Dexter Hazeltine, *Roman and Canon Law in the Middle
Ages,* Cambridge Medieval History, 5:722.
  Fischer, Katherine, trans. The Burgundian Code: Liber
Constitutionum Sive Lex Gundobada, Constitutiones Extravagantes.
3rd series, Vol. 5, of Translations and Reprints from the Original
Sources of History, edited by John L. Lamonte and published by the
Univ. of Penn. history dept. Philadelphia: Univ. of Pennsylvania Press,
1949, 2-3, 5, 6.
[530] Burgund customs and Gallo-roman laws had been codified there.
Cf. G. CHEVRIER, G PIERI, *La loi romaine des Burgondes* (= Jus ro-
manum Medii aevi I 2 b, aa, 4), Mailand, 1969 and H. NEHLSEN, *Lex
Burgundiorum,* in *H.R.G.,* 2, 1978, 1901-1915.
[531] Cf. FOLZ, *De l'Antiquité . . . ,* 110-115.

parallel and [42] separate laws, administrations, and personnel[532]. . . . [43] Burgundy followed this example, and the king Sigismond, Catholic son of the Arian Gondebaud, gathered under the same conditions a council at Epaone in 517. . . . After the death of Clovis the geographic context was modified by the fact that the Frankish kingdom, treated as a private possession, was divided between his four sons, and that the Burgun kingdom was annexed (534) as well as Provence (536)."[533]

"Final establishment of the French monarchy in Gaul. A.D. 536."[534]

With the Burgundians defeated in 532 and annexed in 534 by the Franks for political gain, the Burgundian law code was replaced with the Lex Romana Visigothorum law code to fully cement a uniform jurisdiction of Catholic and Frankish law. Justinian and the Franks then formed an alliance against the Ostrogoths that we viewed earlier. In 536 came the final establishment of the French monarchy in Gaul and the possession of Provence, and this left the Franks in complete control to freely enforce the Lex Romana Visigothorum law code throughout all of Gaul.

---

[532] The Germanic subjects were governed by an especially military administration at the head of which were, in the main garrisons, the "comites gothorum", both civil and military heads at the same time. The Roman subjects were administered in a more complex way but we know by the administrative correspondence of Cassiodore, quaestor of the palace from 507 to 534, the activity of the main services of the palace: master of offices (head of offices), quaestor (correspondence and law), count (finances, state ateliers, distribution of funds).

[533] Pontal, Odette. *Histoire des Conciles Mérovingiens.* N.p.: Éditions du Cerf, 1989, 41-43.

[534] Gibbon, Edward. *The History of the Decline and Fall of the Roman Empire*, (Edited by J. B. Bury. London: Methuen, 1909), 4:128, margin, AMS edition.

APPENDIX II

Dating the Novels of Justinian's Law Code

Compiled by
Heidi Heiks

The numbers by which we cite the Novels or Novellas, also called Constitutions, are those of the Greek Collection of 168 Novels. This numbering of the 168 Novels also defines and corrects the dating of the 168 Novels translated from the Latin by S.P. Scott, otherwise an excellent primary source:

Scott, S. P., trans., ed. *The Civil Law*, Union, NJ: Lawbook Exchange, 2001, 17 Volumes.

The definitive dating used here was taken from the work of a French Doctor of Law:

Noailles, Pierre. *Les Collections de Novelles de L'Empereur Justinien: Origine et Formation sous Justinien*. Paris: Recueil Sirey, 1912.

Pierre Noailles states that the date that is assigned to each Novella is that of the Schoell-Kroll edition:

Schoell, Rudolfus-Kroll, Guilelmus, *Corpus Iurus Civilis, Novellae*, Vol. 3, Berlin, Germany: Apud Wiedmannos, 1895, 1959.

1. January 1, 535.
2. March 16, 535.
3. March 16, 535.
4. March 16, 535.
5. March 17, 535.
6. April 15, 535.
7. April 15, 535.
8. April 15, 535.
9. April 14, 535.
10. April 13, 535.
11. April 14, 535.
12. May 16, 535.
13. October 10, 535
14. Dec. 1, 535
15. August 8, 535.
16. August 8, 535.
17. April 16, 535.
18. March 1, 536.
19. March 17, 536.
20. March 18, 536.
21. March 18, 536.
22. March 18, 536.
23. January 3, 536.
24. May 18, 535.
25. May 18, 535.
26. May 18, 535.
27. July 18, 535.
28. July 16, 535.
29. July 16, 535.
30. March 18, 536.
31. March 18, 536.
32. June 15, 535.
33. June 15, 535.
34. June 15, 535.
35. May 23, 535.
36. January 1, 535.
37. August 1, 535.
38. Feb. 15, 536.
39. April 17, 536.
40. May 18, 536.
41. May 18, 536.

42. August 8, 536,
43. May 17, 537.
44. August 17, 537.
45. August 18, 537.
46. August 18, 537
47. August 31, 537.
48. August 18, 537.
49. August 18, 537.
50. August 18, 537.
51. Sept. 1, 537.
52. August 10, 537.
53. Oct. 1, 537.
54. Sept.18, 537.
55. Oct. 18, 537.
56. Nov. 3, 537.
57. Oct. 18, 537.
58. Nov. 2, 537.
59. Nov. 2, 537.
60. Dec. 1, 537.
61. Dec. 1, 537.
62. Dec. ? 537.
63. March 9, 538
64. Jan. 19, 538.
65. March 23, 538.
66. May 1, 538.
67. May 1, 538.
68. May 25, 538.
69. June 1, 538.
70. June 1 or 4 538.
71. June 1 or 4 538.
72. June 1, 538.
73. June 4, 538.
74. June 4, 538.
75. Dec. ? 537.
76. Oct. 5, 538.
77. ? 538
78. Jan. 28, 539.
79. March 10, 539.
80. March 10, 539.
81. March 18, 539.
82. April 8, 539.

83. May 18, 539.
84. May 18, 539.
85. April 7, 539.
86. April 17, 539.
87. April 18, 539.
88. Sept. 1, 539.
89. Sept. 1, 539.
90. Oct. 1, 539.
91. Oct. 1, 539.
92. Oct. 10, 539.
93. Oct. 10, 539.
94. Oct. 18, 539.
95. Nov. 1, 539.
96. Nov. 1, 539.
97. Nov. 17, 539.
98. Dec. 16, 539.
99. Dec. 13, 539.
100. Dec. 17, 539.
101. August 1, 539.
106. Sept. 7, 540.
107. Feb. 1 541.
108. Feb. 1 541.
109. May 7 541.
110. April 26, 541.
111. June 1, 541.
112. Sept. 10, 541.
113. Nov. 22, 541.
114. Nov. 1, 541.
115. Feb. 1, 542.
116. April 9, 542.
117. Dec. 18, 542.
118. July 16, 5
119. Jan. 20, 544.
120. May 9, 544.
121. April 535
122. March 544,
123. May 546
124. July 544-45
125. Oct.-Jan. 543,
126. ? 546
127. Sept. 548

128. June, 545
129. June, 531,
130. March, 545,
131. March, 545
132. April, 544
133. April, 539
134. May, 556
135. ? 557?
136. April, 535
137. April, 565
138. ?
139. ? 535 or 536
140. ? 566, (Justin)
141. March, 559
142. Nov. 558
143. May, 563
144. May, 572,
(Justin)
145. Feb. 553
146. Feb. 553

147. Feb. 553
148. ? 566 (Justin)
149. Jan. 569,
(Justin)
150. May, 563
151. ? 534
152. June, 534
153. Dec. 541
154. ?
155. Feb. 533
156. ? 539?
157. May, 542
158. July, 544
159. April, 555
160. Before 535
161. Dec. 574,
(Tiberius)
162. June, 539
163. April, 574,
(Tiberius)

164. Dec. 574
(Tiberius)
165. ?
166. 521-523
167. ?
168. 512

We invite you to view the complete
selection of titles we publish at:

www.LNFBooks.com

or write or email us your praises,
reactions, or thoughts about this
or any other book we publish at:

TEACH Services, Inc.
P.O. Box 954
Ringgold, GA 30736

info@TEACHServices.com

.

LaVergne, TN USA
27 July 2010
191121LV00003B/11/P

9 781572 586307